**Collins**

B Health ...re FIRST

Mark Walsh

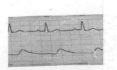

Published by Collins Education

....int of HarperCollins*Publishers*

....Palace Road

Browse ....plete Collins Education catalogue at
www.collinse....cation.com

©HarperCollins*Publishers* Limited 2013

10 9 8 7 6 5 4 3 2 1

ISBN 978-0-00-747980-1

Mark Walsh asserts his moral right to be identified as the author of this work.

British Library Cataloguing in Publication Data

A Catalogue record for this publication is available from the British Library.

Project managed and edited by Anna Clark
Production by Simon Moore
Proof read by Sue Chapple
Index by Jane Coulter
Picture research by Matthew Hammond
Design and typesetting by Jouve India Private Ltd.
Illustrations by Ann Paganuzzi
Cover design by Angela English
Printed and bound in Italy by Lego

Every effort has been made to contact copyright holders but if any have been
inadvertently overlooked, the publishers will be pleased to make the necessary
arrangements at the first opportunity.

All Crown Copyright Material is produced with permission of the Controller,
Office of Public Sector Information (OPSI)

Contents

Acknowledgements

The publishers wish to thank the following for permission to reproduce photographs. Every effort has been made to trace copyright holders and to obtain their permission for the use of copyright materials. The publishers will gladly receive any information enabling them to rectify any error or omission at the first opportunity.

(t = top, c = centre, b = bottom, r = right, l = left)

Cover & p.1 Pipa100/Dreamstime

p.10 Monkey Business Images/Shutterstock, p.8 Monkey Business Images/Shutterstock, p.11r molekuul.be/Shutterstock, p.11l postolit/Shutterstock, p.11c Monkey Business Images/Shutterstock, p.11c Paul Rich Studio/Shutterstock, p.12 Flashon Studio/Shutterstock, p.13 Africa Studio/Shutterstock, p.14 Dmitry Naumov/Shutterstock, p.16 auremar/ Shutterstock, p.17 hartphotography/Shutterstock, p.18t Pressmaster/Shutterstock, p.18b Flashon Studio/Shutterstock, p.19 Monkey Business Images/Shutterstock, p.21t Profimedia.CZ a.s./Alamy, p.21b Aleksey_Ryzhenko/Shutterstock, p.23b Yuri Arcurs/Shutterstock, p.22 Flashon Studio/Shutterstock, p.23t Roxana Gonzalez/Shutterstock, p.25 Yuri Arcurs/ Shutterstock, p.24 somersault18:24/Shutterstock, p.26 Alena Ozerova/Shutterstock, p.27b auremar/Shutterstock, p.27t wavebreakmedia/Shutterstock, p.29 Golden Pixels LLC /Shutterstock, p.28t Darren Baker/Shutterstock, p.28b Janine Wiedel Photolibrary/Alamy, p.31 Barry Lewis/Alamy, p.30 forestpath/Shutterstock, p.32 ejwhite/Shutterstock, p.33 Pressmaster/Shutterstock, p.34 Yuri Arcurs/Shutterstock, p.35 Graham Oliver/Alamy, p.37 © Golden Pixels LLC/ Shutterstock, p.38t Jeff Morgan 05/Alamy, p.38b UrbanImages/Alamy, p.40 Edwin Verin/Shutterstock, p.42 Paul Doyle/ Alamy, p.43t Glyn Thomas Photography/Alamy, p.43b Alistair Laming/Alamy, p.44 giorgiomtb/Shutterstock, p.50 gengirl/ Shutterstock, p.51 PhotoAlto/Alamy, p.55 Angela Hampton Picture Library/Alamy, p.57 Andresr/Shutterstock, p.47 REDAV/Shutterstock, p.48 wavebreakmedia/Shutterstock, p.52 Blaj Gabriel/Shutterstock, p.59 Cultura Creative/Alamy, p.62 LeventeGyori/Shutterstock, p.66 Janine Wiedel Photolibrary/Alamy, p.70 Myrleen Pearson/Alamy, p.73 BSIP SA/ Alamy, p.75l Paula Solloway/Alamy, p.75r RexRover/Shutterstock, p.76 Paula Solloway/Alamy, p.78 Juergen Hasenkopf/ Alamy, p.81 Sally and Richard Greenhill/Alamy, p.83 auremar/Shutterstock, p.85 Science Photo Library/Alamy, p.88 oliveromg/Shutterstock, p.90 Lana K/Shutterstock, p.91t Image Source/Alamy, p.91b Cultura Creative/Alamy, p.92 PjrTravel/Alamy, p.95 Candybox Images/Shutterstock, p.106 Monkey Business Images/Shutterstock, p.109l MJTH/ Shutterstock, p.109r 1000 Words/Shutterstock, p.100 Radoslaw Korga/Shutterstock, p.104l Yuri Arcurs/Shutterstock, p.97 TongRo Images/Alamy, p.104r Tetra Images/Alamy, p.103 Monkey Business Images/Shutterstock, p.112 Juice Images/ Alamy, p.114 Simply Signs/Alamy, p.115 Chris Cooper-Smith/Alamy, p.116 George Impey/Alamy, p.117t Photgrapher unknown/Alamy, p.117l Diego Cervo/Shutterstock, p.119t Art Directors & TRIP/Alamy, p.119b Monkey Business Images/ Shutterstock, p.121 kurhan/Shutterstock, p.123 Graham Oliver/Alamy, p.127r LEDPIX/Alamy, p.127l Stephen Barnes/ Medical/Alamy, p.129 Paul Doyle/Alamy, p.131l Photofusion Picture Library/Alamy, p.124 Alex Segre/Alamy, p.117b NHS Health Scotland, p.120 NHS Health Scotland, p.126 Parentzone Scotland, p.131 Macmillan Cancer Support, p.133l British Heart Foundation, p.133r NHS Health Scotland, p.136 Ronald Sumners/Shutterstock, p.138 Joshua Resnick/ Shutterstock, p.139 Monkey Business Images/Shutterstock, p.142 Vlue/Shutterstock, p.143r Jakub Cejpek/Shutterstock, p.143l Lucie Lang/Shutterstock, p.144 Images of Africa Photobank/Alamy, p.146t Julian Chen/Shutterstock, p.147 Simon Reddy/Alamy, p.148t Sally and Richard Greenhill/Alamy, p.148b Alex Segre/Alamy, p.150 Marco Mayer/Shutterstock, p.151 Jenny Matthews/Alamy, p.152 CBsigns/Alamy, p.154 Science Photo Library/Alamy, p.155 Africa Studio/ Shutterstock, p.158 Janine Wiedel Photolibrary/Alamy, p.159 Petrenko Andriy/Shutterstock, p.160 Monkey Business Images/Shutterstock, p.161t Catalin Petolea/Shutterstock, p.156 Gts/Shutterstock, p.161b Monkey Business Images/ Shutterstock, p.146b bikeriderlondon/Shutterstock, p.157 Science Photo Library/Alamy, p.153 James Turner/Alamy, p.166 iofoto/Shutterstock, p.169 Jim West/Alamy, p.172 Angela Hampton Picture Library/Alamy, p.173 Freya/Alamy, p.174 Paul Doyle/Alamy, p.177 VStock/Alamy, p.178 Golden Pixels LLC/Shutterstock, p.183 Roger Askew/Alamy, p.184 Andy

Dean Photography/Shutterstock, p.188r Diego Cervo/Shutterstock, p.188l Anton Balazh/Shutterstock, p.191 Tyler Olson/ Shutterstock, p.192 i love images / seniors/Alamy, p.186 Andres Rodriguez/Alamy, p.198 Tetra Images/Alamy, p.204 Catchlight Visual Services/Alamy, p.205 Robert Marmion/Alamy, p.211 Graham M. Lawrence/Alamy, p.212 Jack Carey/ Alamy, p.216t BSIP SA/Alamy, p.216b Dragana Gerasimoski/Shutterstock, p.218 Pixel 4 Images/Shutterstock, p.219 Tetra Images/Alamy, p.220 oliveromg/Shutterstock, p.221 Zurijeta/Shutterstock, p.203 Arles France/Alamy, p.206 PhotoAlto/ Alamy, p.207 Wavebreak Media ltd/Alamy, p.208 Pete Titmuss/Alamy, p.217 Jeff Greenberg/Alamy, p.224 Warren Goldswain/Shutterstock, p.228 Anatoliy Samara/Shutterstock, p.229 Kuzma/Shutterstock, p.231 littleny/Shutterstock, p.235 Phase4Photography/Shutterstock, p.236 David Mack/Science Photo Library, p.237t mkmakingphotos/Shutterstock, p.237b Eric Tormey/Alamy, p.238 MaraZe/Shutterstock, p.240 Hercules Robinson/Alamy, p.242 Kzenon/Shutterstock, p.248 Peter Bernik/Shutterstock, p.252 Design Pics Inc./Alamy, p.233 auremar/Shutterstock, p.234 Pressmaster/ Shutterstock, p.241 Jaimie Duplass/Shutterstock, p.253 mangostock/Shutterstock, p.257 Andy Dean Photography/ Shutterstock, p.258 URRRA/Shutterstock, p.261a Photographer unknown/Getty, p.261b BeholdingEye/iStockphoto, p.261c InnerSpace Imaging /Science Photo Library, p.261d BSIP SA/Alamy, p.268 Medimage/Science Photo Library, p.273 Peter Bernik/Shutterstock, p.276 Lisa F. Young/Shutterstock, p.277 Corepics VOF/Shutterstock, p.278 Mikael Damkier/ Shutterstock, p.279 wavebreakmedia/Shutterstock, p.280 John Bavosi/Science Photo Library, p.281 Science Photo Library/Alamy, p.285 Olaf Doering/Alamy, p.290 Alexander Raths/Shutterstock, p.291 Yuri Arcurs/Shutterstock, p.294 PhotoAlto/Alamy, p.296 LeventeGyori/Shutterstock, p.297 LeventeGyori/Shutterstock, p.264 Alex Mit/Shutterstock, p.282 Levent Konuk/Shutterstock, p.286 Agencja FREE/Alamy, p.300 iofoto/Shutterstock, p.302 Paul Doyle/Alamy, p.303 Lisa S./Shutterstock, p.305 Kzenon/Shutterstock, p.306 Justin Kase zsixz/Alamy, p.307 Lisa F. Young/Shutterstock, p.309 Pell Studio/Shutterstock, p.314 Huntstock, Inc/Alamy, p.316 Photgrapher unknown/Alamy, p.317 Poznyakov/ Shutterstock, p.308 Jack Cox in Spain/Alamy, p.310l Bikeworldtravel/Shutterstock, p.310r Paul Drabot/Shutterstock, p.322 Juice Images/Alamy, p.324 Paul Doyle/Alamy, p.325 Jacky Chapman/Alamy, p.326 Michael Dwyer/Alamy, p.328 Paula Solloway/Alamy, p.329 Michael Scheer/Alamy, p.330 Frances Roberts/Alamy, p.331t Chanclos/Shutterstock, p.331b Maskot/Alamy, p.332 John Angerson/Alamy, p.333t Bubbles Photolibrary/Alamy, p.333b Angela Hampton Picture Library/Alamy, p.335 auremar/Shutterstock, p.336 Radius Images/Alamy, p.337 Jon Parker Lee/Alamy, p.339 redsnapper/ Alamy, p.340 Copyright: Ingrid Balabanova/Shutterstock, p.341 Blend Images/Alamy, p.344 Mike Booth/Alamy, p.343b worldinmyeyes.pl/Shutterstock, p.343t Adrian Buck/Alamy, p.347t John Angerson/Alamy, p.347b Alexander Raths/ Shutterstock, p.338 oliveromg/Shutterstock, p.342 67photo/Alamy, p.349 Design Pics Inc./Alamy.

Fig 5.2 p.126 Cancer Research UK, http://www.cancerresearchuk.org/cancer-info/cancerstats/types/lung/smoking/ lung-cancer-and-smoking-statistics, March 2013.

Fig 6.4 p.160 Based on data from *Trends in adult prevalence of obesity*, © OECD, http://www.noo.org.uk/NOO_about_ obesity/trends, accessed September 2012.

Introduction

The aim of this book is to help you develop the knowledge and understanding you will need to complete your BTEC Level 1 or Level 2 First in Health and Social Care qualification. The BTEC First qualification you achieve at the end of your course will have one of the following titles, depending on how many credits you obtain:

▶ Edexcel BTEC Level 1/Level 2 First Award in Health and Social Care

▶ Edexcel BTEC Level 1/Level 2 First Certificate in Health and Social Care

▶ Edexcel BTEC Level 1/Level 2 First Extended Certificate in Health and Social Care.

Your tutor will create a learning programme that gives you opportunities to explore a wide range of health and social care topics and obtain the credits you need for the qualification you wish to gain. It is helpful to find out at the start of your course which BTEC Level 1/Level 2 First qualification you are aiming to achieve and which units you will be studying.

Each chapter in this book covers one unit from the range of BTEC Level 1/Level 2 First Health and Social Care units. The chapters will help you to succeed in the two externally tested units and also cover the assessment criteria that you need to meet when you write your internally assessed BTEC First assignments.

Features of the book

The book closely follows the specification (syllabus) of your BTEC Level 1/Level 2 First Health and Social Care qualification. This means that all of the topics and issues referred to in the course specification are fully covered. You will find the following features in the book:

▶ Chapter opener – each chapter begins with a short list of the learning aims of the unit and the topics that will be covered. This is a reminder of what the unit specification says you need to learn about.

▶ Chapter introduction – this is a short, introductory section at the start of each chapter that tells you what the chapter is going to focus on.

▶ Your assessment criteria – this green box tells you which assessment criteria are being covered by the material you are about to read.

▶ Key terms – the main ideas (concepts) and the language of health and social care are briefly explained in this feature. The key terms that are highlighted in blue in the text are explained in this blue box.

▶ Activities – there is a range of Discuss, Reflect, Participate and Investigate activities in each unit. These are designed to extend your knowledge and understanding by encouraging you to talk about, think about, take part in an activity or find out a bit more about a topic or issue you are covering.

▶ Case study – these are short examples of situations and stories from the world of health and social care. They encourage you to apply your knowledge and understanding to realistic situations that you might encounter if you worked in or used health and social care services.

▶ Assessment checklist – you will find this feature at the end of each chapter. It provides you with an opportunity to think about what you have been studying and to check and record that you have covered everything.

Assessment

BTEC Level 1/Level 2 First Health and Social Care qualifications are assessed through a combination of coursework assignments marked by your tutor and external tests marked by Edexcel-appointed examiners. You are required to demonstrate that you have met the assessment and grading criteria for each unit. The Pass, Merit and Distinction grade criteria for each unit are outlined in the assessment checklist at the end of each chapter. Your tutor may also provide you with a copy of the unit specification that lists all of the assessment criteria for a unit.

I have tried to write a book that helps you to gain an up-to-date and clear understanding of a range of health and social care topics and which also gives you a taste of what to expect from a career in the health and social care sector. Taking an Edexcel BTEC Level 1/Level 2 First in Health and Social Care course will enable you to think about both the theory and practice of care work. Hopefully you will consider taking your interest in health and social care further when you have worked through the book and completed your BTEC First qualification.

Good luck with your course!

Mark Walsh

1 | Human lifespan development

Learning aim A:
Explore human
growth and
development across
life stages

▶ Topic A.1 The different life
stages people pass through
during the life course

▶ Topic A.2 Key aspects
of human growth and
development at each life stage

Learning aim B: Investigate factors that affect human growth and development and how they are interrelated

▶ Topic B.1 Physical factors that affect human growth and development

▶ Topic B.2 Social, cultural and emotional factors that affect human growth and development

▶ Topic B.3 Economic factors that affect human growth and development

▶ Topic B.4 Physical environment factors that affect human growth and development

▶ Topic B.5 Psychological factors that affect human growth and development

▶ Topic B.6 The expected life events that can affect human growth and development and the positive and negative effects of the events on growth and development

▶ Topic B.7 The unexpected life events that can affect human growth and development and the effects of the events on personal growth and development and that of others

▶ Topic B.8 Understanding how to manage the changes caused by life events:

The different life stages people pass through during the life course

Introduction to this chapter

Human growth and development occurs in stages. A person's stage of growth and development affects their health, care and support needs. This chapter tells you about patterns of human growth and development in each life stage. You will also learn about major life events that can affect an individual's personal development.

Key terms

Development: this occurs when a person's skills, abilities and emotions become more sophisticated and complex

Growth: an increase in size or mass

Life course: a series of events and changes that an individual experiences between their birth and their death

The human **life course** is divided into six stages that people pass through.

Life course development

Human beings experience **growth** and physical, intellectual, emotional and social **development** in each main stage of the human life course. These stages are:

- infancy (0–2 years)

- childhood (3–8 years)

- adolescence (9–18 years)

- adulthood (19–45 years)

- middle adulthood (45–65 years)

- later adulthood (65+).

Life stages and change

A person has to go through the six life stages in sequence. They will experience new forms of growth and development in each life stage. This will include physical growth and development as well as intellectual, emotional and social development. Patterns of human growth and development are usually quite predictable. A person can be expected to grow and develop particular skills and abilities in each life stage.

Life stages and continuity

Human growth and development is only partly about the way a person changes in each life stage. You also need to know about factors that have an influence on growth and development in every life stage. These include:

- the **genes** a person inherits from their parents

- the **values** a person learns during childhood

- the **social skills** a person develops during adolescence and early adulthood.

Life stages and skill-building

Human growth and development includes building on a person's existing skills and abilities to develop new ones. For example, an infant must have grown enough to be able to sit up unsupported before they can develop crawling skills. Typically, a child will be able to crawl before they go on to develop the ability to walk. Each of these developments depends on physical growth occurring before they can happen.

DNA makes up our chromosomes

Case study

Sylvia Scott (aged 75) lives alone. She has an active social life and keeps herself busy looking after her garden. Neil is Sylvia's only son. He is 50 years old today and has invited his mum to a birthday lunch at a local restaurant. Neil's wife Sara (aged 48), their daughter Linda (aged 27) and her son Steven (aged 4) are all getting ready to go out for the meal. Steven is struggling to button up his shirt but can now put most of his clothes on by himself. Linda is sitting in the kitchen with her parents waiting for Steven to get ready. She is explaining that she has been to some ante-natal classes to prepare for the birth of her second child in about 12 weeks' time. Sylvia, Neil and Sara are all excited and looking forward to this moment.

1. Which life stage is each member of the Scott family in at the moment?

2. Give two examples of ways in which some members of the Scott family are experiencing physical growth.

3. What kinds of physical skills does Steven need to have to be able to get himself dressed?

Physical growth and development at each life stage

Patterns of physical growth and development

A person's body changes throughout their life, from birth until death. During infancy, childhood and adolescence most individuals experience predictable physical **growth** and achieve developmental norms, or 'milestones'. A developmental norm or milestone is a point when a particular change happens, such as when a child first sits up unaided, begins walking or says their first words.

Table 1. 1 Examples of developmental norms

Age	Ability
3–4 months	Infants can start on solid foods (when they lose the 'tongue-thrust' sucking reflex which is needed for breadfeeding), develop better head control, can roll from side to side, reach for objects
6–9 months	Teething begins, infants learn to sit unaided, lift their heads and look around, use thumb and index finger to grasp objects
9–12 months	Infants can crawl, chew food, use their hands to explore, can walk holding onto parent or furniture ('cruising'), may say a few words, know their name and start to understand their parents' words
12–18 months	Toddlers learn to feed themselves, walk unaided, can understand simple requests – 'give it to me', develop better memory and concentration
18–24 months	Toddlers can run, turn pages of a book, use simple sentences, have temper outbursts and say their own name
10 years (girls) 12 years (boys)	Puberty begins
45–55 years (women)	Menopause occurs

Physical growth and development in infancy

Infants experience rapid physical growth, quickly changing from being small, very dependent babies into much larger, stronger and more capable 'toddlers'. Infants gradually develop **gross motor skills** (sitting up, crawling and walking, for example) and some **fine motor skills** (picking up food and pressing buttons, for example).

Children grow and develop rapidly during infancy and early childhood

Mum, am I normal?

Gross motor skills

The development of gross motor skills begins with the baby gaining control of the neck muscles in order to support the head. Most babies have developed head control and can lift their head up if they are lying on their stomach. They will start to use their leg muscles by kicking, especially when lying on their back or when supported in the bath. Next the baby gains control of their arms, hands and back muscles. By the age of six months, most babies can sit up with some support and can roll over. They will start to use their arms to reach out for toys and other objects and are beginning to bear weight on their legs when held securely by an adult. The development of standing and walking requires muscle strength, balance and co-ordination. By the age of 18 months, most babies walk confidently on their own, but some will still need to hold on to an adult's hand for extra support.

Investigate

Identify a range of different toys and activities that encourage the development of gross motor skills. Give examples of two different toys or activities that could encourage the gross motor skills of:

- *a six-month-old child*

- *a two-year-old child.*

Explain how each toy or activity would encourage gross motor skills at each age.

Discuss

Ask your parents about your own early growth and development. Try to find out whether you followed the expected pattern of development, when you reached different 'milestones' and what their memories are of you as a baby and infant.

Case Study

Trevor and Cristina's daughter, Sophia, is now one year old. She can pull herself up to a standing position and can walk holding on to the furniture. She can sit by herself for long periods of time without any support and enjoys sitting on the floor to play with her toys. Cristina often takes Sophia to the park in her pushchair and pushes her in a baby swing.

1. Identify one activity Sophia does using gross motor skills.

2. How could Cristina encourage Sophia's gross motor skills?

3. What kinds of toys or activities might help Sophia to develop her gross motor skills?

By the age of two years, most children will be able to climb confidently onto furniture and walk up and down stairs, using both feet on each step. Playing outside will give toddlers lots of opportunities to practise these new skills and they will enjoy sit-and-ride toys, running around and learning how to kick a ball. As their gross motor skills continue to develop, children gain more control over their movements. Children need lots of stimulation and opportunities to practise their gross motor skills in a safe environment. Lots of praise and encouragement will also help a child to gain confidence and enjoy developing their physical abilities.

Fine motor skills

Learning to use their hands and fingers is quite a complicated task for babies and infants. It involves skills like:

- *grasping* – learning to hold objects securely and precisely (like a rattle, a pencil or a spoon)

- *hand-eye co-ordination* – learning to make their hands work together with what their eyes can see (like fitting a piece into a jigsaw puzzle or building a tower of blocks)

- *manipulation* – learning to use their hands and fingers to handle objects precisely (like screwing and unscrewing, and threading beads).

The physical changes that infants experience transform their appearance as well as their movement abilities. These changes are also needed for other forms of intellectual, social and emotional development to occur.

Physical growth and development in childhood

Young children gain greater control over their bodies and develop a range of complex physical skills during childhood. Improvements in balance control and co-ordination allow children to develop more complex physical skills, such as skipping, catching a ball and riding a bicycle. A child loses their baby shape in early childhood and gradually develops the body shape and proportions of a small adult. Most children will experience a **growth spurt** in the middle part of childhood.

Adolescence

The process of physical **maturation** that happens in adolescence is called **puberty**. **Hormones** cause the growth spurt and the physical changes that occur during this life stage. The thyroid gland and the pituitary gland are the two main glands that secrete growth and development hormones. The pituitary gland is located at the base of the brain and is only the size of a pea. The thyroid gland is located in the neck. It influences our general growth rate, bone and muscle

development and the functioning of our reproductive organs. During puberty the testes in boys produce the hormone testosterone and the ovaries in girls produce oestrogen and progesterone. These hormones control the development and function of the reproductive organs and secondary sexual characteristics that enable most males and females to produce children, and which give them their adult body shape.

Discuss

In pairs or small groups, share your ideas about outdoor play and make a list of activities that would encourage young children to enjoy the outdoors.

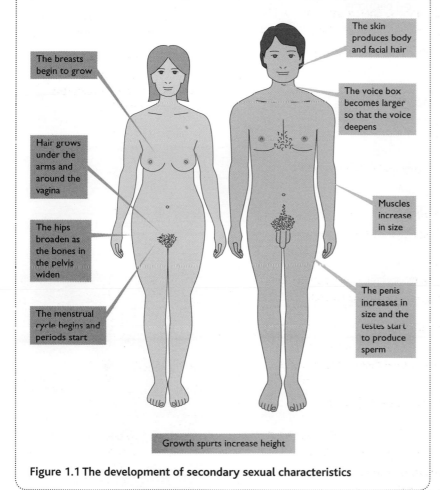

The breasts begin to grow

Hair grows under the arms and around the vagina

The hips broaden as the bones in the pelvis widen

The menstrual cycle begins and periods start

The skin produces body and facial hair

The voice box becomes larger so that the voice deepens

Muscles increase in size

The penis increases in size and the testes start to produce sperm

Growth spurts increase height

Figure 1.1 The development of secondary sexual characteristics

Table 1.2 Physical changes during puberty

Physical changes in girls	Physical changes in boys
Grow taller and heavier	Grow taller and heavier
Grow pubic and underarm hair	Grow pubic, facial and underarm hair
Develop breasts	Penis and testes grow larger
Hips broaden and shape changes	Shoulders and chest broaden, and muscles develop
Menstruation (periods) starts	Voice 'breaks' or deepens

Physical change during early adulthood

Physical changes in adulthood are not always about further growth. This is the stage of the human life cycle when **physical maturity** is achieved. However, a lot of physical development does happen in early adulthood as people use their physical potential and abilities. Most individuals are capable of achieving their maximum physical performance during early adulthood, for example. From about 30 years to 45 years, adults develop more fatty tissue, move more slowly and take longer to recover from their efforts.

Physical change during middle adulthood

From about 45 to 65 years of age, a person may experience hair loss, slower movement, reduced stamina and muscle power, reduced hand–eye co-ordination, deteriorating eyesight and wrinkles as the skin loses elasticity. These are usually referred to as the effects of the human ageing process. Women also experience the menopause during this life stage. This is the ending of menstruation and the natural ability to produce children, sometimes called the 'change of life'. It occurs because a woman's ovaries produce less and less of the hormones oestrogen and progesterone until a point is reached at which the ovaries stop producing eggs. Women experiencing the menopause sometimes suffer unpleasant physical effects of hormone changes. These can include:

- hot flushes and night sweats

- sleep disturbance

- vaginal dryness, itching or discomfort

- cystitis infections

- urgent or more frequent need to urinate.

Some women see the menopause as a signal that they are moving from young adulthood into middle age and that their youthful, reproductive years are over. This can also cause some women to reflect deeply on their past, their role in life and on their future.

Physical activity during middle adulthood has social and emotional, as well as physical, benefits for participants

Physical change in later adulthood

During later adulthood individuals experience a gradual physical decline in both the structure and functioning of their body. These changes are part of the normal **ageing process**. Older adults typically experience:

- reduced heart and lung function

- reduced mobility, often resulting from muscle wastage, brittle bones and stiff joints

- loss of elasticity in the skin and the development of wrinkles

- changes in hair colour (to grey, then white) and texture (finer and thinner)

- changes to the nervous system that may reduce an individual's sense of taste and smell, and can mean that they are less sensitive to the cold, increasing the risk of hypothermia

- some loss of hearing – quiet and high-pitched sounds (and voices!) become more difficult to hear

- eyesight changes because the lens in the eye loses its elasticity; the result is that older people find it harder to focus on close objects

- weakening of bones, also known as **osteoporosis**, as calcium and protein are lost from the bones

- loss of height as intervertebral discs in the spine become thinner and posture becomes bent.

Changes to a person's eyesight are a natural effect of the ageing process

🔑 **Key term**

Ageing process: the process of, and changes that result from, growing older

❓ **Reflect**

Can you think how one or more of these physical changes could affect the care needs of an older person? Why would it be important for a care worker to know about these changes?

🔑 **Key term**

Osteoporosis: a bone disease that leads to an increased risk of fracture

Intellectual, emotional and social development at each life stage

Using the PIES approach

Human growth and development affects every person in a range of ways. As well as growing and changing *physically*, each person experiences intellectual, emotional and social development throughout their life. The so-called PIES approach to development focuses on each of these four areas of human growth and development.

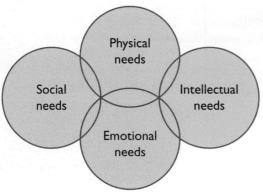

Figure 1.2 PIES

Intellectual development

Intellectual, or **cognitive**, development changes a person's thinking, memory, problem-solving and language skills and occurs in every life stage.

Infancy

Infants begin learning about themselves and the world through their senses (touch, hearing, sight, smell, and taste) and through physical activity. An infant handles, listens to and looks at things and will often put new objects into their mouth as a way of learning about them. By two years of age, most infants point at and can name familiar objects when they see them ('dog' or 'bus' for example) and can join a few simple words together ('go park' or 'shoes on', for example).

Case study

Luke is 18 months old. His mum, Cheryl, spends most time with Luke looking after him at home whilst his dad, Simon, is out at work. Cheryl has recently started taking Luke to a playgroup one day a week. Luke really enjoys this. He likes running around, using the toys and playing alongside other children. Luke likes toys that he can pick up and hold, like teddies and small building blocks, as well as toys that he can push and move about, like toy cars and trains. Luke also likes dogs a lot. He will point and say 'dog' whenever he sees a dog on the television or when he is the park or in his pram.

1. With whom is Luke likely to have formed the strongest attachment relationship?

2. How will going to playgroup help Luke's social development?

3. Is Luke's language development appropriate for his age? Give reasons for your answer.

Early childhood

Children develop the ability to think about objects and concepts that are not actually there in front of them. This allows them to learn numbers, letters of the alphabet and colours, for example. In early childhood, children ask lots of questions about their environment and the society in which they live. By the end of childhood, a child will be able to use adult speech easily and will have vastly improved their knowledge and thinking skills.

Adolescence

Abstract thinking skills develop during adolescence. This allows a person to think about things in a theoretical or hypothetical way. For example, mathematical equations involve abstract thinking, as does thinking about what you would like to do in the future. Children do not have abstract thinking skills so they can't plan ahead in the same way as adolescents.

Early and middle adulthood

People use experience to develop their thinking and problem-solving skills during adulthood. Most adults use abstract thinking, have a good memory and can think very quickly. An adult's intellectual skills and abilities can be developed further through education and training, and by problem-solving at work and in other everyday life situations. Acquiring new knowledge and skills is necessary to cope with the changes that frequently occur in an adult's personal life – such as having children or changes at work.

Key terms

Abstract thinking: the ability to think about and apply complex ideas

Concepts: another term for ideas

? Reflect

How have your memory and problem-solving skills developed since childhood? What kinds of intellectual skills do you have now that you didn't have in childhood?

Later adulthood

Older people maintain and use their intellectual abilities in much the same ways as adults because they need mentally stimulating activities. Thinking speed and response time decline in later adulthood, but usually intelligence and mental ability are not lost. Life experience can, in fact, improve an older person's thinking and problem-solving skills. An older person may, for example, become wiser and may make better judgements as a result of their experiences. Only a minority of older people who develop **dementia-related conditions** lose their intellectual abilities. People with these conditions develop memory problems and become confused more easily. Dementia-related conditions can also result in sufferers gradually losing speech and other abilities that are controlled by the brain.

Emotional development

Emotional development is concerned with a person's feelings. Love, happiness, disappointment and anger are examples of emotions that we gradually learn to recognise, understand and take into account in our relationships with others. Emotional development is a lifelong process that involves:

- becoming aware of your 'self'
- developing feelings about your 'self'
- working out your feelings towards other people
- developing a self-image and personal identity.

Infancy

A child should develop feelings of trust and security during infancy. A secure and consistent **attachment relationship** with parents or main caregivers in the first year of life is needed for this to happen. The parental response to this emotional linking is known as **bonding**. Newborn infants cry when they are frustrated or uncomfortable, and make cooing noises when they are happy. As they develop, infants learn to express their feelings through facial expressions, body movements and, eventually, through speech.

Early childhood

Learning to control feelings like anger, jealousy and frustration, and dealing with disapproval of 'naughty' behaviour is part of emotional development during this life stage. Nurturing a child's emotional

Key term

Dementia-related illnesses: a group of diseases that result in gradual loss of brain function

Investigate

In pairs or as part of a small group, carry out an investigation of the kinds of social and educational opportunities that are provided for older people in your local area. Further education colleges, community education services and the University of the Third Age, as well as private sector providers, may all offer courses and other learning activities for older people. Summarise your findings by suggesting how an older person may benefit from using each of the services you find out about.

Key terms

Attachment relationship: an emotionally close, secure relationship with a parent or carer

Bonding: a very close emotional link between two people

development by offering love, acceptance and respect is also important. Parents, siblings, teachers and friends all play a part in this process. Most children gradually increase their self-confidence, make friendships and become a little more independent at primary school. Children learn to co-operate and can appreciate the viewpoints and feelings of others in ways that infants cannot. This enables children to play together, to join groups and take part in team games.

Adolescence

Adolescence can be an emotionally eventful time. Hormonal changes can cause mood swings and intense emotions. Developing a personal identity, making friendships and experiencing emotional support from peers and family members are important concerns in adolescence. Adolescents often experiment with intimate personal relationships with members of the opposite sex, and sometimes the same sex, as they explore their sexuality and the positive and negative emotions that result from close relationships. Adolescence is a period when individuals develop greater understanding of their own emotions, as well as the thoughts, feelings and motives of others.

Self-concept (or self-image) and **self-esteem** are important developmental issues during adolescence. Self-image is a mental picture that an individual has of themselves. It gradually develops as the person becomes aware of their physical, intellectual, emotional and social abilities and attributes. This awareness is developed through interacting with others. When an adolescent talks about their self-image they often compare themselves with others. Self-esteem also results from the way we compare ourselves with other people. Adolescents who compare themselves negatively with others, thinking they are not as good, attractive or capable as others, are more likely to have low self-esteem. Adolescents who are confident, who accept that they have both strengths and weaknesses, and who feel loved and wanted, tend not to undervalue themselves so much, and usually have higher self-esteem as a result.

Adulthood

Adults are expected to be emotionally mature and to have more self-control and self-awareness than adolescents. Despite this, adulthood can still be emotionally challenging and eventful. Marriage, divorce, parenthood and increasing work responsibility, and the loss of elderly parents, are life events that may affect emotional development during adulthood. For some people, middle age is a period of contentment and satisfaction. For others, it is a period of crisis and concern about what will happen in later adulthood.

Key terms

Self-concept: another term for personal identity

Self-esteem: a person's sense of their own worth or value

Reflect

When was the last time that you felt an emotion really strongly? Which emotion (anger, happiness, anxiety, for example) was this? Did you learn anything about yourself or other people as a result of this experience?

Design

Produce a diagram or a poster that identifies events which can be emotionally challenging during adulthood. You should indicate which emotions might result from each of the key events you identify.

Later adulthood

Older people often reflect on their achievements and past experiences as a way of making sense of their life. This can involve coming to terms with changing family relationships as children move into early and middle adulthood, with the death of partners or friends, and with the ending of previous life roles (work and personal roles). Older people do continue to develop and change emotionally as they experience new life events and transitions, such as becoming grandparents and retiring from work. An older person may also have more leisure time to build relationships with friends and family members. Despite this, insecurity and loneliness can occur if an individual's social contacts are reduced and they become isolated.

Social development

Social development is concerned with the relationships we create with others, the social skills we develop and with **socialisation**.

Infancy

Attachment to and bonding with a parent or carer is needed for a first social relationship to occur. A person's ability to form satisfying friendships and intimate attachments later in their life is strongly influenced by the quality of their very first relationships in infancy. An infant will gradually expand their social circle by forming relationships with other family members and perhaps with neighbours' children. The development of social skills and relationships is strongly influenced by the infant's emerging **communication skills**.

Early childhood

Children need to make relationships with people from outside of their own family to develop socially. A child will develop social skills by learning to co-operate, through communicating and by spending time with new people. As a child grows older they are able to choose their own friends and will want their peers to like and approve of them. Parents and teachers also promote social development by teaching children about acceptable ways of behaving, how to relate to others in everyday situations and why it is important to make and keep good relationships with others.

 Key terms

Communication skills: abilities and behaviours that allow people to interact with each other

Socialisation: the process of learning the attitudes, values and culture, or way of life, of a society

Adolescence

Adolescents strive to achieve a personal identity that distinguishes them from their parents. Relationships with peer groups, close friends and other people outside of the person's immediate family become more important during adolescence. Wearing the right clothes, listening to the right music and being seen in the right places with the right people all become important issues for many adolescents. Entering employment, through part-time work or training, and learning to drive are also ways of developing and demonstrating independence during later adolescence.

Because of their need to fit in and belong, adolescents can be vulnerable to peer group pressure. This can lead some adolescents into uncomfortable activities and situations (such as experimenting with alcohol, drugs and sex), which they find difficult to resist or challenge.

Early adulthood

Leaving home is usually good for a young adult's social development. It often results in an individual making new relationships through their work and social life. Adulthood is also the life stage when people focus on finding a partner and beginning an intimate relationship. Marriage or **cohabitation** can also lead to new responsibilities and an increase in a person's range of friends. Much of adulthood is concerned with trying to find a balance between the competing demands of work, family and friends.

Middle adulthood

Social development during middle adulthood often focuses on an individual trying to achieve their position in society. Middle-aged people also make adjustments to some of their existing relationships as children leave home (the 'empty-nest syndrome'), ageing parents become unwell or infirm and they retire from work. These changes in social relationships can result in changes to an adult's self-concept.

Later adulthood

Many older people are very good at keeping up their friendships and other social relationships. However, loss of health, retirement from work or the death of a partner or close friends can make this difficult. Some older people become isolated as a result. Social development does occur in old age where people have opportunities to participate in social activities and meet others in social situations.

? | Reflect

How do young people in your local area dress and style their hair to fit in with their peers (and differentiate themselves from their parents)?

✎ | Key term

Cohabitation: *'living together' without being married*

Physical factors that affect human growth and development

Which physical factors affect growth and development?

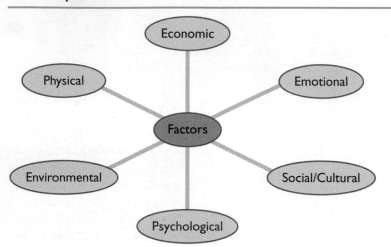

Figure 1.3 Factors affecting human growth and development

The **genes** we inherit, our diet, the amount and type of exercise we undertake, whether we smoke or consume alcohol to excess, and the illnesses and diseases we experience are all examples of physical factors that can affect our growth and development.

Genetic inheritance

The genes that we inherit from our parents play a very important role in controlling our physical growth, appearance and the abilities we develop. Each cell in the human body contains two sets of 23 **chromosomes** – one set from each parent.

Each chromosome can contain up to 4000 different genes. These are the 'instructions' or codes that tell our body's cells how to grow. The genes that control how we grow are a unique combination of our biological parents' genes. A person can do very little to change their physical features and growth potential. Because of your genetic inheritance, you will grow and develop to look like one or both of your parents as your body responds to the 'instructions' in your genes.

Genes also carry a lot of information that affects growth and development throughout life. A person's genes are often responsible for the illnesses, disabilities and diseases that they develop. This is because the risk of getting conditions like heart disease, cancers and strokes can be inherited. A person born into a family with a history of heart disease is at greater risk of developing this condition if they have inherited 'heart

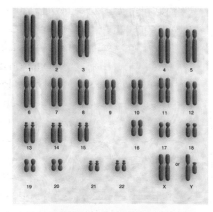

The chromosomes we inherit from our parents contain detailed genetic information that affects our growth and development

disease genes'. Whether this person goes on to develop heart disease or not will depend on many non-genetic factors too. Lifestyle, for example, will be a key influence for a person in this position

Lifestyle choices

A person's lifestyle, expressed through their attitudes, behaviour and choices, can have a significant impact on their health and development. The lifestyles of people who enjoy good health and wellbeing can be very different to those of people who are in poor health or whose lifestyle increases the risk of them experiencing health problems. An individual who eats a balanced diet that is sufficient to meet their growth and energy needs, who exercises regularly and who avoids smoking, substance misuse and excessive consumption of alcohol has a healthy lifestyle. An

Diet is one of the lifestyle choices that affect human growth and development

individual whose lifestyle choices lead them to consume an unbalanced diet and excessive amounts of alcohol, and to misuse of substances – while avoiding all exercise – is at much higher risk of experiencing illness, disease and development problems.

Illness and disease

Many of the illnesses that we experience are short-term and treatable. Coughs, colds and even broken limbs can all be cured with the right medicine and treatment, and don't have any lasting impact on growth or development. However, some illnesses and diseases can have much more serious consequences. Genetic diseases, such as haemophilia, Down's syndrome and cystic fibrosis, are all life-long conditions that cannot be cured and which have an impact on a person's growth and development. Infectious diseases, such as tuberculosis, meningitis and HIV, can also cause significant and permanent damage to a person's health and development, and may prove fatal if left untreated. Degenerative conditions, such as Alzheimer's disease, multiple sclerosis and arthritis, tend to affect people's health and development opportunities in adulthood or later adulthood. As well as having a severe physical impact, degenerative conditions such as these can also have a major impact on a person's social relationships, result in emotional distress and destroy their intellectual abilities.

 Investigate

Use library sources or the Internet to find out about the genetic causes of haemophilia, Down's syndrome and cystic fibrosis, and the effects of each condition on growth and development.

Social, cultural and emotional factors that affect human growth and development

The influence of play

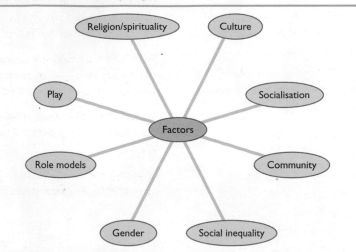

Figure 1.4 Social and cultural factors affecting human growth and development

During the early stages of development, infants and young children play a lot. Play promotes development in a number of ways. For example, children's play changes from the solo and **parallel play** of infancy to **associative** and **co-operative play** during childhood. Children use play to extend their social relationships, develop interaction and co-operation skills, and to develop their imagination. Play also provides lots of opportunities to develop gross and fine motor skills, and to build physical strength and stamina.

Culture

We often take **cultural** influences, such as the way an individual dresses, their diet and the types of relationships they form, for granted – we think they are just the 'normal' or right way of doing things. However, in a multicultural society like the United Kingdom people do develop differently due to cultural differences.

A person's culture also includes their religious and spiritual beliefs. Religions such as Islam, Judaism, Hinduism and Christianity provide believers with guidance on how best to live their lives. Many religions also set out rules about health, lifestyle and moral issues ranging from relationships and marriage to diet, personal hygiene and abortion. In a similar way, an individual's health beliefs, behaviour and relationships can be strongly influenced by the attitudes, values and traditions of the community that they belong to.

Key terms

Associative play: *play based on imitation and pretending*

Co-operative play: *a form of play that involves children working together for the same purpose*

Culture: *the shared beliefs, values, language, customs and way of life of a group of people*

Parallel play: *this happens when children play alongside, but not directly with each other*

What type of play is this?

Investigate

Use the Internet, the library or other sources of information to investigate cultural differences in diet, family relationships or the influence of religion on an individual's development. You should identify a cultural group different to your own, find out about the type of diet, family relationships or religious beliefs associated with this group and describe how this might influence the development of a person from that cultural group.

Gender

A person's sex refers to whether they are biologically male or female. Gender refers to the behaviour society expects from men and women. In Western societies girls are socialised to express 'feminine' qualities such as being kind, caring and gentle. This leads to assumptions that women should look after children, cook and do non-manual work. In contrast, boys are socialised to express 'masculine' characteristics such as being boisterous, aggressive and tough. This leads to assumptions that men should go out to work, do physical, manual jobs and be decision-makers. Parents, schools, friends and the media all play a part in gender socialisation.

The gender expectations that an individual experiences influence the way their identity develops, how they relate to others and the opportunities that may be open to them. The idea that boys and men should experience better opportunities than girls and women – especially in education and employment – because they are the 'superior sex' is not as powerful as it once was. However, gender does still play an important part in an individual's intellectual, social and emotional development because ideas about socially acceptable ways for men or women to behave remain very powerful in society.

Role models

The media, including newspapers, television, radio and the Internet, can have a powerful effect on the ideas and images that people develop about themselves and each other. Parents are often concerned about television programmes showing violence or negative behaviour that may affect their children's development. The use of gender, racial and ageist stereotypes and celebrity role models is also a concern for people who see the media as having an influence on the development of children and young people. At the same time as having a potentially negative influence on an individual's development, the media can also be used positively to deliver health education and promote healthy living.

Social isolation

Individuals who are socially isolated tend to lack family relationships and a support network of friends and neighbours. People can become socially isolated when they age and get infirm, when they experience mental health problems, and when they lack the social skills and self-confidence to make effective relationships. Social isolation can also result from bullying during childhood and adolescence. A socially isolated person is likely to feel stressed, depressed, lonely and have low self-esteem.

Key terms

Gender: a term used to describe the social and cultural expectations of males and females

Role model: a person who has the qualities or characteristics that others admire, want to have and imitate

Social skills: the talking, listening and relationship skills a person needs to communicate and interact with others

Socialisation: the process of learning the values, ideas, practices and roles of a society

Stereotype: a simplified, over-generalised view or description.

Do these pictures show gender stereotypes?

Economic factors that affect human growth and development

More than money?

Personal development can be affected by a number of economic or money-related factors. In particular, economic factors have a strong influence on the kinds of opportunities that a person is able to enjoy in each life stage.

Key term

Poverty: having insufficient money to afford everyday items such as food, heating and housing costs

Income and wealth

Income is the money that a household or individual receives. People receive money through working, pension payments, welfare benefits and other sources such as investments. The amount of income that an individual has, and the things they spend it on, can have a big impact on their personal development because it affects the quality of life available to them. People with a good income are likely to have better educational and leisure opportunities, and will live in better circumstances than people who have insufficient income and who may be in **poverty**. Having better opportunities and little or no money-related stress puts some individuals and families in a position to make the most of their abilities and potential. The reverse is the case for poorer people.

Poverty and material possessions

People who have a very low income and who experience poverty are more likely to suffer ill-health and to have restricted opportunities for personal development. The following quotation explains this.

'Poverty means staying at home, often being bored, not seeing friends, not going to the cinema, not going out for a drink and not being able to take the children out for a trip or a treat or a holiday. It means coping with the stresses of managing on very little money, often for months or even years. It means having to withstand the onslaught of society's pressure to consume ... Above all, poverty takes away the building blocks to create the tools for the future – your 'life chances'. It steals away the opportunity to have a life unmarked by sickness, a decent education, a secure home and a long retirement. It stops people being able to plan ahead. It stops people being able to take control of their lives.'

(C. Oppenheim and L. Harker (1996) *Poverty: The Facts*, 3rd edn, Child Poverty Action Group)

Employment status and occupation

Having paid employment is the way most adults in the United Kingdom obtain their income. However, some jobs provide better incomes, better working conditions and have a greater status than others. A person's employment status determines their **social class**; people in higher status employment are allocated to higher social class groups. As well as providing income, a person's job may influence their self-concept, their intellectual development, and their social and emotional development. Having a high status occupation and stimulating work is likely to have a positive effect on personal development. Working in very difficult or stressful conditions, a low status job or in an environment where employers and colleagues are not supportive or friendly may have a negative effect on self-esteem and personal development.

Key term

Social class: *people with the same economic, social or educational status*

The type of work a person does affects their income and status in society

Case study

Kieran Goff, aged 42, is a solicitor. He has never been unemployed. Kieran worked part-time in shops and on building sites while he was studying to become a solicitor. He is very proud of his employment record and of the high status that his job gives him. This is particularly important for Kieran because he comes from an estate where very few people went to college or university and where over half of the men are unemployed at any one time. Kieran was determined to escape from this situation. He believes that he has succeeded in life because he worked very hard and was very determined to achieve his goals. Kieran still sets himself challenges and says that he is 'driven to succeed'. He believes that he can do most things if he sets his mind to it.

1. How would you describe Kieran's self-esteem?

2. In what way does Kieran's job affect his self-concept?

3. Which aspect of Kieran's personal development has been affected most by his determination to become a solicitor?

NEETs

NEET is an abbreviation or shortened term used by the government to refer to young people aged 16 to 24 who are 'Not in Education, Employment or Training'. In 2007, 20% of young people in England, Wales and Scotland were NEETs. In Northern Ireland this was 14%. NEETs are sometimes seen as 'teenage drop outs' and are associated with crime and teenage pregnancy, particularly by politicians and parts of the media. Children who truant or who are excluded from school are most likely to become NEETs and are then more likely to experience youth and long-term unemployment, low self-esteem and have a higher risk of developing mental health problems.

Physical environment factors that affect human growth and development

Physical environment factors

A range of factors within the physical environment can affect human growth and development. These include the quality of a person's housing, as well as air and noise pollution.

Housing conditions

A person's housing provides them with physical shelter and protection. This is important for physical health and development. For example, lack of adequate heating, dampness and overcrowding can lead people of all ages to develop respiratory (breathing) disorders, stress and mental health problems. Children who live in overcrowded homes are more likely to be victims of accidents. People with low incomes sometimes have to choose between buying food and heating their homes. The consequence of not having enough heating can be hypothermia (a fall in body temperature to below 35°C; normal body temperature is 37°C). It is also important to note that a person's home also provides them with a sense of emotional wellbeing and psychological security, so housing can affect an individual's emotional development too.

Rough sleeping has a very bad effect on both physical and mental health

Case study

April is three years of age. She lives with her mum in a small cottage three miles from the nearest town. April's mum is an artist who works at home, creating pictures and cards that she sells at local markets. Despite being a talented artist, April's mum earns very little money from her work and relies on child benefit and income support to pay the bills. The cottage where they live is damp and isolated. As a result, April frequently gets colds and chest infections, is underweight and has no friends of her own age. April's mum is worried about her daughter's health and has started looking for somewhere new to live, closer to town, as she believes that their current living conditions are harming April's health and development.

1. Explain why the housing conditions April lives in may have a negative effect on her health and development.

2. How is April's mum trying to influence the way in which she develops?

3. Describe two features of a new home that would be good for April's health and development.

? Reflect

What is healthy housing? Identify the features you feel are important in making a person's housing 'healthy'.

Pollution

Usually, though not always, **pollution** involves the release of high concentrations of a harmful substance, such as human sewage or chemicals, into the environment. Pollution can remain in the environment for a long time, causing health problems for whole populations for many years.

Pollutants can affect the air, sea, waterways and land. Factories and cars that produce carbon-based fumes are common sources of air pollution. People often associate pollution with the smoke and fumes that we can see in the environment. However, some air pollutants are less visible. For example, 'acid rain' is ordinary rainwater that has become acidic after picking up residues of sulphur and nitrogen oxides that are produced by cars, power stations and other factories, often located long distances away from where the rain falls. Acid rain is thought to make respiratory problems, such as asthma, worse because it irritates surface membranes in the lungs.

Noise pollution

Noise pollution occurs when human or machine-made sound disrupts the activity or balance of a person's everyday life. Transport systems (particularly cars, airplanes and trains) are the main source of noise pollution. People who live in densely populated residential areas may also experience noise pollution, especially if they live near to industrial buildings.

Noise pollution lowers the quality of life of those people who are exposed to it. **Chronic** (long-term) exposure to excessive noise is linked to **tinnitus**, increased stress levels, disturbed sleep patterns and hearing loss. The World Health Organisation (2008) has also produced research linking noise pollution to premature death from heart disease that is triggered by exposure to excessive levels of noise. It estimated that 3030 of the 101,000 deaths from coronary heart disease in the UK in 2006 were caused by chronic noise exposure. The WHO guidelines on noise pollution say that chronic exposure to noise of 50 decibels or more – light traffic noise, for example – may lead to cardiovascular problems. People who are exposed to 42 decibels or more are likely to experience sleep disturbance.

Key term

Pollution: contamination of natural surroundings (including the air, water and landscape) with poisonous or harmful substances

---

Sources of noise pollution

1. Car engines and alarms
2. Airplanes
3. Trains
4. Audio entertainment systems
5. Power tools and construction work
6. Office machinery
7. Factory machinery
8. Domestic appliances
9. Lighting hum
10. Barking dogs
11. Noisy people

Key terms

Chronic: another term for 'ongoing' or 'long-term'

Tinnitus: a noise, typically ringing, buzzing or whistling sounds, heard in the head or in one or both ears, even though there is no obvious cause of the sound

Psychological factors that affect human growth and development

Psychology and human development

Psychological factors influence a person's feelings about themselves.

Family relationships

The family is often seen as the foundation of society because of the key role it plays in human development. Our family relationships ensure that we are provided for, supported and protected as we grow and develop. For example, an individual's family:

- *provides* them with informal education and **socialisation** during infancy and childhood

- *supports* them emotionally, socially and financially from infancy through to adulthood

- *protects* their health and wellbeing by giving informal care, advice and guidance in every life stage.

Relationship problems

Relationship problems are likely to have an impact on a person's social and emotional development. Relationships in the family can become stressful for a range of reasons. Tensions that arise in a couple's relationship may cause both partners a lot of stress and can also have an impact on their children. Problems with the behaviour of children and teenagers can also cause difficulties that everyone in the family feels.

Negative family relationships can affect a person's emotional development and wellbeing.

Growing up in care

Children who grow up in care are more vulnerable to the problems and challenges of adolescence. Dealing with sexuality, peer pressure and the general confusions of puberty can be much more difficult without the support of a parent or close family. As a result young people who grow up in care are more likely to experience teenage pregnancy, to become

Key term

Socialisation: the process of learning the values, ideas, practices and roles of a society

Investigate

Using an Internet search engine, find the Who Cares? Trust website and look through 'Helping Children in Care to Thrive'. This provides information and stories about the experience of young people growing up in care.

involved in alcohol and substance misuse, to be excluded from school and to achieve fewer and lower grade qualifications. Children and young people who grow up in care situations also worry about the **prejudices**, discrimination and bullying that can result when others view them in a negative way. Supportive foster parents and teachers can provide stable relationships for children in care; many of those who grow up with foster parents or in care homes believe that their lives improved when they were taken into care.

Friendship patterns and relationships with partners

Friendships play an important role in a person's social and emotional development. As we move into early childhood, we increase our range of friendships. Friends can feel especially important during adolescence when young people are trying to forge an identity separate from their parents. During this life stage, peer groups become influential in a person's social and emotional development. Adolescents often want to belong to a group of like-minded friends and have a strong need to be liked, respected and accepted by their peers. In adulthood, friendships remain important because they usually form the basis of an individual's social life outside of the family. Friendships in later adulthood can be a vital source of companionship and connection to a person's past.

Throughout life, an individual's personality, social skills and emotional development are all shaped by their friendships. Friendship enables people to feel they belong, are wanted and liked by others and that there are people they can turn to for support. However, if an individual is bullied or rejected by their friends or peer group, they can lose self-confidence and suffer low self-esteem.

Stress

Stress is what we feel when we are challenged or threatened by the demands that other people or situations place on us. The more we feel unable to cope, the more stressed we become. Extreme stress can lead to a range of physical and mental health problems. These include eczema, asthma, high blood pressure and migraines, as well as anxiety and depression.

Stress can be experienced during any life stage. A high stress level will have an impact on a person's emotional development because of the negative feelings that it causes. A person's social development may be affected if their stress level causes difficulties in their relationships with others.

Key term

Prejudice: a negative, hostile belief about an individual, group or issue that is based on a lack of knowledge, wrong or distorted facts

Reflect

Make a list of all the current and past friendships that have influenced your personal development. Try to identify how each friend has influenced you — positively or negatively.

Reflect

What are the most common sources of stress nowadays? List all the sources of stress that you can think of. What are the best ways of reducing stress? Identify as many stress-reduction strategies as you can.

Understanding life events

Life events are turning points in life that impact on the individual's personal development. Some life events, such as starting school, getting a job and getting married, occur in a predictable or expected way. Other life events, such as serious illness, divorce and redundancy, are unexpected. Every individual's development is affected by the life events they experience. The impact of life events can be:

- *positive* – such as when a person gets married, starts school or succeeds in getting a job that they want. In situations like this, a person's self-confidence and emotional wellbeing may be boosted.

- *negative* – such as when a partner, relative or close friend dies. In a situation like this, a person's emotional wellbeing may decline due to the sadness and grief that they feel as a result of their loss.

Life events can result in significant change in a person's life because of the need to adapt to or overcome them.

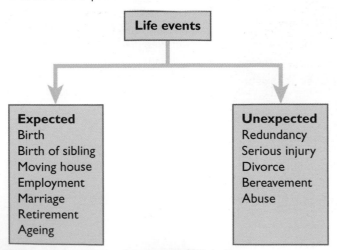

Life events

Expected
Birth
Birth of sibling
Moving house
Employment
Marriage
Retirement
Ageing

Unexpected
Redundancy
Serious injury
Divorce
Bereavement
Abuse

Figure 1.5 Expected and unexpected life events

Key term

Life event: an important, significant change that affects the course of a person's development

Reflect

Make a list of the main events that you think have affected your personal development since early childhood. Which of these life events were expected and which were unexpected?

Starting, being in and leaving education

Starting school or nursery is one of the first expected life events that a child experiences and is very significant for personal development. Beginning nursery or primary school:

- promotes physical and intellectual development through learning and play

- provides opportunities for social and emotional development through friendships and regular contact with other children and adults.

A child's self-confidence, relationships, communication skills, and knowledge and understanding of the world around them will all change as a result of going to nursery and starting school. However, some children see this as a negative life event because they are anxious about leaving the security of their parents. Despite some tears and tantrums, most children do adjust and come to see going to nursery and school in a positive way.

Moving house or location

Moving house is a stressful life event for many people. It can mean a break with the past and perhaps with friends, neighbours and the security of familiar surroundings. Home is usually a place that people associate with safety, security and stability in their lives. The practical demands of organising the removal of possessions, arranging finance to cover the cost of moving, and perhaps buying a house or flat, can all make this feel more emotionally difficult.

> **? Reflect**
>
> *Can you remember what your first day at primary school was like? If not ask a parent or other carer how you reacted on your first day and how you changed as a person during your first year at school.*

> **? Reflect**
>
> *Make a list of the reasons why a person may move house. Think about reasons why people choose to move as well as reasons why people are forced to move. In each case, describe the possible impact that moving might have on an individual who has to move house for the reason you have identified.*

Entering and being in employment

Everybody finishes studying at school, college or university at some point in their life. Most people then enter employment. Starting work affects personal development because it:

- requires people to behave more independently without the support of parents or teachers

- can involve training and the development of work-related skills that promote intellectual development

- can lead to new social relationships and social skills through time spent with work colleagues

- leads to changes in self-confidence and identity as an individual gains experience, gets promoted and achieves higher status positions in their field of work.

Living with a partner, marriage and civil ceremony

Marriage is a life event that generally occurs in early adulthood. Couples are usually very positive about their future together when they first get married. However, both individuals have to adapt to their new relationship and marital roles, and may find that their relationships with friends and family members change as a result of their marriage. Moving in together or entering a civil partnership may have similar effects on personal development.

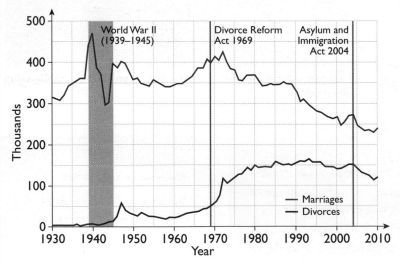

Source: Office for National Statistics (2010)

Figure 1.6 Number of marriages and divorces in England and Wales, 1930–2010

 Investigate

What does the data in Figure 1.6 reveal about the patterns of marriage and divorce in England and Wales between 1930 and 2010?

Parenthood

The birth of a child is a life event for both the parents and the brothers and sisters of the baby. New relationships are formed and existing relationships, between parents and older brothers and sisters, change as a result of the birth. For many children, the birth of a **sibling** is an exciting and happy event. However, some children become jealous and feel a need to compete for their parents' affections.

For many people becoming a parent is a very emotional moment that motivates them to try to be the best possible mum or dad. However, for others, parenthood can be an unwelcome burden that causes them stress, mental health difficulties or leads them to neglect or abuse their child because they cannot cope with the pressures of parenthood. New parents also have to adapt their own roles and relationship to cope with the needs of a dependant child. Some people are able to offer their partner practical and emotional support, strengthening their relationship. Other people find that they are unable or unwilling to do this, leading to relationship difficulties and even the breakdown of the marriage. Parenthood can result in a major change in a person's identity as they adapt to their new 'mum' or 'dad' role.

Parenthood can be both a very positive and a very challenging life event

Retirement

Retirement is a third life event linked to a person's working life. For people who have been very committed to their work, and whose work provided their social life, retirement can result in too much time to fill and the loss of contact with work friends. Retirement can also cause financial problems. State and occupational pensions usually provide less money than a salary. For many older people, retirement can be the beginning of financial hardship. For other people who have planned for their retirement and who have other interests and friendships, retirement can offer new opportunities, provide more time to enjoy hobbies and more time to enjoy the company of friends and family. These people may welcome retirement as a positive life event.

🔑 Key terms
Sibling: a brother or sister
Retirement: the point at which people end their working career

Unexpected life events and their effects on personal growth and development

Understanding unexpected life events

Imprisonment can have a major effect on a person's emotional and social development

Unexpected life events, such as sudden bereavement, illness, injury or imprisonment often involve a loss of some sort and may occur at unpredictable moments in a person's life.

Death of a partner, relative or friend

Feelings of bereavement usually accompany the death of a partner, relative or friend (or even a pet) and can affect a person's social and emotional development. Sometimes a person's death may be anticipated

Key term

Bereavement: the deep feelings of loss that people experience when someone to whom they are emotionally attached, such as a partner, relative or friend, dies

Reflect

Which aspects of a person's development are most likely to be affected by bereavement and loss?

because of their old age or a terminal illness. In other cases, however, a person's death can be sudden and unexpected. Bereavement can result in:

- **acute** emotional distress (confusion, crying, anger)

- loss of self-confidence and emotional insecurity as the person adjusts to life without their partner, friend or relative

- the loss of friendships and other social contacts if the person who died played a significant part in the individual's social life.

Most people are able to adjust to their loss once they have grieved for the person who has died. However, bereavement can also have long-term effects that are damaging to a person's emotional wellbeing, mental health and social relationships if they are unable to adapt to life without their loved one.

Key term

Acute: sudden and usually short-term

Case study

Laura and Ian decided to go on holiday to Costa Rica as a way of celebrating their first wedding anniversary. They were really enjoying their first week away, taking part in snorkelling and diving trips, and just enjoying themselves on the beach. At the beginning of their second week, Ian and Laura went out for a meal to a beachside restaurant. Both had some wine to drink and agreed that this was their best holiday together. On the walk back to their hotel, Ian persuaded Laura that they should go for a quick swim in the sea. Neither of them knew the beach or that there were dangerous tides in the area. Ian quickly got into trouble. Laura lost sight of him in the waves but managed to get herself back to the beach despite the strong tide pulling her out to sea. Ian's body was washed up on another beach the next morning. Laura says that she thinks about the incident every day and is still grieving for Ian. She hasn't returned to work since the incident six months ago, takes anti-depressant tablets to help with her mood and is beginning to lose touch with friends who have tried hard to support her.

1. What kind of life event has Laura experienced?

2. Describe the impact of Ian's death on Laura's emotional wellbeing.

3. Which care practitioners might be able to provide help and support for Laura?

Accidents and injury, ill-health

An unexpected, serious injury can have a dramatic effect on a person's health, development and lifestyle. Serious injury can affect:

- physical development and wellbeing, particularly if the injury or illness affects a person's ability to look after themselves or live independently

- intellectual development if the injury or illness affects a person's ability to learn or use their existing skills

- emotional development if the person is traumatised by the injury or illness, or experiences problems in adapting to the change in their life

- social development if the individual finds that their relationships with others change because they, or their friends, are unable to adapt to their new situation.

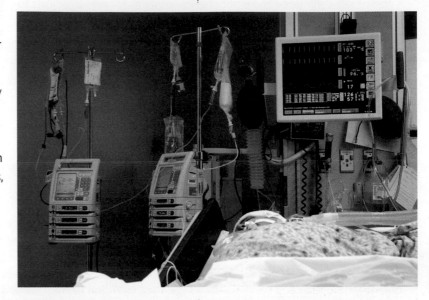

Accidents that cause serious injury can affect a person's development at any stage of their life. If an injury is serious it may cause a permanent or a temporary problem, depending on the potential for recovery. Some serious injuries can result in a long-term disability, such as loss of sight, hearing or the loss of a limb. This may mean that the person has to adapt their skills and lifestyle – if they are no longer able to move, pick up and hold things or manage personal hygiene and toilet needs without assistance, for example. Friends, family and colleagues may also have to adjust their relationship with the person to take account of the disabled person's new situation.

Imprisonment

Adults who are sent to prison experience disrupted personal relationships and family lives, often leading to relationship and family breakdown. Imprisonment tends to have a negative effect on a person's self-esteem and self-concept. There are higher rates of mental health problems within the prison population, some of which result from the shock and stress of imprisonment. Prisoners tend to smoke more than average, eat poorly and take less exercise than the population as a whole.

 Investigate

Use the Internet or library resources to investigate the impact that a spinal injury can have on an individual's health and wellbeing. Use your findings to produce a short leaflet or poster that describes the physical, intellectual, emotional and social effects that this kind of serious injury can have.

On release, many former prisoners find their employment opportunities are reduced and that they have few sources of social support to help them readapt to ordinary life. This can lead to a repeating cycle of reoffending and reimprisonment.

Exclusion and dropping out of education

Being excluded from school and dropping out of education are linked to:

- higher rates of unemployment and low-paid work

- a higher risk of teenage pregnancy

- a higher risk of becoming involved in alcohol and substance misuse

- higher rates of behavioural and mental health problems

- higher rates of offending and criminal convictions

- lower self-esteem and poor self-image.

Children and young people who are excluded from school or who drop out of education early are often already experiencing high levels of family disruption and social disadvantage. Their exclusion from school may, in fact, result from existing behavioural problems, abuse or substance misuse that have not been addressed.

Promotion, redundancy, unemployment

Work can also affect personal development when a person loses their job because they are made **redundant**. Redundancy can lead to:

- loss of self-confidence and self-respect

- loss of status and identity

- increased stress levels

- problems with sleeping, eating and mood

- loss of social relationships with work colleagues

- increased strain in personal and family relationships.

Losing a valued job can take away a person's usual routine, the structure of their day and leave them wondering about their own worth and abilities. However, even though the loss of a job may be unexpected, some people find that it is a positive turning point in their life where they are able to identify a new direction and pursue new opportunities.

 Key term

Redundancy: this happens when an employer decides that a job is no longer required and ends the employment of the person who does that job

Understanding how to manage the changes caused by life events

Types of support

Major events in people's lives, such as going to school, starting work, marriage, divorce and bereavement, can result in significant change and disruption to a person's everyday life, relationships and identity. To deal with, and even benefit from, life events an individual needs to identify sources of support, and ways of coping and adapting. The four main types of support available are:

1. **formal support** from trained care professionals and care organisations

2. **informal support** from family, friends, partners and colleagues

3. *emotional* support in the form of supportive relationships, guidance and listening

4. *physical* support in the form of practical help and assistance.

Sources of support

Family support is often the first form of help that people seek when they experience a major life event. Families may be able to provide physical and emotional support at times of stress, change and crisis, and are the source of a lot of informal care for people in all age groups. People need support from their families at different stages in their lives. Marriage is a major life event in which parents (or other relatives) may provide both emotional and financial support for their adult children, for example. Similarly, parenthood and bereavement are occasions when family members may need to support each other emotionally, practically and financially.

Voluntary groups and organisations

Some individuals experiencing difficult life events may make use of the support services and professional skills offered by community groups and voluntary organisations. Support can be obtained from organisations such as the Citizens Advice Bureau, Relate (the marriage guidance agency) and MIND (the mental health charity), for example. These organisations enable people to obtain information and guidance, and provide opportunities for people to talk through the different options available to them.

Professional support

Professional support can also be obtained from health and social care workers, such as district nurses and social care workers, who are trained and qualified to deal with complex difficulties. Where people need financial help and advice, support is available from professionally qualified advisers, banks, building societies and government departments such as the Department of Social Security.

Faith-based organisations

Faith-based organisations, such as churches, mosques, synagogues and other religious groups, provide support to members of their local community who are experiencing social and emotional problems. The services of voluntary and faith-based groups are usually free or low-cost. The services offered are wide-ranging and include advice and guidance, information-giving, counselling as well as a range of practical help to meet specific needs.

Key term

Faith-based organisations: *religious organisations that provide support and assistance for people in need*

Discuss

In a small group, or with a partner, discuss the support needs a person may have if they were faced with each of the major life events listed below. Write down examples of the types of support that may help a person to cope with each situation:

- *the break up of a marriage or long-term relationship*
- *leaving school or college with no job to go to*
- *family moving to a new area of the country*
- *being involved in a car crash*
- *sudden loss of eyesight*
- *being promoted to a very responsible position at work*
- *leaving home to go to university or to live with friends*
- *the birth of a first child*
- *being made redundant*
- *failing to get the exam grades that are needed for a job*
- *the death of a close relative or friend*
- *being diagnosed with a serious illness*
- *the onset of puberty*
- *winning the National Lottery jackpot*
- *being sent to prison*
- *starting employment*
- *moving from primary to secondary school*
- *getting married*
- *getting into serious debt*
- *a parent develops Alzheimer's disease*
- *retiring from work after 40 years in the same job.*

2 | Health and social care values

Learning aim A:
Explore the care values that underpin current practice in health and social care

▶ Topic A.1 Defining and demonstrating care values

Learning aim B:
Investigate ways of empowering individuals who use health and social care services

▶ Topic B.1 Empowering individuals

Defining and demonstrating care values

Introduction to this chapter

Health and social care values underpin good practice in all areas of health and social care work. This unit will introduce you to:

- a number of important health and social care values

- the importance of care values in health and social care practice

- ways of applying care values in practice to empower individuals who use services.

What are care values?

Care values are beliefs about the right ways to treat people who use care services. Health and social care workers need to understand and demonstrate a number of different care values in practice, including confidentiality, dignity and respect.

Confidentiality

Confidentiality is a key care value for all health and social care workers. Confidentiality involves making sure that only people who need to know, or have a right to know, have access to confidential information relating to an individual or their care needs.

Confidentiality is not about keeping things secret. It is about sharing, transmitting and storing information about individuals in ways that are appropriate to their care needs. This means that confidential information can be shared with care team colleagues if they need to know. Beyond this, a health or social care worker must consult the individual and respect their wishes about who should be informed or given access to information about them. The different types of information that health and social care workers are expected to treat as confidential concern issues like an individual's:

- physical and mental health status and history

- personal details to do with their identity, such as religion and sexual orientation

- physical measurements such as weight and height

- test and investigation results, such as blood and urine tests, and x-rays

- family information to do with relationships and personal history

- financial and legal matters.

Your assessment criteria:

1A.1 Identify how care values are used to support users of services

2A.P1 Describe how care values support users of services, using relevant examples

1A.2 Demonstrate the use of care values in a selected health and social care context

2A.P2 Demonstrate the use of care values in selected health and social care contexts

Key term

Confidentiality: protecting the privacy of information

Reflect

Have you ever been given some information 'in confidence'? What do you think the person giving you the information expected of you when they said this?

Safe storage of records

Confidential information about individuals who use care services should be safely and securely stored, either in a manual (paper-based) or electronic (computer-based) record-keeping system. In care settings where manual record-keeping systems are used, the physical security of information can be protected by:

- keeping confidential information in a locked cupboard or cabinet in an area of the workplace that is discreet and only used by specific members of staff

- making sure that visitors to the care setting are not allowed into any area where records are stored or may be seen

- never leaving care records, notes or reports open in public areas of the care setting and ensuring that staff cannot be overheard when making or receiving telephone calls about individuals or care-related issues.

Confidential information relating to individuals is now often created and stored electronically on computer-based devices. Computers, mobile phones and memory sticks are examples of electronic information storage systems. **Encrypting** files protects the security of this kind of confidential computer-based information. The only people who can access this material are those with approved passwords or security codes. Health and social care workers can ensure information in electronic storage systems remains safe and secure by:

- always protecting and never sharing their computer password or security code with others at work

- ensuring that they close files and log-off properly when they have finished reading or adding information to an individual's computer-based files

- changing their password or security code regularly and never writing it down

- working on one record at a time and saving work regularly to ensure that information is not entered in the wrong record, or is lost if they are distracted or called away

- only using an individual's initials and giving minimum personal information about them in a 'public' communication

- using only computers and other devices provided by their employer to record and store confidential information about individuals.

 Key term

Encrypting: putting information into a coded form

Not discussing confidential information

There are times in care work when it is important to keep information about service users to yourself. For example, if a child at the your placement nursery swore at you and misbehaved one afternoon, you would be breaching confidentiality to reveal this to your friends or partner. Similarly, if an individual asks you questions about someone's health or personal circumstances, you should not give them any confidential information. You should not breach confidentiality in situations where an individual has a right to privacy or where their comments or behaviour do not cause anybody harm or break the law. If health or social care workers gossip or talk publicly about events or issues that happen at work, they are betraying the trust of service users and co-workers.

Not sharing information without written permission

Health and social care workers should assume that information relating to an individual's health, social problems or personal circumstances is confidential. As a consequence, they must not share this information with others unless they receive the explicit, usually written, consent of the individual. There are many circumstances where a health or social care worker will come under pressure to share confidential information with others who are not entitled to know it. This may happen, for example when:

- a partner, relative, friend or neighbour of an individual phones or asks in person for confidential information about them or their care and support

- a police officer, council official or employer, for example, requests confidential information about an individual's health, wellbeing or circumstances.

Health and social care workers should always decline to give confidential information about an individual to these or any other people or organisations unless they have the written permission of the individual to do so. The best thing to do in situations like this is for the health or social care worker to make a note of the request and to refer it to their manager or supervisor who can then decide how best to deal with it.

Members of a care team often need to share information about service users' care and treatment

When must confidentiality be broken?

Occasionally, the normal rules about confidentiality have to be broken. This happens when the need to protect an individual, or to protect others, overrides the need to keep information private. The information may be something a care worker knows about a person or something they have witnessed. For example, confidentiality must be broken when:

- a person is at risk of harm, such as showing suicidal behaviour

- a person has committed, or is about to commit, a crime

- the health or safety of others is at risk

- abuse of a child or adult is disclosed or suspected

- a court orders certain information to be disclosed.

In these situations a health or social care worker should share confidential information with other people, such as co-workers, the police or with a doctor, who can act to keep the person, or other people, safe.

Investigate

Go to http://www.nmc-uk.org to find out what the Nursing and Midwifery Council tell nurses and midwives about the importance of confidentiality in health care practice.

Discuss

Read the following confidentiality situations. For each scenario, explain:

1. why confidentiality may be important to the individual

2. the dilemma facing the health or social care worker

3. whether you would break confidentiality and why.

- *Darren has an appointment with the school nurse for a BCG booster injection. He's worried that it will make him ill. He says that he's just taken some ecstasy and pleads with the nurse not to tell anyone.*

- *Jennifer goes to her GP for contraceptive pills. She asks her GP not to tell her parents. She is 14 years old.*

- *Eileen has terminal cancer. She tells her district nurse that she's had enough of living and is going to end her own life tomorrow. She says it is her choice and asks the district nurse not to interfere.*

- *Yasmin tells her new health visitor that her boyfriend is violent towards her. She asks the health visitor not to say anything to anyone as she is frightened of what might happen. Yasmin and her boyfriend have a three-month-old baby.*

- *Lee turns up at a hostel for the homeless. He says that he has run away from home because his father has been beating him. He asks the social worker not to contact his family. He is 16 years old.*

- *A man with a stab wound arrives at the hospital casualty department. He won't give his name and asks the nurse not to phone the police. He says that he will leave if she does. He is bleeding heavily.*

Dignity

Dignity in relation to care involves treating people as individuals and enabling them to maintain the maximum possible level of independence, choice and control over their own lives.

Dignity in practice

Health and social care workers should always treat the individuals they provide care or support for in a dignified way. For example, an individual should always have privacy when personal care is being provided. Most people would feel it is undignified to be exposed to the view of others when they are being dressed, undressed, taken to the toilet or helped to wash. Health and social care workers can take simple precautions such as closing doors, keeping curtains drawn and not leaving individuals partially dressed when others may walk in or see them. Knocking before entering a room and checking that it is alright to come in is much more respectful than simply throwing the door open and carrying out tasks without asking.

Preserving someone's dignity through appropriate actions is a very important way of showing the person that you value them as an individual. It also shows that the health or social care worker acknowledges the individual's rights, whatever their needs, problems or personal difficulties.

Respect

Showing respect for individuals and their families is a very important part of health and social care work. Everybody who uses a health or social care setting or service should be valued and respected, whatever their physical characteristics or their social or cultural background. People feel respected when:

- they are treated as equals while having their individual needs, wishes and preferences recognised

- their beliefs, culture and traditions are acknowledged as an important part of who they are

- health and social care workers use inclusive, non-discriminatory language that avoids **stereotypes**, **prejudices** and **stigmatised** words

- health and social care workers are non-judgemental and discuss a person's particular needs, problems and concerns in an open-minded way

- others show interest in their cultural and religious traditions and take part in an appropriate way in celebrating festivals and events that are significant for them and their community.

Your assessment criteria:

1A.2 Demonstrate the use of care values in a selected health and social care context

2A.P1 Describe how care values support users of services, using relevant examples

2A.P2 Demonstrate the use of care values in selected health and social care contexts

Key terms

Prejudice: unreasonable or unfair dislike or negative beliefs about an individual or group of people

Safeguarding: protecting an individual against danger, damage or injury, for example

Stereotype: a simplified, over-generalised view or description of a person that doesn't take into account their individual characteristics or differences (e.g. 'all young women are …')

Stigmatised: marked out or described as bad or negative in some way

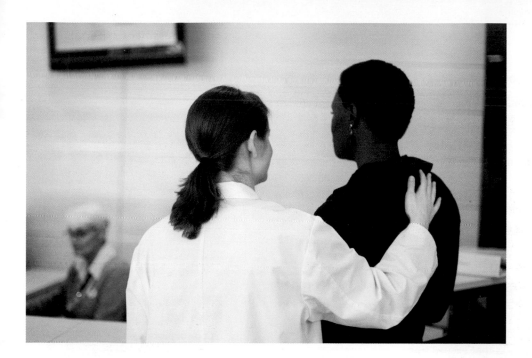

Safeguarding individuals

Most adults can protect themselves from threats of harm – they are not vulnerable to abuse or neglect – and can meet their own daily living and care needs. However, some adults and children who use health and social care services may need safeguarding. This means that these individuals are, for a variety of reasons, at greater risk of (or may have already experienced) abuse or neglect, or are unable to meet their own needs independently. To safeguard individuals from danger and harm, health and social care workers should:

- be aware of any signs or indicators of abuse or exploitation

- establish supportive, trusting and respectful relationships and ensure individuals feel safe and able to communicate their concerns or disclose distress

- ensure that their own health and hygiene does not pose a threat to the health and safety of others, and that they manage their personal safety at work

- follow the infection control, moving and handling, accident and waste disposal procedures set out in their employer's health and safety policies

- make use of any risk assessments that have been carried out to minimise health and safety hazards

- respond appropriately to security risks in the workplace

- report health and safety, and security issues to relevant people.

Your assessment criteria:

1A.1 Identify how care values are used to support users of services

2A.P1 Describe how care values support users of services, using relevant examples

1A.2 Demonstrate the use of care values in a selected health and social care context

2A.P2 Demonstrate the use of care values in selected health and social care contexts

Key term

Safeguarding: *protecting an individual against danger, damage or injury, for example*

Investigate

Go to the Social Care Institute for Excellence (http://www.scie.org.uk) website and put the term 'safeguarding' into the search box to find out more about safeguarding vulnerable adults in care and community settings.

Duty of care

Health and social care workers owe a **duty of care** towards those they support and care for. This means that a care worker should do all they reasonably can, at all times, to act in the best interests of these people. Health and social care workers do this by:

- putting the needs and interests of clients at the centre of their thoughts and actions

- always ensuring that what they do, or don't do, will not be harmful to the health or wellbeing of the people they support or care for.

Health and social care workers fulfil their duty of care by:

- developing the knowledge, understanding and skills needed to perform their work role well

- working within their own level of competence and not taking on or agreeing to carry out tasks that exceed this

- following the agreed ways of working within their care setting that are outlined in their employer's policies and procedures

- following current and relevant **codes of practice** relating to their area of health or social care work.

Duty of care dilemmas

Health and social care workers sometimes face a dilemma because their duty of care towards an individual conflicts with the individual's rights. For example, a care worker has a duty of care to:

- ensure an individual's rights are always upheld

- always act in the best interests of the individual.

However, what should a care worker do if a service user decides to do something that the care worker considers dangerous, or not in the person's best interests? This might involve taking part in an adventure activity like horse riding, rock climbing or bungee jumping, or it could be something as simple as wanting to go out alone for a walk or to the shops. Alternatively, it might involve a very serious life-changing decision, such as to try independent living or refusing treatment.

Ideally, the care worker will be able to find a way of balancing the individual's right to make their own choices with the risks involved in the activity. In a situation where the care worker is not sure what to do, they should always seek advice and support from their manager or supervisor before making a decision.

Your assessment criteria:

1A.1 Identify how care values are used to support users of services

1A.2 Demonstrate the use of care values in a selected health and social care context

2A.P1 Describe how care values support users of services, using relevant examples

2A.P2 Demonstrate the use of care values in selected health and social care contexts

🔑 Key terms

Code of practice: *a document setting out standards for practice*

Duty of care: *responsibility for the safety and wellbeing of another person*

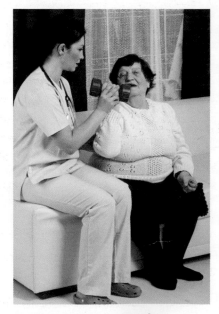

Person-centred approaches tailor treatment to meet each individual's particular needs

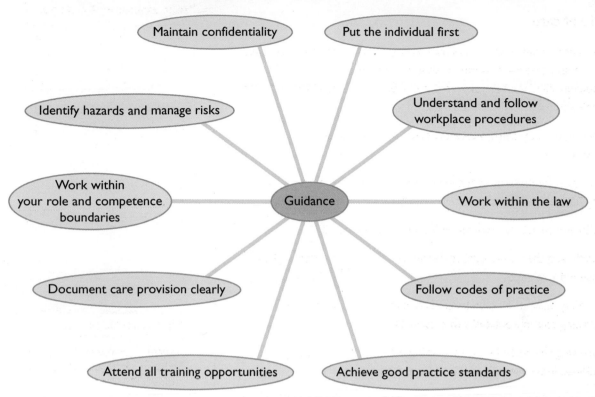

Figure 2.1 Guidance for care workers on duty of care dilemmas

Person-centred approaches to care delivery

Health and social care workers who adopt a **person-centred approach** aim to deliver care and support that respects each person's values, needs and preferences, and which offers them real choice. The principle underlying any person-centred approach to care or support is that the individual plays a central role. Individuals are involved, as much as they are able and want to be, in every aspect of their care or support. This may include the assessment of their needs, care delivery or support planning. All policies, procedures and care practices in a person-centred care setting should put the people receiving care or support at the centre of day-to-day activity.

Health and social care workers who use a person-centred approach to practise focus on understanding:

- who the person they are caring for or supporting is

- who the important people are in the person's life

- what they and other members of the care team can do in partnership with the individual to achieve a better life for that person, now and in the future.

Every individual has a different life story, needs, wishes and values, so it is important to understand these as a way of putting the person at the centre of the care planning and delivery process.

 Key term

Person-centred approach: *care that focuses on an individual's particular needs and wishes*

Empowering individuals

Empowering vulnerable people

Health and social care workers play an important role in service users' lives. Often, this is because care service users are unable to meet their own health or daily living needs without support. However, health and social care workers should always try to ensure that individuals receiving care and support don't become too dependent on them. If this happens, an individual may lose important self-care and decision-making abilities that are needed for independent living. Health and social care workers can empower people who have care needs by:

- promoting active and full participation, taking any potential difficulties into account

- planning person-centred care, considering individual rights, preferences, needs, likes and dislikes

- working in partnership with individuals receiving care or support to promote their autonomy

- promoting and supporting choice

- adapting their communication skills.

Promoting active and full participation

An active participation approach in health and social care involves treating the people who use services as active partners in the care-giving process. This is a 'working with' approach rather than a 'doing things to' approach. Active participation prevents individuals from becoming passive recipients of care or support services. To encourage active participation, health and social care workers need to:

- put the individual's goals, wishes and preferences first to promote their wellbeing

- use positive working practices to focus on what the individual *can do*

- find and adapt resources, services and facilities that meet the individual's particular PIES needs

- work in partnership with the individual and other important people including family and professionals.

When it happens, active participation benefits the individual in various ways (see Figure 2.2 on page 55).

(see Figure 2.2 on page 55).

Your assessment criteria:

1B.4 Describe how an individual's circumstances can be used to create a care plan that empowers the individual

2B.P3 Describe ways in which care workers can empower individuals using relevant examples from health and social care

2B.P4 Explain why it is important to take individual circumstances into account when planning care that will empower an individual, using relevant examples from health and social care

---

Key terms

Active participation: *enabling and supporting an individual's direct involvement in planning and meeting their care needs*

Empower: *giving the opportunity or power to do something*

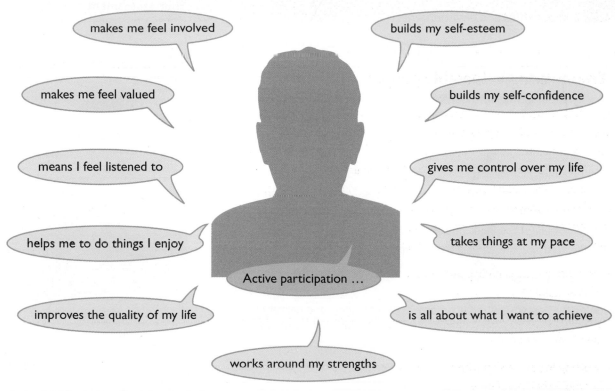

Figure 2.2 How active participation helps me

The speech bubbles around the central figure read:
- makes me feel involved
- builds my self-esteem
- makes me feel valued
- builds my self-confidence
- means I feel listened to
- gives me control over my life
- helps me to do things I enjoy
- Active participation …
- takes things at my pace
- improves the quality of my life
- is all about what I want to achieve
- works around my strengths

Case study

Kyle is 24 years old, has physical and learning disabilities, and lives at home with his parents. He attends a day centre each day. One weekend a month, and for one week every two months, he stays at a local residential care home to give his parents a break. Kyle's mobility is limited and he tires quickly. Kyle uses signing to communicate and has some verbal skills. The people who know him say that he has a good sense of humour, is great fun to spend time with, and only becomes cranky when he is tired. He is also determined and patient, has a meticulous approach to detail, and is creative. His key worker has been working on a support plan with Kyle and his parents. Kyle has expressed a wish to get a job working with plants, as he loves growing things. He knows that to do this he will need to get a qualification. Kyle's key worker and his parents helped him to research this and they have found a course at a local college.

1. What strengths, skills or interests does Kyle have that his key worker could focus on as part of an active participation approach to working with him?

2. What barriers do you think may exist to Kyle's active participation?

3. How would Kyle's care worker help reduce these barriers?

Adapting activities and environments

An individual's physical, sensory or learning disabilities, or their mental health problems, dementia and other conditions may limit their ability live independently. The barriers that individuals face in meeting their own needs and living independently can sometimes be overcome by adapting activities and environments. For example, adapting buildings and a person's home can empower those with mobility problems or other physical disabilities to live independently. Adapted equipment and technology can also be used to enable individuals with learning disabilities to take part in care or daily living activities. Health and social care workers should always consult the individuals they work with to find out about the kinds of assistance or support that the person requires to overcome barriers to participation.

Planning person-centred care

Adopting a person-centred approach to care planning and delivery is an effective way of encouraging active participation. Person-centred approaches make health and social care workers focus on the needs, wishes and abilities of each individual. Person-centred relationships are also empowering for those receiving care because:

- users of services are treated as individuals with specific needs, interests and preferences that are recognised and valued by health and social care workers

- every individual is seen as deserving of respect, regardless of their personal or social characteristics.

The main aim of a person-centred approach is to ensure that the individual receiving care or support is placed at the centre of the process. The person should be involved in all aspects of their care or support, including assessment of their needs, the planning of care or support and the delivery of any services or interventions. A **care plan** should always contain information on:

- an individual's assessed care needs

- the person's circumstances and current level of support

- the required outcomes (what they need to keep them safe and healthy)

- the individual's views about the desired outcomes (what they want)

- planned forms of support or interventions

- timescales for implementing and reviewing the care plan.

Your assessment criteria:

1B.4 Describe how an individual's circumstances can be used to create a care plan that empowers the individual

2B.P3 Describe ways in which care workers can empower individuals using relevant examples from health and social care

2B.P4 Explain why it is important to take individual circumstances into account when planning care that will empower an individual, using relevant examples from health and social care

Key term

Care plan: a document that details an individual's care needs and wishes, how these will be met, and who is involved in meeting those needs

Reflect

Can you think of reasons why individualised care plans are always part of the person-centred approach to care?

A person-centred care plan will also contain information about the:

- individual's views regarding their needs and circumstances

- the individual's own priorities

- the individual's strengths, interests, likes and dislikes

- way the individual wants to live their life

- ways the individual prefers to have their needs met

- people who are important to the person and who provide their support network.

Care plans that are not person-centred tend to focus on the services that an organisation can provide, rather than on the services the person needs or prefers. These service-focused care plans don't take account of individuality or an individual's preferences. This can result in impersonal care and a disempowering approach that neglects an individual's needs. All person-centred policies, procedures and care practices should put the people receiving care or support at the centre of day-to-day activity.

Overcoming difficulties in promoting person-centred care

Person-centred care that focuses on the particular needs of an individual is generally seen as positive: something that health and social care workers should aim to deliver. However, health and social care workers may face a number of difficulties in promoting and delivering care that is person-centred. For example, barriers to person-centred care can result from:

- a lack of funding to pay for the equipment or other resources needed by an individual

- difficulty in finding suitably qualified or experienced staff to deliver specialist care or support services

- the competing needs of other service users who also require the time, attention and skills of health and social care workers and whose care has to be paid for out of a limited budget

- the physical limitations of a care or domestic environment that cannot be adapted or modified to meet an individual's needs.

Health and social care workers should always consult and work closely with individuals to offer care and support services that are enabling and empowering. However, care planning and delivery must also take into account the availability of resources and the challenges of adapting to an individual's circumstances and problems.

Working in partnership

Ideally, the relationship between a health and social care worker and an individual using care services should be a partnership. The individual receiving care should feel equally involved in, and empowered by, this relationship. This means that the focus of the relationship should be on collaboration and consultation – working with and on behalf of individuals, not doing things for or to them. There are a number of different types of partnership in health and social care work. These include partnerships with:

- colleagues or co-workers
- practitioners from other agencies
- people receiving care or support
- the partners and families of the people receiving care.

Partnerships with individuals receiving care should be empowering so that people can make as many decisions as they wish and do as much as they can for themselves. Encouraging and supporting individuals to be involved in their own care and support, and to take as much control as possible is a crucial way of helping them to maintain their skills and self-esteem.

Promoting and supporting choices

Like most people, you probably take it for granted that you should have the opportunity to make choices in different areas of your everyday life. This isn't the case for some people when they make use of health or social care services. Being presented with choices can be a new and confusing experience for some service users. Other people may be denied choices or can be prevented from making their own decisions because of the way health and social care workers and care organisations function. As a basic principle, individuals receiving care or support should always be encouraged to make their own choices and decisions on the basis of their own wishes and preferences. Health and social care workers can promote and support service user empowerment and choice by:

- finding out each individual's likes and dislikes
- providing active support while encouraging each individual to do what they can for themselves
- giving people different options for both large and small-scale decisions
- adapting activities and the care environment to meet the individual's specific needs, and helping them to take part as much as possible in care, leisure or domestic activities.

Your assessment criteria:

1B.4 Describe how an individual's circumstances can be used to create a care plan that empowers the individual

2B.P3 Describe ways in which care workers can empower individuals using relevant examples from health and social care

2B.P4 Explain why it is important to take individual circumstances into account when planning care that will empower an individual, using relevant examples from health and social care

 Discuss

Imagine that you were admitted to hospital and were dependent on others to meet your basic care needs. Which aspects of your care and everyday life would you want, or expect, to be given choices about? Discuss this with a class colleague or in a small group.

In order to support an individual to make an informed choice a health or social care worker needs to:

- understand the individual's needs and abilities

- provide the person with relevant information

- explain how each choice may benefit or suit the individual

- explain what the person may lose by making each choice

- ensure that they are objective in the way they present each choice

- give the individual time to consider their options

- check that the person understands each choice available to them.

Case study

Lianne arrived at Mrs Al Hammed's house to help her have a bath. She had never met Mrs Al Hammed before since she was standing in for her colleague Deirdre, who was on holiday. Mrs Al Hammed, who was not expecting to see a new person, was in bed when Lianne let herself in. Lianne thought that Mrs Al Hammed was 'a bit grumpy' and later said that she 'didn't speak to me in a polite way'. Lianne and Mrs Al Hammed were soon at odds over whether she should take a bath.

Lianne had already run the bath, had chosen some clothes for Mrs Al Hammed and had collected together some towels and toiletries. She then said 'you need to have a bath now' to Mrs Al Hammed who remained in bed. Mrs Al Hammed said something in reply that Lianne didn't understand. She could see that Mrs Al Hammed 'looked a bit annoyed with me'. Lianne asked Mrs Al Hammed to 'co-operate' telling her 'I'm just doing my job'. Despite this Mrs Al Hammed remained in bed. Lianne left after Mrs Al Hammed said 'leave my house'; she later reported 'the problem' to her supervisor.

1. Identify the care values that Lianne should have used in her interaction with Mrs Al Hammed.

2. How, if at all, has Lianne offered Mrs Al Hammed a choice in the way her care is provided?

3. Suggest ways in which Lianne could have empowered Mrs Al Hammed in this situation.

Adapting communication skills

People from a diverse range of social and cultural backgrounds use UK health and social care services. As well as speaking different languages and having differing cultural beliefs, users of health and social care services have diverse communication needs. An individual may, for example, have a hearing or visual impairment, a health problem or a learning disability that affects their ability to communicate effectively with others. Other users of care services may speak English as a second or additional language, and may have a different preferred language.

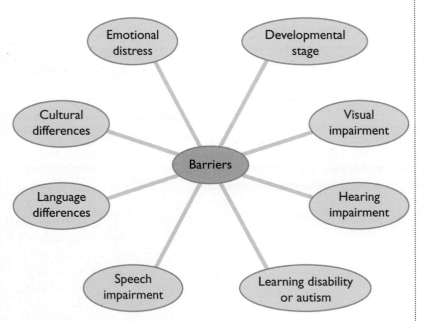

Figure 2.3 Barriers to effective communication

Health and social care workers need to know about the ways in which these factors can act as barriers to communication (see Table 2.1 on page 61). It is important for the health or social care worker to use an individual's preferred method of communication, or to make use of communication support services and specialist equipment to enable the individual to communicate effectively. Refer to Chapter 3, pages 79 and 80, for more information on overcoming communication barriers.

Your assessment criteria:

1B.4 Describe how an individual's circumstances can be used to create a care plan that empowers the individual

2B.P3 Describe ways in which care workers can empower individuals using relevant examples from health and social care

2B.P4 Explain why it is important to take individual circumstances into account when planning care that will empower an individual, using relevant examples from health and social care

 Investigate

Dysarthria is a speech disorder resulting from neurological, or brain, injury. Use library or Internet resources to find out how dysarthria affects an individual's communication ability.

Table 2.1 Barriers to communication and their impact

Type of barrier	Impact on communication
Developmental stage	A person's developmental stage could limit their ability to communicate and may be a barrier to effective communication if this is not taken into account when choosing words. Don't use long sentences, complex words or unusual phrases with young children or individuals with learning disabilities, for example.
Sensory deprivation and disability	Visual impairment may reduce a person's ability to see faces, written signs and leaflets. Hearing impairment may limit conversation. Conditions such as cerebral palsy, stroke, cleft palate, Down's syndrome and autism tend to limit a person's ability to communicate verbally and non-verbally, and difficulties interpreting non-verbal communication are typical of autism.
Language and cultural differences	The UK is a multicultural country with a mix of different ethnic groups and a range of language communities. English may be a second or even third language for some children and adults, and may not be spoken or understood at all by others. Communication in written and spoken English may not be easy or even possible for people in this situation. Similarly, people from different cultural groups may interpret non-verbal behaviour in different ways, misunderstanding messages.

How can you overcome communication barriers?

Barriers to communication can often be overcome, or are at least reduced, when a care worker:

- is able to use the individual's preferred method of communication

- makes use of appropriate communication support services or equipment.

If a child or adult has difficulty communicating in English, or has sensory impairments or disabilities that affect their communication skills, specialist communication support may be needed. Learning a few words of another person's language or developing some basic sign language skills can also really help a care worker to establish a positive, supportive relationship with a service user, their relatives or with colleagues.

Your assessment criteria:

2B.P4 Explain why it is important to take individual circumstances into account when planning care that will empower an individual, using relevant examples from health and social care

2B.M2 Discuss the extent to which individual circumstances can be taken into account when planning care that will empower them, using relevant examples from health and social care

---

 Discuss

In a small group, identify as many ways as you can of helping people to overcome language and cultural differences that may be a barrier to communication in a care setting. Think about different forms of communication as well as specialist skills that could be drawn on to promote effective communication between speakers of different languages and backgrounds.

Case study

Mrs O'Sullivan, aged 78, is being admitted to a residential care home for a three-week respite period for the first time. Alex, a support worker, has been given the job of meeting and showing Mrs O'Sullivan around. Alex knows that Mrs O'Sullivan has become deaf because of injuries she received in a car accident.

On arrival Mrs O'Sullivan is accompanied by her daughter and by a social worker. When Alex introduces herself to Mrs O'Sullivan, her daughter answers by saying, 'You are wasting your time. She doesn't communicate any more.'

Alex feels that she should persevere and starts her communication by making eye contact with Mrs O'Sullivan and by using non-verbal signals such as smiles. Alex hopes Mrs O'Sullivan will start to respond to her.

1. Suggest reasons why Mrs O'Sullivan may communicate less often than she used to.

2. What could Alex do to maximise communication with Mrs O'Sullivan during her brief visit?

3. What kinds of extra help and support might improve Mrs O'Sullivan's ability to communicate effectively during her three-week respite break?

Investigate

Visit the websites of the Royal National Institute for the Deaf (www.RNID.org.uk) and the Royal National Institute for the Blind (www.RNIB.org.uk). Find out about the range of services that these groups provide for people who have sensory impairments. Produce a summary of the different forms of communication support that are available to people with visual or hearing impairments.

The goals of empowerment

There is no single agreed way of empowering individuals who use health and social care services. In fact, the meaning of the term' empowerment' is often debated by health and social care workers and those who receive care services. Does it just mean providing 'help' for people or is it supposed to involve making a real difference to an individual's life? Despite the different meanings it may have, the goal of empowerment is something that health and social care organisations and their employees typically see as a good thing. Health and social care practice that aims to empower users of health and social care services generally aims to:

- promote the independence of individuals
- respect and support individuality
- promote the overall wellbeing of individuals
- encourage and support participation in all aspects of care and support.

Health and social care workers seek to empower individuals by:

- finding ways of supporting people to make decisions for themselves
- supporting people to express themselves as fully as possible
- encouraging feedback on the services that are being provided
- building trusting relationships with individuals.

Figure 2.4 identifies a range of other positive practices that can also be used to promote empowerment in health and social care settings.

Your assessment criteria:

1B.3 Identify ways in which care workers can empower individuals

2B.P3 Describe ways in which care workers can empower individuals using relevant examples from health and social care

Figure 2.4 Positive practices that promote empowerment

63

Assessment checklist

To achieve level 1, my portfolio of evidence must show that I can:

Assessment criteria	Description	✓
1A.1	Identify how care values are used to support users of services	☐
1A.2	Demonstrate the use of care values in a selected health and social care context	☐
1B.3	Identify ways in which care workers can empower individuals	☐
1B.4	Describe how an individual's circumstances can be used to create a care plan that empowers the individual	☐

To achieve a pass grade, my portfolio of evidence must show that I can:

Assessment criteria	Description	✓
2A.P1	Describe how care values support users of services, using relevant examples	☐
2A.P2	Demonstrate the use of care values in selected health and social care contexts	☐
2B.P3	Describe ways in which care workers can empower individuals, using relevant examples from health and social care	☐
2B.P4	Explain why it is important to take individual circumstances into account when planning care that will empower an individual, using relevant examples from health and social care	☐

To achieve a merit grade, my portfolio of evidence must show that I can:

Assessment criteria	Description	✓
2A.M1	Discuss the importance of the values that underpin current practice in health and social care, with reference to selected examples	☐
2B.M2	Discuss the extent to which individual circumstances can be taken into account when planning care that will empower them, using relevant examples from health and social care	☐

To achieve a distinction grade, my portfolio of evidence must show that I can:

Assessment criteria	Description	✓
2A.D1	Assess the potential impact on the individual of effective and ineffective application of the care values in health and social care practice, with reference to selected examples	☐
2B.D2	Assess the potential difficulties in taking individual circumstances into account when planning care that will empower an individual, making suggestions for improvement	☐

3 | Effective communication in health and social care

Book about mini-beasts.

Learning aim A:
Investigate different forms of communication

▶ Topic A.1: Effective communication

▶ Topic A.2: Alternative forms of communication

Learning aim B:
Investigate barriers to communication in health and social care

▶ Topic B.1: Barriers to communication and how to overcome them

Learning aim C:
Communicate effectively in health and social care

▶ Topic C.1: Communicating with groups and individuals

Effective communication

Introduction to this chapter

Health and social care workers require effective communication skills in order to work with the diverse range of people they meet in care settings. This unit will introduce you to:

- different forms of communication
- factors that affect communication in care settings
- ways of overcoming barriers to effective communication.

You will have the opportunity to observe and discuss the communication skills of others and to demonstrate your own communication skills.

Your assessment criteria:

1A.1 Identify different forms of verbal and non-verbal communication

2A.P1 Describe different forms of verbal and non-verbal communication

2A.M1 Explain the advantages and disadvantages of different forms of communication used, with reference to a one-to-one and a group interaction

2A.D1 Assess the effectiveness of different forms of communication for service users with different needs

The communication cycle

Communication is about making contact with others and being understood. You will not be assessed on your understanding of the communication cycle but it is helpful to know about the process of sending 'messages' as this underpins both verbal and non-verbal communication. We all communicate, or 'send messages' continuously. Figure 3.1 describes the communication cycle.

Discuss

With a class colleague, identify the point where the communication cycle breaks down when a) one person speaks in a language the other cannot understand and b) one person doesn't listen properly to what the other is saying.

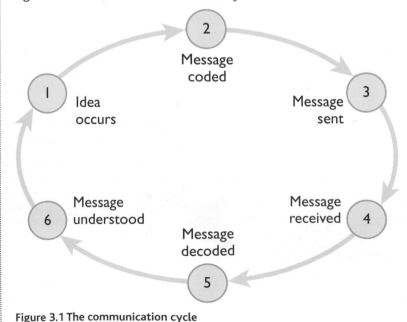

1 Idea occurs
2 Message coded
3 Message sent
4 Message received
5 Message decoded
6 Message understood

Figure 3.1 The communication cycle

Figure 3.1 shows that a communication cycle occurs when:

1. A person has an idea

2. They code their 'message' (using words or non-verbal means).

3. They send their message to someone else (by speaking, for example).

4. A second person then receives the message (by hearing what has been said or by noticing non-verbal communication, for example).

5. The second person **decodes** the message.

6. The message is understood.

Once the original message has been understood, the cycle will be repeated if the second person replies or responds. Repetitions of the communication cycle occur every time we have a conversation and are an essential part of our relationships.

 Key term

Decode: making sense of the information contained in a message

---

Case study

Charlie is 2 years of age. He enjoys helping his mum in the kitchen when she is making a meal. When she says, 'Can I get some fruit for you Charlie?' he puts his arms in the air and says, 'Me, me!' while smiling at her. His mum responds by picking him up and saying, 'Okay, you take something yourself this time, Charlie.'

1. How does Charlie's mum communicate with him in this example?

2. How does Charlie communicate non-verbally with his mum in response to her question?

3. Describe how a cycle of communication occurs in this example.

Forms of communication

Health and social care workers use different forms of communication during their working day (or night). These include the **verbal** communication skills of talking, writing and listening and various forms of **non-verbal** communication skill, such as touch, eye-contact and facial expression. A care worker has to use both verbal and non-verbal communication when they:

- give or receive information about the care that is being provided for an individual

- provide emotional support to a individual or member of their family

- carry out an assessment of an individual's care needs.

Your assessment criteria:

1A.1 Identify different forms of verbal and non-verbal communication

2A.P1 Describe different forms of verbal and non-verbal communication

 Key terms

Non-verbal: wordless forms of communication

Verbal: communication using words

Verbal communication

Verbal communication occurs when one person speaks and another person listens. A person's ability to communicate verbally develops in childhood and is generally very good by the time they reach adulthood. Health and social care workers communicate effectively when they:

- speak clearly, pronouncing words correctly and sounding the end of words

- select appropriate language when communicating formally or informally

- avoid using slang, jargon, technical terms and regional words

- select age-appropriate language, particularly when talking with children

- control the pace, tone and pitch of their speech

- use non-discriminatory language

- use active listening skills.

The communication cycle demonstrates that effective verbal communication is a two-way process. Speaking *and* listening must occur for two people to communicate. Listening is much harder than speaking, and there is more to this skill than just waiting for the other person to stop talking.

Non-verbal communication

As well as communicating through speech, people use a variety of forms of non-verbal communication (see Table 3.1). Some of these forms of communication are referred to as body language. This is because they involve the individual using their body and appearance to communicate in some way. For example, a care worker's behaviour, appearance and attitude send messages to people who receive care (as well as to colleagues) about what they think and feel. Similarly, a person's body language may tell a care worker that they are uncomfortable or experiencing pain, even when they say 'I'm okay'. Non-verbal communication provides a channel of communication that is 'always on'. Important aspects of non-verbal communication include:

- facial expression and eye contact

- touch or physical contact

- gestures and proximity.

Your assessment criteria:

1A.1 Identify different forms of verbal and non-verbal communication

2A.P1 Describe different forms of verbal and non-verbal communication

Investigate

When you have a chance to watch a group of people talking or socialising together, observe the way they use their bodies to communicate. Try to work out what they are 'saying' non-verbally.

How are these girls communicating non-verbally?

Table 3.1 Forms of non-verbal communication

Non-verbal communication	What it involves	Examples
Facial expression	Movements of the face that express a person's feelings	• Smiling • Frowning
Touch or contact	Physically touching or holding a person	• Holding someone's hand • Placing a hand on a person's arm or shoulder to reassure them
Gestures	Deliberate movements of the hands to express meaning	• Thumbs-up gesture to show agreement or pleasure • Shaking a fist to show anger or aggression
Proximity	The physical closeness between people during interactions	• Being very close may be seen as reassuring and accepting • Alternatively, this may make the person feel uncomfortable and threatened • People need less personal space (proximity) when they have a close, trusting relationship
Eye contact	Looking another person directly in the eyes	• Short or broken eye contact can express nervousness, shyness or mistrust • Long unbroken eye contact can express interest, attraction or hostility

Contexts of communication

Individual and group communication situations are the two main contexts in which health and social care workers use the communication cycle.

Individual communication

Health and social care workers talk to people who use care services, their relatives and work colleagues on a one-to-one basis many times each day. Sometimes this involves **formal communication**, though **informal communication** might be used when the care worker speaks to a colleague who is also a friend or when they know a patient or relative very well. Effective one-to-one communication requires:

• listening skills

• information-giving skills

• questioning skills.

Your assessment criteria:

1C.5 Demonstrate communication skills through one interaction in health and social care, identifying the forms of communication used

2C.P5 Demonstrate communication skills through interactions in health and social care, describing their effects

Key terms

Formal communication: *official or correct forms of communication*

Informal communication: *a casual, relaxed conversation, written note or text message, for example, that doesn't stick to the formal rules of communication*

Health and social care workers need to be able to help people talk about and express their concerns. They do this by:

- using open questions that give people a chance to talk at length, rather than to give a one-word response – 'How are you feeling today?'

- checking their understanding of what the person says to them by asking questions like 'Can I just check that you meant...'

- using **empathy** to show they understand.

One-to-one communication skills are needed for basic everyday interactions. They are also needed to establish and maintain supportive relationships with people who use care services and with work colleagues.

Participate

Role plays provide an opportunity for you to develop and practice basic communication skills in a safe, simulated situation. With a class colleague or in a small group, role-play one or more of the following situations:

- *A parent approaches a nursery nurse about obtaining a place for their child at the nursery. The parent wants to know what the nursery can offer, how the child will be looked after and what the costs will be. The nursery nurse must use verbal and non-verbal communication skills to provide appropriate information and reassurance.*

- *A patient is waiting to see their GP. The receptionist knows there is a 30-minute delay. The receptionist has inform the patient about this while also reassuring the patient that they will see the GP as soon as possible. The patient is restless, irritable and anxious. Both participants are allowed to speak but should concentrate on communicating non-verbally.*

- *A person has come for an interview at a homeless persons' unit. The housing officer needs to find out the person's details and how their accommodation needs can best be met. The homeless person is reluctant to discuss their past but wants to get off the streets because they are frightened. Both parties must use verbal and non-verbal communication skills in the interaction.*

Groups

People belong to a range of different groups including family, friendship and work groups. Health and social care workers communicate in group situations when they participate in:

- report or handover meetings where an individual's needs are discussed

- case conferences and discharge meetings

- therapeutic and activity groups

- meetings with relatives and managers of care organisations.

Your assessment criteria:

1C.5 Demonstrate communication skills through one interaction in health and social care, identifying the forms of communication used

2C.P5 Demonstrate communication skills through interactions in health and social care, describing their effects

 ## Key term

Empathy: *understanding and entering into another person's feelings*

? Reflect

Is there such as thing as 'talking properly'? What do you think about this issue?

Care workers use a range of communication skills in the work setting

The communication skills we use in group contexts are slightly different to those we use in one-to-one situations. One of the main differences is that people have to learn how and when to take turns at speaking and listening, sometimes compromising. Communication in groups can sometimes feel challenging, competitive and negative if a few members of the group dominate. However, groups can also be supportive, co-operative and productive when members respect each other, are inclusive and share information. People who are effective group members:

- make verbal contributions to the group

- listen to other group members

- respond positively to the group leader

- are open about themselves

- don't try to distract others or disrupt the main purpose of the group

- have a positive and constructive approach to other group members

- arrive on time and stay until the end of the group's meetings.

Alternative forms of communication

What are alternative forms of communication?

Do you ever communicate without speaking or using body language? Most young people do this frequently when **text messaging**. Some individuals who use health and social care services have to make use of alternative forms of communication because they have disabilities or illness conditions that prevent them from making or hearing speech, or using body language.

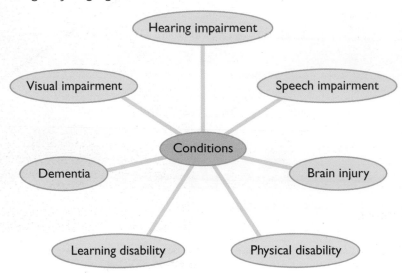

Figure 3.2 Examples of conditions that can prevent conventional use of speech and body language

People who are unable to communicate in conventional ways sometimes use alternative communication systems to send and receive messages:

• People with visual impairments often use their sense of touch to read documents written in Braille. The combinations of raised dots represent letters that can be touch-read by people who understand the Braille system.

• People with hearing impairments or learning disabilities sometimes use lip reading and sign language. Sign language systems include finger spelling (dactylography), British Sign Language and Makaton.

• A range of graphical signs and symbols is also widely used in health and social care settings to warn people of health and safety hazards, provide directions and to give information to people who are unable to speak or understand English.

Your assessment criteria:

1A.2 Identify different forms of alternative communication for different needs, using examples from health and social care

2A.P2 Describe different forms of alternative communication for different needs, using examples from health and social care

Key term

Text messaging: exchanging brief written text between mobile phones or portable communication devices

Key term

Makaton: a language system that uses signs and symbols to enable people who can't speak to communicate

Some users of health and social care services are speakers of languages other than English. Health and social care workers who are unable to speak the service user's language sometimes make use of an interpreter (English to Hindi, for example) who is able to explain what they are saying in the person's own language. Similarly, specialist translators are sometimes employed to translate documents from one language to another to overcome this kind of communication barrier.

Key term

Interpreter: a person who coverts an individual's speech, intentions and feelings from one language into another while (or just after) the individual speaks

Signs, symbols and objects of reference

Signs and symbols are used in many care settings to communicate basic information quickly. Bliss symbols are one system that is used to help people with communication, language and learning difficulties to express themselves using a speechless language. Similarly, some service users carry a personalised booklet, known as a communication passport, that contains practical information about their communication needs and preferences. This can help care workers to adapt their own communication methods to meet the person's needs. Where a person has some communication ability but requires help, an advocate may be used to support the person's efforts to communicate or to communicate on their behalf.

Objects of reference are items such as toys, clothes, jewellery or other everyday objects that represent something else. That is, they have a special meaning for somebody. For a child, a cuddly toy may represent comfort and safety. For a couple, their wedding rings may represent love and commitment. An older person may treasure their photographs because they represent and reawaken memories of family, friends and relatives. Health and social care workers need to be aware of the significance that objects of reference can have for people because they can play an important part in a person's identity and emotional life.

What is this common sign communicating?

Key terms

Objects of reference: objects that have a particular meaning for a person (such as a special brooch, ring or statue)

Symbol: an item or image that is used to represent something else

Barriers to communication and how to overcome them

Your assessment criteria:

1B.3 Outline the barriers to communication in health and social care

2B.P3 Describe the barriers to communication in health and social care and their effects on service users

A variety of factors, including hearing and visual impairment, can be barriers to communication in care settings

What are barriers to communication?

A number of factors can affect an individual's ability to communicate effectively (see Figure 3.3). These factors are sometimes also known as barriers to communication because they prevent or interfere with the person's ability to send, receive or understand a message.

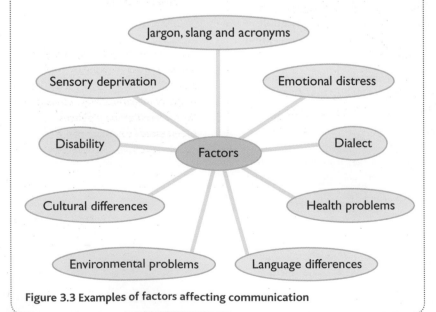

Jargon, slang and acronyms

Sensory deprivation

Emotional distress

Disability

Dialect

Factors

Cultural differences

Health problems

Environmental problems

Language differences

Figure 3.3 Examples of factors affecting communication

 Discuss

Identify an occasion when you were unable to communicate effectively because of one or more of these factors.

Environmental barriers

A physical environment that is noisy, uncomfortable, has poor lighting or which lacks privacy reduces an individual's ability to communicate effectively with others. Noisy environments affect our ability to listen and concentrate. Poor lighting can affect our ability to notice non-verbal communication and could reduce a hearing-impaired person's ability to lip read. An environment that is cramped or too small may cause people to feel frustrated and anxious, leading to aggressive or negative behaviour. Environments that lack privacy discourage people from expressing their feelings and problems.

Physical barriers and illness

Visual and hearing impairment can act as a barrier to effective communication. Health and social care workers should be alert to the additional communication needs of people with sensory impairments and disabilities. Problems with sight or hearing can mean that signs can't be seen, leaflets can't be read or conversations can't be heard, for example. Conditions such as Cerebral Palsy, Down's syndrome and autism also tend to limit an individual's ability to communicate verbally and to interpret the non-verbal communication of other people.

Mental illness

Some mental health conditions, such as depression or schizophrenia, may affect an individual's ability to communicate because they reduce the person's ability to send and receive messages effectively. Similarly, when a person is angry, aggressive or upset they may find it difficult to communicate and others may misunderstand their communication.

Physical illness

Illness and injuries can cause people to withdraw, feeling that they don't wish to see other people or talk about themselves. Medication and operations may also affect an individual's ability to speak, concentrate or use non-verbal methods of communicating.

 Investigate

Using the internet or other library sources, investigate the needs of people with one of the following conditions:

- *visual impairment*
- *hearing impairment*
- *cerebral palsy*
- *Down's syndrome*
- *autism.*

Start your investigation by going to a support group website for each type of condition. Produce a leaflet, poster or magazine story outlining the communication problems experienced by people with the condition you are investigating.

Your assessment criteria:

1B.3 Outline the barriers to communication in health and social care

2B.P3 Describe the barriers to communication in health and social care and their effects on service users

Language barriers

Britain is a multicultural country. Within the mix of different ethnic groups, people speak a range of languages. English may be a second or even third language for some people and may not be spoken or understood at all by others. If health and social care organisations only produce and display information in English and workers only speak English, some people will find it very difficult to find and use the services they need.

Similarly, people from different cultural groups interpret non-verbal behaviour in different ways and may have a differing sense of humour. This can lead to messages being misunderstood by, or making no sense to, the person on the receiving end.

Jargon, slang and use of acronyms

Jargon is technical language that is understood by people in particular industry or area of work. Health and social care workers often use jargon to communicate with each other quickly. **Slang** is an informal type of language that is used by a particular group of people. Teenagers sometimes use forms of slang to communicate with each other which their parents and teachers don't understand. **Acronyms** are abbreviations that stand for longer phrases. Jargon, slang and acronym all have one thing in common – they are forms of language that only makes sense to people with specialist knowledge. A person who doesn't have this specialist knowledge won't understand a message that includes jargon, slang or acronyms.

Dialect

A **dialect** is a version of a language. People who speak English using a Glagwegian dialect or a Liverpudlian dialect will pronounce the same words differently and may use some words that are local and specific to the area where they live. A person who isn't from the same area may not understand a local dialect.

Key terms

Acronym: a word formed from the initial letters of a series of words, such as NHS (National Health Service)

Dialect: a form of language spoken in a particular area

Jargon: specialised technical language used by a profession or group of people that may not be understood or used by others

Slang: Informal, non-standard words or abbreviations used by members of a particular group

---

Reflect

Can you think of any slang terms that are used by young people in your local area? Do you think that adults or other young people from a different area would know what these terms mean?

Overcoming barriers to communication

Barriers to communication can often be overcome, or are at least reduced, by making changes to the environment or approach to communication.

Preferred language and method of communication

Health and social care workers should accommodate the language needs and communication preferences of service users by:

- using each person's preferred language (directly or through an interpreter or signer)

- adapting their communication strategies to the language needs and preferences of the person.

Learning a few words of another person's language or developing some basic sign language skills can really help a care worker to establish a positive relationship with the person receiving care.

Health and social care workers often seek support from those with specialist communication skills to find out how they can best meet the needs of individuals who are unable to communicate in conventional ways. For example, special interest groups for visually and hearing impaired people provide information and services that are designed to help people with these disabilities to overcome communication barriers.

Adapting the environment

Making changes to the physical environment can improve the effectiveness of communication:

- replacing poor lighting with brighter lighting

- sound-proofing rooms, reducing background noise or creating quiet areas

- putting up multilingual posters and displaying signs clearly

- fitting electronic devices such as induction loop systems.

Health and social care workers can make the best of the care environment by:

- making sure they can be seen clearly when communicating

- facing both the light and the person at the same time

- making sure their mouth is visible when speaking

- minimising background noise

- using their eyes, facial expressions and gestures to communicate.

 Investigate

Visit the websites of the Royal National Institute for the Deaf (www.RNID.org.uk) and the Royal National Institute for the Blind (www.RNIB.org.uk) to find out about the range of services that these groups provide for people who have sensory impairments. Produce a summary of the different forms of communication support that are available to people with visual or hearing impairments.

? **Reflect**

Who do you think might benefit from each of the environmental changes listed on the left?

Effective non-verbal communication

Using posture in a positive, confident and non-intimidating way, making good use of facial expressions to communicate emotions and interest, and the appropriate use of gestures are all ways of involving service users in the communication process. Effective non-verbal communication can be used to communicate a range of emotions and is reassuring to people who may otherwise struggle to understand speech and written language. A care worker's behaviour and demeanour sends messages to services users about how much they care for and respect them, for example.

Case study

Read the following scenarios. For each of them explain briefly:

1. the barriers to effective communication

2. how these barriers could be overcome.

- Salvo is a patient in the medical ward of a large District General Hospital. His diabetes has got worse and he has now lost his sight. Salvo finds this very distressing and tends to stay close to his bed for fear of getting lost in the ward. He is becoming worried that he will not be able to get to the toilet in time on his own.

- Edith is 56 years old and has recently suffered a stroke. This has left her paralysed down her right-hand side and she is unable to speak. Edith cannot put her thoughts into words or understand words that are written down. She can understand some of what is said to her. You have been asked to find out what meals Edith would like to choose from next week's menu. You have been given a printed menu that patients normally fill in themselves.

Your assessment criteria:

1B.4 Identify ways in which barriers to communication may be overcome for individuals with sensory loss

2B.P4 Using examples, explain ways in which barriers to communication may be overcome and the benefits to service users of overcoming these barriers

2B.M2 Explain how measures have been implemented to overcome barriers to communication, with reference to a selected case

2B.D2 Evaluate the effectiveness of measures taken to remove barriers to communication, with reference to a selected case

Benefits to individuals when barriers are removed

Enabling every individual who uses health and social care services to communicate using their preferred language and method of communication is a challenge for health and social care workers. However, it is always important to do this as it:

- increases access to health and social care services

- improves the quality of health and social care delivery

- reduces emotional distress

- increases involvement in interactions

- raises levels of self-esteem

- reduces frustration.

? Reflect

What are the connections between effective communication and person-centred care? Think about the reason one might depend on the other!

Communicate effectively in health and social care

Communicating effectively

Effective communication in care settings helps both health and social care workers and people who use care services to form good relationships and to work well together. People communicate most effectively when they:

- feel relaxed

- are able to **empathise** with the other person

- experience warmth and genuineness in the relationship.

Effective communication also requires the care worker to develop and use a range of skills, abilities and communication techniques (see Figure 3.4).

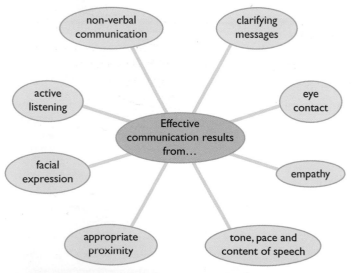

Figure 3.4 Effective communication results from...

Key term

Empathise: putting yourself in the place of the other person and trying to appreciate how they experience the world

Active listening

A person who uses active listening pays close attention to what the other person is saying and notices the non-verbal messages they are communicating. People who are good at active listening also tend to be skilled at using minimal prompts. These are things like a nod of the head, 'Mm' sounds and encouraging words like 'yes, I see' or 'go on'. Skilful use of minimal prompts encourages the person to keep speaking or to say a little more.

Case study

Eileen Morgan has worked in a pre-school nursery for the last 15 years. During this time she has developed very good relationships with the children she cares for. Students who come to the nursery on work placement notice that the children really like to talk to Eileen. This is partly because Eileen listens more than she talks when she is interacting with a child. Eileen is also very encouraging when a child comes to speak to her. She smiles a lot, focuses on their face, but also notices what they are doing. She says this helps her to understand what the child is feeling. She gives each child plenty of time to talk, staying quiet when the child pauses and uses sounds like 'mm', 'uh huh', and little phrases like 'I see', 'that's good' and 'tell me more' to encourage them.

1. How is Eileen using active listening skills when she interacts with children at the nursery?

2. Why does Eileen try to notice what a child is doing when they are talking to her?

3. Give an example of a minimal prompt used by Eileen to encourage children to express themselves.

Use of body language and proximity

People use different forms of body language to communicate feelings and to support what they are actually saying (see pages 68 to 75). Effective communicators often use the SOLER behaviours (see Figure 3.5) when they are talking to another person. These are not hard-and-fast rules that must always be obeyed, but they do encourage more open communication.

> Face the other person **S**quarely
>
> Adopt an **O**pen posture
>
> **L**ean towards the other person
>
> Maintain **E**ye contact
>
> Try to be **R**elaxed while paying attention

Figure 3.5 SOLER behaviours

Your assessment criteria:

1C.5 Demonstrate communication skills through one interaction in health and social care, identifying the forms of communication used

2C.P5 Demonstrate communication skills through interactions in health and social care, describing their effects

2C.M3 Select and demonstrate communication skills through interactions in health and social care, explaining their effectiveness

2C.D3 Select and demonstrate skills through one-to-one interactions in health and social care, evaluating their effectiveness and making recommendations for improvement

---

? | Reflect

People communicate messages in a variety of non-verbal ways. This activity requires you to discreetly observe people communicating non-verbally with each other.

Identify a public place where you can observe people communicating, a café, fast food restaurant or station for example.

Use a table with columns for 'Person', 'Description of non-verbal behaviour' and 'What was being communicated'. Watch for and record examples of non-verbal behaviour. In the table, explain what the people you observed could have been communicating non-verbally.

An awareness of **proximity** or the amount of personal space that a person requires is also an important feature of effective communication. Sitting or standing too close to someone can make them feel uncomfortable and intimidated. Sitting too far away might seem unfriendly and can make the person feel isolated. Health and social care workers often adjust their proximity by moving their chair or their position in response to the person's body language. It can also be a good idea to ask, 'Is it okay if I sit here?'

Facial expressions and eye contact

The human face is very expressive and is an important source of non-verbal communication. A person's face usually reveals their feelings. However, sometimes people are able to disguise their true feelings, presenting a socially acceptable 'face'. Effective communicators are able to read and interpret other people's facial expressions and are also good at using facial expressions to convey their own emotions.

A person's eyes, and the eye contact they make, can be good indicators of their feelings. Long, unbroken eye contact can indicate either hostility or attraction, for example. A person who makes eye contact for a longer time and who widens their eyes is likely to be seen as friendly, especially if they also smile. Effective communicators use eye contact to let people know they are paying attention, to establish trust and provide reassurance.

Key term

Proximity: physical closeness

Reflect

Can you think of an example from your own experience where a person's facial expression told a different story to their verbal message?

Participate

In pairs role-play a difficult interaction between a social worker talking to a client about their welfare benefits, or a nurse talking to a patient about how they feel. Take it in turns to be the care worker and the person using care services. You should:

- *sit opposite each other in chairs of equal height*
- *interact for about four minutes*
- *let the care worker start and lead the conversation.*

The service user should try not to listen and the care worker should try to get them to listen using verbal and non-verbal means. The care worker must not touch or shout at the listener. The listener must stay seated.

After each person has played the care worker role, take it in turns to tell each other what you liked and disliked about the activity. Write a short comment on what it felt like not to be listened to and identify the main factors that inhibited the communication cycle.

Repeat the activity but this time the service user should do the talking and the care worker should use the SOLER behaviours (Figure 3.5) to promote effective communication. Take it in turns to share what you liked and disliked about this part of the activity. Write a short comment on how the SOLER behaviours affected communication between you.

Your assessment criteria:

1C.5 Demonstrate communication skills through one interaction in health and social care, identifying the forms of communication used

2C.P5 Demonstrate communication skills through interactions in health and social care, describing their effects

2C.M3 Select and demonstrate communication skills through interactions in health and social care, explaining their effectiveness

2C.D3 Select and demonstrate skills through one-to-one interactions in health and social care, evaluating their effectiveness and making recommendations for improvement

Appropriate language, tone and pace

A person's choice of words, as well as the way they speak, influences the effectiveness of their communication. The pace, **tone**, **pitch** and volume of the speaker's voice are important. For example, it is never a good idea to shout (or to talk so loudly that the listener believes you are shouting). This kind of behaviour is likely to draw attention away from the verbal message. Mumbling, speaking too quickly, failing to complete sentences and using a hostile or aggressive tone will also impair the effectiveness of communication.

It is important to speak clearly and at a pace the other person can follow. Effective communicators also avoid using slang, jargon and acronyms to prevent misunderstandings. Speaking in a measured, clear and reasonably paced manner will help listeners to hear and understand. A relaxed, encouraging and friendly tone of voice also helps the speaker to convey warmth, sincerity and appropriate respect for the listener.

 Key terms

Pitch: the sound quality of a person's voice (e.g. 'she spoke in a low-pitched voice')

Tone: the emotional quality of a person's voice (e.g. 'he used an aggressive tone')

Reflect

How is a person's speech affected when they are nervous? What happens to the tone and pace of their speech, for example?

Clarifying or repeating

An effective communicator may clarify or repeat aspects of what the other person has said during a conversation as a way of checking their understanding. They might, for example, repeat some of the speaker's words back to them or summarise a part of the person's message. This can sometimes help the communicators to explore the key issues in more detail.

Alternatively, an effective communicator may say something like, 'Can I just check that you meant...?' in order to clarify their understanding. However, it is important not to repeat or clarify too often in a conversation as this will interrupt the speaker's flow and might make them think you are 'parroting' them.

Discuss

Identify a care situation in which it would be helpful to clarify or repeat parts of what an individual says. Describe this to a class colleague and share ideas on why this might be beneficial to both the care worker and service user.

Care workers need to adapt their communication skills to meet the needs of each person they work with

Participate

In pairs, role play a nursery nurse talking to a parent who is concerned about health and safety at nursery. You should:

- *Sit opposite each other in chairs of equal height*

- *Interact for about four minutes.*

The parent should talk about health and safety concerns at the nursery. The nursery nurse should listen, using SOLER behaviours, also repeating and clarifying what the parent has said every so often.

After each person has played the care worker role, take it in turns to tell each other what you liked and disliked about the activity. Write a short comment on how repeating and clarifying affected communication between you.

85

Assessment checklist

To achieve level 1, my portfolio of evidence must show that I can:

Assessment criteria	Description	✓
1A.1	Identify different forms of verbal and non-verbal communication	☐
1A.2	Identify different forms of alternative communication for different needs, using examples from health and social care	☐
1B.3	Outline the barriers to communication in health and social care	☐
1B.4	Identify ways in which barriers to communication may be overcome for individuals with sensory loss	☐
1C.5	Demonstrate communication skills through one interaction in health and social care, identifying the forms of communication used	☐

To achieve a pass grade, my portfolio of evidence must show that I can:

Assessment criteria	Description	✓
2A.P1	Describe different forms of verbal and non-verbal communication	☐
2A.P2	Describe different forms of alternative communication for different needs, using examples from health and social care	☐
2B.P3	Describe the barriers to communication in health and social care and their effects on service users	☐
2B.P4	Using examples, explain ways in which barriers to communication may be overcome and the benefits to service users of overcoming these barriers	☐
2C.P5	Demonstrate communication skills through interactions in health and social care, describing their effects	☐

To achieve a merit grade, my portfolio of evidence must show that I can:

Assessment criteria	Description	✓
2A.M1	Explain the advantages and disadvantages of different forms of communication used, with reference to a one-to-one and a group interaction	☐
2B.M2	Explain how measures have been implemented to overcome barriers to communication, with reference to a selected case	☐
2C.M3	Select and demonstrate communication skills through interactions in health and social care, explaining their effectiveness	☐

To achieve a distinction grade, my portfolio of evidence must show that I can:

Assessment criteria	Description	✓
2A.D1	Assess the effectiveness of different forms of communication for service users with different needs	☐
2B.D2	Evaluate the effectiveness of measures taken to remove barriers to communication, with reference to a selected case	☐
2C.D3	Select and demonstrate skills through one-to-one interactions in health and social care, evaluating their effectiveness and making recommendations for improvement	☐

4 | Social influences on health and wellbeing

Learning aim A: Explore the effects of socialisation on the health and wellbeing of individuals

▸ Topic A.1 Primary and secondary socialisation

▸ Topic A.2 Effects of socialisation

Learning aim B: Understand the influences that relationships have on the health and wellbeing of individuals

▸ Topic B.1 Influences of relationships on individuals

Learning aim C: Investigate the effects of social factors on the health and wellbeing of individuals

▸ Topic C.1 How social factors influence health and wellbeing

Primary and secondary socialisation

Your assessment criteria:

1A.1 Identify agents involved in the primary and secondary socialisation processes

2A.P1 Explain the influence of agents of primary and secondary socialisation

Introduction to this chapter

People are social animals. We need and develop relationships with those around us, forming important emotional bonds with members of our families and with friends. The people we are close to, especially those we spend time with during infancy and childhood, are very influential in shaping our attitudes, behaviour and beliefs. This chapter focuses on different types of social relationship, as well as a range of broader social factors that influence human development, health and wellbeing.

🔑 Key terms

Agent (of socialisation): an individual who is involved in socialising others as a result of their work role or personal relationship

Norms: the rules of socially appropriate behaviour in a society

Primary socialisation: the process through which infants and children begin learning the norms or expectations of society; this usually happens within their family

Secondary socialisation: the process of learning attitudes, values and social norms outside of the family, usually through education, work and friendship relationships

Social skills: the talking, listening and relationship skills a person needs to communicate and interact with others.

Socialisation processes

Socialisation is the process of learning values, ideas, practices and roles; it is about becoming a socially aware and socially skilled member of a society. As a newborn baby, you came into the world with no sense of self and no knowledge of the rules of your society. You didn't know about acceptable behaviours, or how you should relate to others. You learnt this through **primary** and **secondary socialisation**.

Primary socialisation

Your primary socialisation as a member of society began within your family during infancy and early childhood. A child's family (parents, carers and siblings) are known as **agents** of primary socialisation. They usually teach an individual:

- the **norms** or expectations of society

- attitudes and values about what is right and wrong

- basic **social skills**, like the importance of saying 'please' and 'thank you'

- ways of speaking and behaving towards others.

Young children are taught how to behave normally so that they can fit in, becoming accepted members of social groups and our broader society. Primary socialisation also has an important influence on a child's ways of thinking and their expectations of people outside of their family.

Primary socialisation involves teaching basic care skills as well as social skills

Case study

Jan is a nursery nurse. She works in an early years playgroup with children aged three to five years of age. Jan sets up a range of indoor and outdoor play activities and supports the children who take part in them. Jan also helps the children to manage their personal hygiene, to get their shoes and coats on and off and encourages them to talk and behave in socially acceptable ways. As part of this, she praises the children when they make a 'good choice' but also points out when they have made a 'bad choice' in the way they behave or relate to others.

1. Identify two ways in which Jan is socialising the children at nursery.

2. Describe how Jan teaches the children the difference between 'right' and 'wrong'.

3. Explain why it is important that Jan demonstrates appropriate behaviour and tells the children about ways of speaking and relating to others.

 Discuss

How might the media (TV programmes and adverts, radio, magazines and books) and other young people (at school or college perhaps) also play a part in the socialisation of adolescents? Give an example of how each of these factors might influence a young person's development.

Secondary socialisation

Secondary socialisation occurs from later childhood onwards and continues to the end of an individual's life. It involves learning a range of new skills and attitudes, and also modifying our existing attitudes, values and behaviours. Agents of secondary socialisation include:

- friends

- peer groups

- the media

- teachers and youth workers

- faith leaders (such as priests, imams and rabbis, for example)

- social workers

- employers and work colleagues.

We develop and change as individuals as a result of going to school, getting a job and spending time with non-family members, for example. Schools, the mass media, workplaces, friends and peer groups all play an important part in our secondary socialisation, shaping the person we become. This process continues throughout our lives.

Case study

Emma is in her second year of nurse training. Her interest in nursing developed from watching hospital dramas on television when she was younger. Emma has since learnt that real-life nursing is much harder work and less glamorous than the programmes led her to believe. She is currently working in an assessment unit for older people with medical problems. Heidi, the ward sister, is Emma's workplace mentor and assessor. Emma has learnt a lot from watching and listening to Heidi. She says that she would like to be as confident and compassionate as Heidi is when faced by difficult care situations and when dealing with relatives and other senior staff in the hospital.

1. How did the media influence Emma's socialisation as a nurse?

2. What role has Heidi played in Emma's professional socialisation?

3. How has Emma's contact with Heidi helped her to develop as a nurse?

Your assessment criteria:

1A.1 Identify agents involved in the primary and secondary socialisation processes

2A.P1 Explain the influence of agents of primary and secondary socialisation

How does socialisation happen?

Socialisation processes are sometimes deliberate and easy to observe. For example, when a parent tells a child what to do or when a person is penalised or punished in some way for breaching social norms, socialisation is happening. Parents and carers, as well as siblings and other people who have a close relationship with a young child, may:

- explain how or why a child should behave (say 'please' or 'think you')

- show the child what to do (holding cutlery or a cup properly, for example)

- model behaviour (greeting people, being friendly towards others).

In all of these cases the agent of socialisation is trying to shape or develop the child's attitudes, values and behaviour to enable them to fit in with social norms. Socialisation can also occur in more subtle ways too; when a young person learns from the example being set by a parent or sibling or when they are given praise for behaving in a way that conforms to what is expected and acceptable in society.

? Reflect

How might a person's work role and experiences influence their social development? Give a couple of examples to show how work roles and experiences could affect an individual's social skills and relationships.

💬 Discuss

Reflect on your own experience as a child or your more recent experiences with young children (as a parent, carer or sibling, perhaps) and try to identify ways in which:

- *you experienced some form of socialisation by other family members*

- *you acted as an agent of socialisation.*

Share your examples and experiences with class colleagues. How do you think your own experiences of socialisation have shaped you as a person?

Effects of socialisation

Socialisation outcomes

A wide range of socialising agents contribute to the socialisation processes that run through the whole of the human life course, having a major impact on an individual's personal identity, relationships and behaviour. Socialisation influences who we become and how we learn to fit into society, as well as many of our lifestyle choices and behaviours.

Gender roles

A person's sex refers to whether they are biologically male or female. Gender refers to the behaviour society expects from men and women. The gender expectations that are imposed on girls and boys during childhood and adolescence have a powerful impact on the kind of people men and women become. In Western societies girls are socialised to express so-called feminine qualities, such as being kind, caring and gentle. This leads to assumptions about gender roles, such that women should look after children, cook and do non-manual work. In contrast, boys are socialised to express accepted masculine characteristics such as being boisterous, aggressive and tough. This leads to assumptions that men should go out to work, do physical, manual jobs and be decision-makers. Parents, schools, friends and the media all play a part in gender socialisation.

The gender expectations that an individual experiences influence the way their identity develops, how they relate to others and the opportunities that may be open to them. The idea that boys and men should experience better opportunities than girls and women – especially in education and employment – because they are thought to be the 'superior sex' is not as powerful as it once was. However, gender does still play an important part in an individual's intellectual, social and emotional development because ideas about socially acceptable ways for men or women to behave remain very powerful in society.

Attitudes, values and social norms

Parents are a key socialising influence on children during the early years of life. In particular, children learn basic **attitudes**, **values** and **norms** from parents throughout childhood and into adolescence. Children absorb and learn a set of attitudes and values from their parents or carers through:

- what they hear their parents say

- observing the way their parents react and behave

- listening to what their parents tell them about how they *ought* to behave and think.

Your assessment criteria:

1A.2 Outline the main effects of socialisation on the health and wellbeing of individuals

2A.P2 Describe the effects of socialisation on the health and wellbeing of individuals

2A.M1 Explain the effects of primary and secondary socialisation on the health and wellbeing of individuals, with reference to relevant examples

2A.D1 Evaluate the impact of primary and secondary socialisation on the health and wellbeing of individuals, with reference to specific examples

Key terms

Attitude: a way of thinking and behaving that expresses beliefs

Gender: the social and behavioural expectations that are associated with males (masculine) and females (feminine) in society

Norms: expected patterns of behaviour and belief

Role: an expected pattern of behaviour

Values: ideals that a person believes are important

Discuss

What does 'growing up as a girl' involve in today's society? How are the expectations placed on girls different to those of boys? Has this changed much since the time when your mother and grandmother were your age? Share and discuss ideas about this with class colleagues.

For example, if children see their parents expressing **prejudiced** attitudes about a minority group, they are likely to see this behaviour (and the attitudes being expressed) as acceptable. Children are not born with prejudiced attitudes towards others – they learn or acquire them through what they see, hear and experience from others.

Social norms and behaviour

Parents teach their children a set of social norms and what is acceptable behaviour by responding to their child's own behaviour with approval or disapproval. Part of this involves teaching a child 'manners' and 'good behaviour'. Parents use a variety of methods to do this including encouragement, explanation and even punishment. Many parents also model (demonstrate) what they see as acceptable social behaviours so that the child copies. These norms then become a feature of the child's social behaviours inside and outside of the family.

A parent who encourages and reinforces tolerant behaviour in their child is more likely to raise a tolerant child than a parent who does not value tolerance or who neglects this aspect of their child's behaviour. Similarly, where a child's parents show little respect or are hostile to those in positions of authority (such as teachers, social workers or police officers), the child is likely to absorb this kind of attitude. Where this happens the child may express what they have learnt in hostile or disrespectful relationships with authority figures.

Making moral choices

During childhood children learn to base their judgments about right and wrong, and good and bad, on rules (**morals**) that they have been taught by people who have authority in their lives, such as parents, teachers and religious leaders. Children generally obey rules if this means that they will avoid being punished or that they will receive rewards. The standards of morality that are taught or demonstrated by parents tend to have a big influence on young children who wish to be a 'good boy' or 'good girl'. As children move into adolescence, making moral choices becomes more complicated as other factors like **peer group pressure**, religious and other beliefs, and role models all influence thinking and behaviour. Moral rules passed on by parents seem less helpful when adolescents are faced with the complexities of adult life; they are more likely to use principles like truth, equality and social justice to make their decisions.

Your assessment criteria:

1A.2 Outline the main effects of socialisation on the health and wellbeing of individuals

2A.P2 Describe the effects of socialisation on the health and wellbeing of individuals

2A.M1 Explain the effects of primary and secondary socialisation on the health and wellbeing of individuals, with reference to relevant example

2A.D1 Evaluate the impact of primary and secondary socialisation on the health and wellbeing of individuals, with reference to specific examples

Key terms

Morals: *principles of right and wrong*

Prejudice: *a biased, unfounded and usually negative belief about a group of people*

Peer group: *typically a group of people of about the same age who see themselves (and are seen by others) as belonging together in some way*

Peer group pressure: *the emotional and moral influence that a* peer group *can have on an individual's behaviour*

Reflect

Can you remember how you were socialised into developing 'manners' and 'good behaviour' by your parents? How would you socialise a child of your own to behave at the dinner table? Think about what you feel is important, socially acceptable behaviour and how you would develop this in your own child.

Lifestyle and behaviour

Most people live as part of a family at some point in their early life. Parents are very powerful role models and influence development and lifestyle choices in both deliberate and subtle ways. A range of other socialisation factors can also influence an individual's lifestyle choices. These include, for example:

- when and in what way an individual enters employment or experiences unemployment, particularly when young

- a person's choice of career and the subsequent choices they make in developing their career

- whether a person chooses to use illegal substances, misuse alcohol or smoke cigarettes, which are all likely to have a damaging effect on health

- whether a person marries or develops a long-term relationship and the extent to which this contributes to their health and wellbeing

- an individual's religious beliefs or involvement in an alternative lifestyle (such as communal living, environmentalism or veganism, for example)

- the extent to which a person participates in sport and exercise and uses medical services to maintain their health and wellbeing.

The way in which these and other factors interact to influence personal development will vary. However, as a general rule, a person's lifestyle and the impact this has on their health, development and wellbeing is strongly affected by socialisation processes.

The impact of socialisation on health and wellbeing

Primary and secondary socialisation can shape an individual's health and wellbeing in many different ways. The positive impacts of socialisation could include:

- learning effective social and relationship-building skills

- developing self-confidence and self-esteem

- learning effective practical skills to deal with everyday life situations

- developing positive, constructive attitudes and values

- learning basic problem-solving and coping skills.

However, not everybody has positive early socialisation experiences. Neglectful, inconsistent or ineffective parenting can lead to the development of poor social skills and negative self-esteem, for example. Similarly, bad experiences of education or work situations in which colleagues are unsupportive, critical or even hostile can undermine a person's self-confidence, leading to a variety of emotional difficulties and mental health problems.

Relationships, health and wellbeing

People form different types of relationship at different stages of their life. Family relationships tend to be most important during infancy and childhood. There is then a gradual shift in adolescence as friendships become more important, though emotional support from within the family – or from other supportive carers – is also essential for adolescent development. A whole range of new personal and working relationships are formed as the individual progresses into adulthood.

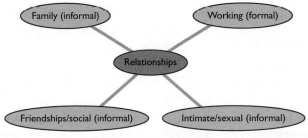

Figure 4.1 Different types of relationship

Family relationships

There are many different types of family structure. Whatever type of family structure a person lives in, their relationship with their parent(s) will play a big part in their development, health and wellbeing. Relationships with **siblings** are also important within family relationships. An individual's feelings about their family and the skills they develop (or don't develop) in relating to others within the family play an important part in the relationships they develop with others outside of the family during each life stage.

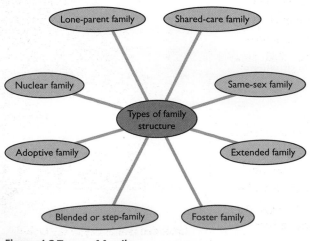

Figure 4.2 Types of family

Key term

Siblings: brothers and sisters in the family

An individual's family relationships develop and change as they move through different life stages. Family relationships are usually seen as special because of the biological connections and close emotional bonds between family members. However, while family relationships can be a source of love, protection and mutual support, negative family relationships that involve abuse, neglect or violence can result in physical hurt or psychological and emotional damage. Family relationships are often complex and many people have both good experiences of family relationships that support their personal development and some difficult and challenging experiences.

Table 4.1 Types of family structure

Type of family	Key characteristics
Nuclear family	Two heterosexual parents and dependent child(ren)
Extended family	Nuclear family plus additional relatives living together
Single-parent family	Single parent and dependent child(ren)
Reconstituted family	Two parents with dependent children from previous relationships and/or their own child(ren)

Nuclear families

A nuclear family is based around two heterosexual parents and their dependent children living together in the same household. A nuclear family tends to have some contact with other relatives who may also live in nuclear families but not in the same household. Though they have family connections to other relatives, nuclear families tend to be seen as independent, self-sufficient units. This doesn't mean that the parents in a nuclear family will necessarily provide all of the care for children. Some nuclear families use childminders, grandparents or other child care services to look after children during working hours, for example. However, on the whole, the parents do have the main responsibility and spend most time caring for their children.

Extended families

Extended families are nuclear families that are extended by the presence of grandparents or other relatives living in the same household, all part of the same family unit. Extended families were much more common in the United Kingdom in the nineteenth and early twentieth centuries. Despite this, extended families are still present in the United Kingdom, particularly in South Asian, Chinese and some other minority ethnic communities.

Extended families typically include grandparents as well as parents and children

One of the benefits of living in an extended family is that there are more adults around to provide assistance with domestic activities and child care. Extended families can be very supportive, boosting family members' self-esteem and giving feelings of security. However, living closely with lots of relatives can also be stressful and may lead to higher levels of anxiety where there are disagreements, tensions in relationships or communication problems between family members.

Single-parent families

The single-parent family is one of the fastest growing, though not the most common, type of family structure in the United Kingdom. It consists of a single parent (usually the mother) and at least one dependent child. The parent living with the child may share custody and responsibility for child care with the child's other parent. Though it is not always the case, many single-parent families have previously been part of a nuclear or extended family. Separation, divorce or the death of one partner may be the reason why a single-parent family is formed. Changes in social attitudes, particularly a decline in the stigma associated with being an 'unmarried mother', have made one-parent families and the birth of children outside of marriage more socially acceptable. Single-parent families are no less secure or supportive than other types of family. However, single-parent families may experience stress where the parent feels unsupported or is under a great deal of pressure to cope with all of the parental responsibilities alone. Similarly, where children feel abandoned or unsupported by a parent who has left the family, they may become less trusting, have lower self-esteem and feel less secure than children living in a supportive two-parent family.

Reconstituted families

Reconstituted families are also known as reconstructed, blended and, more popularly, as step-families. What all of these ideas have in common is the notion of two families merging into a new family. The 'merger' that occurs when a reconstituted family is created usually involves two partners bringing dependent children from their previous relationships into a new family situation. A reconstituted family may also develop further when the new partners produce children themselves.

Approximately 10 per cent of children live with a step-parent in the United Kingdom and many enjoy a safe, happy and supportive family environment that contributes to their health, wellbeing and personal development. However, reconstituted families are often poorer than other types of families and relationships between step-parents and step-children can be emotionally difficult. The self-concept of each member of a reconstituted family is likely to be changed by the 'merger' and the new set of relationships that develop.

Your assessment criteria:

1B.3 Outline the different types of relationships that have an impact on the health and wellbeing of individuals

2B.P3 Describe the influences that different types of relationships have on the health and wellbeing of individuals

Key term

Stigma: disapproval of personal characteristics, behaviour or beliefs

Reflect

How do you think people view single parents? In your opinion has the stigma associated with being part of a single parent family changed? What are your own thoughts about the impact that having only one parent at home has on children's health, wellbeing and development?

For some individuals, life in a reconstituted family can have a negative effect on their emotional development and wellbeing, especially if they struggle to come to terms with the loss or ending of their original, birth family and subsequently reject opportunities to form new relationships with step-parents or step-children.

Working relationships

Working relationships are different to other forms of relationship because the relationship serves a particular, non-personal purpose – it is about getting a particular job done. Most working relationships are formed between individuals who are not of equal status; one person usually has more power or authority in the relationship than the other. Relationships between teachers and students, between employers and employees and between work colleagues are examples of working relationships.

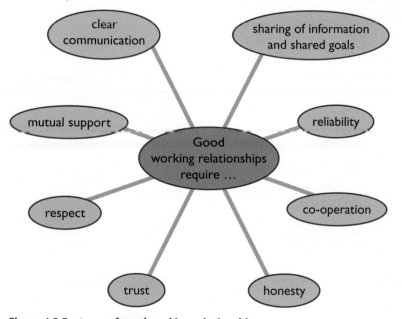

Figure 4.3 Features of good working relationships

? | Reflect

Why do you think respect, trust and mutual support are particularly important aspects of work relationships in health and social care settings?

Effective work relationships tend to be based on good communication, trust and respect between the people involved. Positive working relationships contribute to social, emotional and intellectual development and wellbeing because they can lead to:

- higher self-esteem

- positive self-image

- development of new skills and understanding

- a positive sense of self-worth

- a clear sense of personal identity.

Teacher–student relationships

Learning is the specific focus of relationships between teachers and students. Relationships with class teachers and nursery workers become important in children's lives from the point at which they begin attending nursery or primary school. A child needs to trust their teacher or nursery worker to establish the kind of relationship that enables them to develop their communication skills, self-confidence and self-esteem. A lack of trust and a negative, unsupportive relationship is likely to hamper the child's social, emotional and intellectual development and wellbeing.

The relationship between a student and teacher becomes more of a partnership during adolescence. Both parties have an interest in promoting learning and general intellectual development. The teacher may still have more authority in the relationship but learning cannot occur without the student's willing and active participation. A good working relationship between student and teacher is likely to contribute positively to the self-esteem, self-confidence and self-concept of both individuals and provides the basis for the student's intellectual development and emotional wellbeing.

Employer–employee relationships

The employer–employee relationship is an example of a **formal relationship**. That is, it is based on a set of rules and expectations about how people should relate to each other because of their employment relationship. The employer has more power and authority, directing the activities of the employee. Employment relationships can affect an individual's self-image, their social skills and their intellectual development – depending on the type of work they do and the development opportunities they are given. A person's relationship with their employer may also influence their attitudes, values and behaviour as well as their self-concept. A negative relationship with an employer, or the experience of being made redundant, may cause an individual to experience high stress levels and can be damaging to their self-esteem and sense of security.

Work colleagues

Some work colleagues are peers. That is, they are people of equal status and similar background. People involved in these types of working relationships may also be friends. Effective relationships with peers and other work colleagues are important because people often need to co-operate in work situations. Being liked and valued by work colleagues also increases an individual's self-confidence and self-esteem. However, in work environments where bullying and other negative behaviours occur, an individual's self-esteem may be undermined. The higher stress levels that result can also lead to emotional and mental health problems.

Your assessment criteria:

1B.3 Outline the different types of relationships that have an impact on the health and wellbeing of individuals

2B.P3 Describe the influences that different types of relationships have on the health and wellbeing of individuals

✎ Key term

Formal relationship: a relationship based on a set of established rules, such as the employer–employee relationship

? Reflect

Think about your own relationships with teachers. Have they all been positive and productive? If not, what has been missing from those that were less successful?

Work colleagues sometimes disagree but must always respect each other to prevent bullying from occurring

Social relationships

Social relationships are voluntary, made out of choice by individuals who are not related to each other, largely because they enjoy each other's company. Friendships and membership of religious and **secular** groups are examples of social relationships.

Friendships

Friends are people we generally see as likeable and dependable, and with whom we can communicate easily. People form friendships for a variety of reasons, such as common attitudes, values and interests, and a need for emotional support and companionship. Friendships tend to boost a person's self-esteem and self-confidence, and help to develop social skills. Overall, friendships make an important contribution to an individual's emotional and social wellbeing, and the formation of their self-concept.

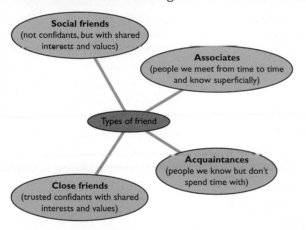

Figure 4.4 Types of friendship

Early friendships

Throughout childhood, friendships play an important part in developing a child's self-esteem. Being liked and accepted by other children is very important for self-confidence and self-image. By contrast, children who struggle to make friends or who are rejected or bullied are likely to suffer low self-confidence and to have lower self-esteem because they become aware of this lack of social acceptance. This can damage the child's long-term social and emotional wellbeing and they may develop a negative self-concept as a result.

Friendships become increasingly important and are often more intense during adolescence. Boys and girls now begin to form opposite-sex friendships, in contrast to childhood when friendships are mainly with members of the same sex. Girls tend to belong to smaller friendship groups and have emotionally intense friendship relationships, whereas boys tend to belong to larger friendship groups in which members share common practical or sporting interests.

Your assessment criteria:

1B.3 Outline the different types of relationships that have an impact on the health and wellbeing of individuals

2B.P3 Describe the influences that different types of relationships have on the health and wellbeing of individuals

2B.M2 Explain the influences that different types of relationships have on the health and wellbeing of individuals

Key term

Secular: non-religious

? Reflect

Can you recall your first (or early childhood) friends? What did you do together? How do you think that your early friendships affected your development during childhood?

Belonging to a friendship group provides an adolescent with an important sense of belonging and social acceptance outside of their family. Some adolescents who lack social skills, who have significantly different values to their peers or who are physically different in some way can be ostracised or left out of friendship groups. This can be damaging to self-esteem and to social and emotional development generally. Similarly, adolescents who lack self-confidence and self-esteem may find themselves vulnerable to peer group pressure within friendship groups. This can lead some young people into activities, such as drinking, petty crime, drug use or sex, that make them feel uncomfortable but which they go along with to remain a member of the group.

Adult friendships

Adult friendships tend to be carefully chosen and based on shared interests and values. They usually last longer if both parties meet each other's emotional needs for support, loyalty and honesty in the relationship. Adult friends can be very important for social development and emotional wellbeing as they provide the basis for a supportive social network. Friends are particularly important when an individual experiences significant life events, such as divorce, unexpected illness or stress, when they need people to offer emotional support. The loss of friends can lead to loneliness, isolation and feelings of insecurity.

Your assessment criteria:

1B.3 Outline the different types of relationships that have an impact on the health and wellbeing of individuals

2B.P3 Describe the influences that different types of relationships have on the health and wellbeing of individuals

? | Reflect

People with learning difficulties such as autism and enduring mental health problems, like depression, can struggle to make and maintain adult friendships. How do you think this might affect an individual's social and emotional development or their wellbeing?

Case study

Ffion, Nia and Eleri are all 32 years of age. They have known each other since they started primary school at five years of age. The three women are all now married, have two children each and live in different parts of the United Kingdom. Living hundreds of miles from each other hasn't got in the way of their friendship. All three communicate regularly, sending text messages a couple of times a week and speaking quite frequently on the phone. Ffion still lives in the part of Wales where the three friends grew up. When Nia and Eleri visit their families at Christmas and in the summer, the women also arrange to go out for a meal or to have a barbeque at Ffion's house. Ffion, Nia and Eleri discuss personal feelings and seek advice from each other when they have problems. All trust one another and believe they have an honest, supportive and genuine friendship that they can rely on, whatever else is happening in their lives.

1. Which aspects of the women's wellbeing and development are likely to have been affected by their friendship?

2. Explain why the friendship between these three women is likely to have had a positive effect on each individual's self-concept.

3. Using the information provided, identify possible reasons why the friendship between the three women has been successful and has lasted so long.

Intimate and sexual relationships

People generally start to be come interested in personal relationships in their early teens. Adolescents tend to fall in and out of love quite frequently as they experience 'crushes' or infatuations during puberty. This can be emotionally painful, but most teenagers use these experiences to learn more about the emotional aspects of relationships and to extend their understanding of their own needs and preferences. Girls tend to seek and engage in romantic, intimate and, to a lesser extent sexual, relationships at a younger age than boys. For many teenagers their first intimate relationship is an intense emotional experience rather than a sexual one.

Intimacy in adolescence

Intimate relationships do develop out of sexual attraction, though sexual intercourse is not necessarily a part of teenagers' intimate relationships. Kissing, hand-holding and other forms of physical contact are more frequently used to express physical and emotional attraction during this life stage. Intimate personal relationships tend to be short-lived during early adolescence but become longer with greater emotional and physical involvement in later adolescence. These longer-term relationships are based on greater emotional maturity and a stronger sense of personal identity. They also help to prepare young people for future relationships with the partners they will meet as adults.

Intimacy in adulthood

Sexual relationships are a normal part of intimate personal relationships during all phases of adulthood. For most adults, engaging in sexual activity with a partner expresses both physical and emotional needs. Sexuality often becomes a feature of an individual's self-concept during adulthood. During adulthood people typically search for a partner, developing emotionally and physically intimate relationships with one or more individuals before they form a long-term, usually monogamous, relationship. While some people avoid sexual relationships outside of marriage, many other people form intimate relationships before, or without, getting married. The physical and emotional intimacy of a close personal and sexual relationship contributes to an individual's social and emotional development and wellbeing. Unprotected sex, promiscuity and extramarital affairs may damage an individual's existing relationship and personal development because of the risk of unwanted pregnancy, sexually transmitted disease and the emotional distress that this can cause to existing partners. Adults who find themselves in sexually abusive relationships are also likely to experience significant emotional distress and sometimes physical injury, as well as low self-esteem.

Positive and negative influences of relationships on health and wellbeing

People form different types of relationship at different stages of their life. Family relationships tend to be most important during infancy and childhood. Friendships become important during adolescence and intimate personal relationships are significant during early adulthood, for example. Relationships have a positive impact on health and wellbeing when they are consistent and supportive. These types of relationships are good for health and wellbeing because they:

· provide emotional security through trust

· promote self-confidence and self-esteem

· influence the development of self-concept

· help us to develop our social skills.

Relationships that are abusive, neglectful or unsupportive tend to have a negative effect on an individual's health and wellbeing. People who don't have supportive relationships can experience loneliness and low self-esteem, as well as a range of mental health problems that result from being treated badly and not having their needs met by others who are important to them. Researchers have shown that people who lack close, supportive relationships are much more likely to experience depression.

Your assessment criteria:

2B.D2 Compare the potential positive and negative influences of different relationships on the health and wellbeing of individuals

Investigate

Is there a befriending scheme for vulnerable people in your local area? Using local library or Internet resources, find out what this offers and who uses it. If there is no local scheme, go to The Befriending Scheme at http://www.thebefriendingscheme. org.uk and watch the short film in which people explain what they enjoy about a scheme in Sussex.

How social factors influence health and wellbeing

Society, health and wellbeing

Health and social care workers are aware that a range of social factors influence people's experiences of health and wellbeing. Research studies that show the links between social factors and health refer to patterns of experience within a large population of people, such as a social class. There may be individuals within a social class whose health experience doesn't follow the general trend or pattern. However, the key point to understand is the general pattern or trend that is revealed by the research.

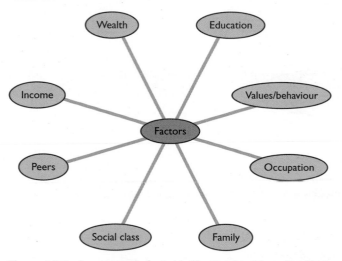

Figure 4.5 Socio-economic factors affecting health and wellbeing

Social influences on health and wellbeing

A range of **socio-economic factors** can influence health, wellbeing and development across the life course (see Figure 4.5).

Income and wealth

Income refers to the money that a family or individual receives on a regular basis. People receive money through working, pension payments, welfare benefits and other sources such as investments. Wealth refers to the assets and resources that people own. People with high incomes tend to build up greater levels of wealth than people on low incomes.

An individual's (or a family's) income and wealth, and the things they spend it on, affect their quality of life and health choices. As a result, people from wealthy families tend to have better opportunities to make the most of their potential and to reduce their health risks than people from low-income families.

 Key term

Socio-economic factors: non-biological influences, such as relationships, lifestyle (socio) and money-related (economic) factors, which influence an individual's living circumstances, personal development and experiences

Education, values and behaviour

Educational experiences are part of secondary socialisation. Friends, peers and teachers at school or college all influence an individual's attitudes, values and behaviour in relation to health and lifestyle.

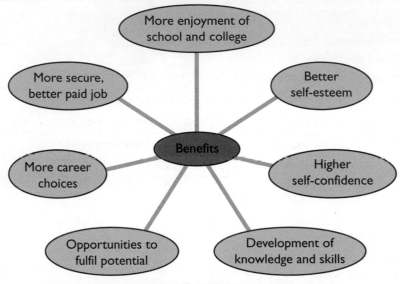

Figure 4.6 The benefits of a good education

Some people learn a lot at school, succeed in exams, make good friends and see education as a positive influence on their personal development and wellbeing. Educational success and strong friendships are very good for self-esteem and self-image and give the knowledge and understanding to make good health and lifestyle choices. However, not everybody enjoys school and not everybody succeeds. Failure and bad experiences in education can lead some people to develop a negative self-image, low self-esteem and may damage a person's sense of wellbeing.

Occupation and social class

Paid employment is the way in which most adults in the United Kingdom gain their income. However, some jobs provide a better income and working conditions and have a greater status than others. A person's employment status determines their **social class**. People in higher status employment are allocated to higher social class groups, and vice versa. As well as providing income, a person's occupation may influence their self-concept, their personal development and expose them to work situations that impact on their health and wellbeing.

Having high status employment, comfortable surroundings and stimulating work is likely to have a positive effect on health and development. Working in difficult or stressful conditions, in a low status job or in an unsupportive environment may have a negative effect.

Your assessment criteria:

1C.4 Identify the effects of social factors on the health choices of individuals

2C.P4 Describe how social factors can affect the health and wellbeing of individuals

2C.M3 Explain how social factors can affect the health and wellbeing of individuals, with reference to relevant examples

Key term

Social class: a group of people who are similar in terms of their wealth, income and job

People in the UK who have a higher than average income also tend to experience better than average health and wellbeing

Table 4.2 Effect of social class on health choices and outcomes

Aspect of health and wellbeing	Social patterns
Smoking rates	• Highest rates amongst manual groups, lowest in higher social classes. • Social disadvantage seen as cause of persistent class patterns.
Alcohol consumption	• People in higher income brackets drink most. • Higher social classes experience greatest risk of alcohol-related illnesses.
Diet	• People in higher social classes have better quality diet. • People in lower social classes eat more processed foods, and have higher obesity rates.
Exercise	• Men and women in lowest social classes with manual jobs are most physically active. • People in higher social classes are most likely to participate in sport or exercise for leisure.
Health care	• People in higher social classes are more likely to use preventive health services. • People in lower social classes are less likely to access hospital care.

Gender

Gender refers to the social expectations placed on men and women in society. Gender is linked to health behaviour; men being associated with more physically demanding, dangerous and risk-taking behaviours and women with more nurturing and caring activities. Both the different social expectations of men and women and their differing opportunities in society are linked to their diverse experiences of health and wellbeing. Women tend to experience more illness than men – and seek health care more often – but men die sooner, have higher rates of heart disease and are more likely to have fatal accidents than women.

Table 4.3 Effects of gender on health choices and outcomes

Aspect of health and wellbeing	Social patterns
Smoking rates	• Men are more likely to smoke than women. • Young mothers on low incomes are more likely to smoke than other women.
Alcohol consumption	• More men (40%) exceed recommended daily intake than women (23%). • Alcohol-related deaths for men are double those of women.
Diet	• Women are more likely to eat a balanced diet containing unprocessed wholefoods. • Men eat more meat, chips and cake than women.
Exercise	• Men take more exercise than women but too few people meet recommended levels of exercise. • Men are more likely to be overweight than women but women have higher rates of obesity.
Substance misuse	• Overall decline in substance misuse since 1998. • Men are more likely to misuse substances and experience negative health effects than women.
Health care	• Women visit GP more frequently and have higher rates of hospital in-patient stays. • Range of health services targeted at women is greater than those targeted specifically at men.

Culture

Culture is a complex and wide-ranging social influence on health and wellbeing; it can affect our dietary choices, the types of relationships we form and our general health beliefs, for example. We often take these cultural aspects for granted – we just think of them as being the 'normal' or right way of doing things. However, in a multicultural society like the United Kingdom cultural differences do result in different patterns of health and wellbeing. Minority ethnic groups in the UK are more vulnerable to ill health in general than white British people, for example. There are also significant differences in the types of physical and mental health problems experienced by members of different minority ethnic groups.

Family and peers

The family is often seen as the foundation of society because of the key role it plays in human development. The relationships we have with parents, brothers and sisters ensure that we are provided for, supported and protected as we grow and develop. For example, an individual's family:

- *provides* them with informal education and socialisation during infancy and childhood

- *supports* them emotionally, socially and financially from infancy through to adulthood

- *protects* their health and wellbeing by giving informal care, advice and guidance in every life stage.

Peer groups influence a person's social and emotional development and affect their sense of wellbeing. Adolescents often want to belong to a group of like-minded friends and have a strong need to be liked, respected and accepted by their peers.

Throughout life, an individual's personality, social skills and emotional development are all shaped by their friendships and peer group relationships. These relationships enable people to feel they belong, are wanted and liked by others and that there are people they can turn to for support. However, if an individual is bullied or rejected by their friends or peer group, they can lose self-confidence, feel very stressed and suffer low self-esteem.

Media

The media, including newspapers, television, radio and the Internet, have a powerful effect on the ideas and images that people develop about themselves and their health behaviour. Parents are often concerned

Your assessment criteria:

1C.4 Identify the effects of social factors on the health choices of individuals

2C.P4 Describe how social factors can affect the health and wellbeing of individuals

2C.M3 Explain how social factors can affect the health and wellbeing of individuals, with reference to relevant examples

Investigate

Use the Internet, the library or other sources of information to investigate cultural differences in diet, family relationships or the influence of religion on an individual's health and wellbeing. You should identify a cultural group different to your own, find out about the type of diet, family relationships or religious beliefs associated with this group and describe how this might influence the health and wellbeing of a person who belongs to the group you have chosen.

Discuss

With a class colleague, make a list of the different groups or communities living in your local area. Do members of these groups have any beliefs or make lifestyle choices that are different to your own? How might these have an impact on their members' health and wellbeing?

about fast-food advertising and television programmes that might have a negative effect on their children's health and wellbeing. However, at the same time as having a potentially negative influence on health, development and wellbeing, the media can also be used positively to deliver health education and to promote healthy living.

The media has a strong influence on how we think and behave in relation to health and wellbeing

Living conditions

A person's living accommodation provides them with physical shelter and protection. This is important for physical health and development. For example, lack of adequate heating, dampness and overcrowding can lead people of all ages to develop respiratory disorders, stress and mental health problems. Children who live in overcrowded homes are more likely to be victims of accidents.

People with low incomes sometimes have to choose between buying food and heating their homes. The consequence of not having enough heating can be hypothermia (a fall in body temperature to below 35°C – normal body temperature is 37°C). It is also important to note that a person's home provides them with a sense of emotional wellbeing and psychological security, so housing can affect an individual's emotional development too.

Effects of social factors on health and wellbeing

The links between social factors, such as social class and gender, health choices and their effects on health outcomes have been identified by health and social care researchers. Tables 4.2 and 4.3 summarise some of the patterns of health experience that provide evidence of social influences on health and wellbeing.

Your assessment criteria:

2C.M3 Explain how social factors can affect the health and wellbeing of individuals, with reference to relevant examples

2C.D3 Evaluate the link between social factors and the health and wellbeing of individuals, and the impact on health and wellbeing, with reference to relevant examples

💬 **Discuss**

What is 'healthy housing'? Identify the features you feel are important in making a person's housing healthy.

Assessment checklist

To achieve level 1, my portfolio of evidence must show that I can:

Assessment criteria	Description	✓
1A.1	Identify agents involved in the primary and secondary socialisation processes	☐
1A.2	Outline the main effects of socialisation on the health and wellbeing of individuals	☐
1B.3	Outline the different types of relationships that have an impact on the health and wellbeing of individuals	☐
1C.4	Identify the effects of social factors on the health choices of individuals	☐

To achieve a pass grade, my portfolio of evidence must show that I can:

Assessment criteria	Description	✓
2A.P1	Explain the influence of agents of primary and secondary socialisation	☐
2A.P2	Describe the effects of socialisation on the health and wellbeing of individuals	☐
2B.P3	Describe the influences that different types of relationships have on the health and wellbeing of individuals.	☐
2C.P4	Describe how social factors can affect the health and wellbeing of individuals	☐

To achieve a merit grade, my portfolio of evidence must show that I can:

Assessment criteria	Description	✓
2A.M1	Explain the effects of primary and secondary socialisation on the health and wellbeing of individuals, with reference to relevant examples	☐
2B.M2	Explain the influences that different types of relationships have on the health and wellbeing of individuals	☐
2C.M3	Explain how social factors can affect the health and wellbeing of individuals, with reference to relevant examples	☐

To achieve a distinction grade, my portfolio of evidence must show that I can:

Assessment criteria	Description	✓
2A.D1	Evaluate the impact of primary and secondary socialisation on the health and wellbeing of individuals, with reference to relevant examples	☐
2B.D2	Compare the potential positive and negative influences of different relationships on the health and wellbeing of individuals	☐
2C.D3	Evaluate the link between social factors and the health and wellbeing of individuals, and the impact on health and wellbeing, with reference to relevant examples	☐

5 | Promoting health and wellbeing

Learning aim A:
Explore the purpose, types and benefits of health promotion

▶ Topic A.1 Health promotion

▶ Topic A.2 Benefits of health promotion to both the health and wellbeing of the individual and the nation

Learning aim B:
Investigate how
health risks can be
addressed through
health promotion

▶ Topic B.1: Targeting selected
health risks

Health promotion

What is health promotion?

Have you ever set yourself a goal of 'being healthier' or 'getting fit'? A common time to do this is just after Christmas, when people often feel they've had too much to eat or drink. Other people change their diet and do their best to get fit when the summer is approaching or when they have a big occasion, like a wedding, to attend. We've probably all wanted to improve our health and wellbeing at one time or another, though it is best to have a healthy lifestyle all year round. The area of care practice that focuses on healthy lifestyle and health improvement is known as **health promotion** work, or health education work. Health promotion involves providing information and education containing **health messages** to individuals, to various social groups, to a whole community or, on a larger scale, to the wider nation.

Key terms

Health messages: key points of information or advice about health behaviour or outcomes

Health promotion: the process of enabling people to increase control over and to improve their health

Who is responsible for health promotion?

Most of the large-scale health promotion work is carried out by government agencies, such as the Department of Health, the Health Protection Agency or the National Health Service. They use different media to put health messages across. You have probably seen many different health promotion campaigns in newspapers and magazines, on television or in booklets and posters.

You may also have come across them at your local leisure centre, sports ground, health centre, library, shopping centre, health food shop, school, college, in a care home, nursery, or at a youth club. Some of these campaigns may be aimed at people of your age group or background, while others may target different groups in the population.

Purpose and aims of health promotion

The purpose of health promotion activity is to provide people with information, education and advice that will enable them to make lifestyle choices to improve their health and wellbeing. Health promotion activity often focuses on lifestyle issues and behaviours that present a risk to health. For example, smoking, poor diet, lack of exercise, alcohol and drug misuse and unprotected sex are all important health promotion issues.

Your assessment criteria:

1A.1 State what is meant by health promotion, identifying the purpose and aim(s) of one health-promotion activity

1A.2 Outline how health promotion is used to benefit individuals

2A.P1 Describe health promotion and the purpose and aims of three different health promotion-activities

Key terms

Department of Health: the part of national government responsible for health and social care services

Health Protection Agency: the agency that protects UK public health by providing support and advice to the NHS, local authorities, emergency services and government bodies

Media: the means of communicating health messages (via radio, television, Internet, newspapers, magazines, for example)

Reflect

Can you recall any health promotion campaigns or materials that have had an impact on your health choices or behaviour? Think about the focus and purpose of the materials and the reasons why you were influenced by them.

However, health promotion activity isn't just about health dangers and giving warnings. Increasingly, it is about promoting positive health. For example, you may see health promotion activities that focus on how to:

- lose weight safely

- get the most from local health services

- lead an active life after disability

- keep warm in winter

- eat healthily

- prepare for retirement

- benefit from exercise

- maintain personal hygiene

- prevent dental problems

- get the best out of sport and leisure facilities

- maintain desired weight in pregnancy.

Health promotion activity should be carefully planned in order to be effective. The aims of any health promotion work must be clearly identified from the outset. These might include:

- raising awareness of health and wellbeing issues

- reducing risk, preventing accidents or reducing levels of ill-health

- improving fitness levels

- improving life expectancy.

The specific aim of a health promotion activity could, for example, be to:

- reduce the number of road accidents in an area

- encourage healthy eating habits

- give people the knowledge and skills to improve their personal safety

- reduce the number of people smoking

- reduce levels of binge drinking or excessive alcohol consumption.

Road safety campaigns like this one provide brief information and advice that aims to save lives

Your assessment criteria:

2A.P2 Describe how different types of health promotion are used to benefit the health and wellbeing of individuals and the nation

2A.M1 Discuss how different types of health promotion are used to benefit the health and wellbeing of individuals and the nation, using selected examples

Types of health promotion activity

Health promotion activities can occur in a number of different ways. These include giving individuals information, advice and guidance about ways to improve their health, wellbeing or safety and much larger scale health promotion campaigns that are directed at the whole population or at specific groups.

Health risk advice

Health professionals often encourage the individuals they work with to make lifestyle changes as a way of improving their health and wellbeing. A health professional may have given you, or somebody you know, advice on ways of improving your health or sense of wellbeing. 'Do more exercise', 'lose some weight' or 'stop smoking' might form part of a health promotion message during a **consultation** with a health professional, for example.

As well as raising awareness of health risks by giving information and advice, these workers also:

- identify lifestyle issues that may lead to health problems and encourage people to adopt healthier lifestyles

- develop health improvement plans that focus on improving personal health, physical fitness and general wellbeing

- monitor health and wellbeing through **screening** and other health assessments, and provide services such as **immunisation** to prevent ill-health.

Health promotion occurs when care workers provide information, advice and guidance and when instructors demonstrate safe fitness techniques

Key terms

Consultation: an appointment or meeting

Immunisation: the act of creating immunity by introducing a small, controlled dose of an infection into a person's body

Screening: a strategy used in a population to detect disease in individuals who currently don't have any signs or symptoms of the disease

Health professionals such as GPs (family doctors), community nurses, occupational therapists and physiotherapists may work with individual service users to set targets for health improvement. They do this after undertaking a thorough assessment of the person's current health status.

Many people are very motivated to adopt a healthier lifestyle if they believe that it will reduce their risk of health problems, such as heart disease, obesity or cancer. However, sometimes an individual may struggle to make the necessary lifestyle changes or find that motivation to achieve their targets starts to slip. It is then part of the health professional's role to provide support and encouragement as needed.

Health promotion activity that informs people of health risks may also be provided through:

- peer education groups in schools, colleges or youth groups – this usually involves advisors from a similar age group and background providing information and advice on health and wellbeing issues, such as personal relationships, substance misuse or sexual health, for example

- advice from the police and fire service – on personal safety, crime and accident prevention issues

- testimonies – from people affected by health problems or issues such as substance misuse, unhealthy eating or diabetes for example, who are able to use their own experience to highlight specific health issues and identify ways in which others can avoid these problems.

Your assessment criteria:

2A.P2 Describe how different types of health promotion are used to benefit the health and wellbeing of individuals and the nation

2A.M1 Discuss how different types of health promotion are used to benefit the health and wellbeing of individuals and the nation, using selected examples

Key terms

Prevalent: *widespread or commonly occurring*

Vaccine: *a biological preparation that improves immunity to a particular disease*

Investigate

Use the Internet, your local library or health promotion services to find examples of crime or accident prevention campaigns that give expert advice as a way of promoting health, safety and wellbeing. Try to identify the specific aim or purpose of the campaign and think about who the campaign is targeting. Do you think expert advice is effective as a form of health promotion?

Case study

Vicky is a district nurse. She visits a large number of older people who live in their own homes and who are cared for by relatives or partners. When Vicky visits, these carers often complain to her about a range of health problems of their own, such as back pain, depression and stress. Vicky is wondering how to begin some health promotion work with this group of socially-isolated carers.

1. Who is the target group for Vicky's health promotion work?

2. What would be the purpose and aims of health promotion work targeted at this group of people?

Health promotion campaigns

Governments, usually through the Department of Health, often use large-scale health promotion campaigns to raise national awareness of health risks and lifestyle issues such as healthy eating, drug misuse and HIV infection. Newspapers, magazine and television adverts, as well as booklets, leaflets, posters, websites, emails and text messages, are used to communicate information about a variety of health risks to the whole population, or large sections of it. The purpose is to give people information about health risks and encourage everybody who may be at risk to take responsibility for making healthier or safer lifestyle choices.

Some large-scale health promotion campaigns, such as the Christmas anti-drink–driving campaign and the summer skin cancer awareness campaigns, are carried out every year. Other regional initiatives relating to safe drinking, road safety or personal safety, for example, may be targeted at a local population by the local NHS, police or fire service because there is a specific need for information in that area.

Medical interventions

Health care practitioners provide a range of medical interventions that are designed to prevent people from becoming ill and to eliminate disease in the population. For example, illness prevention services include:

- *immunisation* with **vaccines** against significant childhood infectious diseases such as polio, diphtheria and measles; against viruses, such as HPV (Human papillomavirus) that affects sexually active men and women, and influenza (flu) that affects many older people; and against tropical diseases, such as malaria, that can affect overseas travellers visiting areas where the virus is **prevalent**

- *screening* programmes that are used to detect diseases such as cervical, breast and bowel cancers which have few signs or symptoms in the early stages of their development. The aim of screening is to identify disease early enough to treat people and, hopefully, prevent them becoming unwell. Common screening tests for adults include blood pressure measurement, blood cholesterol tests, cervical smears (for cervical cancer) and mammograms (for breast cancer).

This woman is having a mammogram, a common form of screening for breast cancer.

? Reflect

Think about a national health promotion campaign that you have seen in the past. Where did you see the information? Reflect on the health messages of the campaign and think about how it affected your own health and lifestyle choices.

Table 5.1 Typical childhood immunisation programme

Vaccine	When given
• Diptheria • Tetanus • Pertussis (whooping cough) • Polio • Hib (*Haemophilus Influenzae*) • Pneumococcal infection	2 months
• Diptheria • Tetanus • Pertussis (whooping cough) • Polio • Hib (*Haemophilus Influenzae*) • Meningitis	3 months
• Diptheria • Tetanus • Pertussis (whooping cough) • Polio • Hib (*Haemophilus Influenzae*) • Meningitis • Pneumococcal infection	4 months
• Meningitis C and Hib	Around 12 months
• MMR (Measles, mumps, rubella) • Pneumococcal infection	Around 13 months
• Diptheria • Tetanus • Pertussis (whooping cough) • Polio • MMR	3 years
• Human papillomavirus (cause of cervical cancer)	Girls aged 12 to 13 years
• Diptheria • Tetanus • Polio	13–18 years

Investigate

Look at the immunisation programme. Research three of the diseases that are identified in Table 5.1. Use the information to make a leaflet or poster that informs parents about the dangers of these diseases.

Benefits of health promotion to the health and wellbeing of the individual and the nation

Who benefits from health promotion activity?

The health promotion activities of government agencies and health care practitioners are designed to improve the health and wellbeing of:

- individuals with specific health problems or needs

- communities or social groups with particular health problems or needs

- the nation as a whole.

Benefits for the individual

The health risk advice given to individuals by health care practitioners and the campaigns that are targeted at individual members of particular communities or social groups are designed to:

- increase understanding of health issues

- motivate individuals to take greater personal responsibility for their health and wellbeing

- reduce the risk of experiencing disease or injury by encouraging people to make different lifestyle choices or change their behaviour

- improve quality of life by boosting health and wellbeing

- increase life expectancy by promoting a healthier and safer lifestyle.

Benefits for the nation

Governments and local agencies that have health and social care responsibilities invest in health promotion activities because it can be an effective way of improving the health and wellbeing of communities and the nation as a whole. Large-scale health promotion campaigns and medical interventions like vaccination and screening programmes that are supported by governments and local health services can:

- reduce levels of illness and disease in the population as a whole

- help to tackle inequalities in health and illness experienced in different sections of the population

- reduce crime and accident levels (related to road safety, drug use and alcohol-related violence, for example), both locally and nationally

Your assessment criteria:

1A.2 Outline how health promotion is used to benefit individuals

2A.P2 Describe how different types of health promotion are used to benefit the health and wellbeing of individuals and the nation

Regular exercise has a beneficial effect on both health and wellbeing

? Reflect

Why would it be beneficial to the nation if health promotion activities managed to reduce obesity levels in the UK?

- increase participation in vaccination and screening programmes within targeted sections of the population

- raise awareness of and help to tackle current and emerging health and wellbeing concerns within the UK population (obesity levels, heart health, drug use and sexually transmitted disease, for example)

- reduce the financial cost to the NHS and government of having to treat preventable health problems (diet, smoking and alcohol-related conditions, for example)

- reduce the cost to society, the police, courts and prison service of dealing with alcohol, drug and road safety-related crime and disorder incidents.

The benefits of participation in exercise and sport

Some people really enjoy sports, going to the gym or doing exercise classes. You might be one of them. Or you might be one of the large number of people who don't do enough exercise. Health care practitioners and government health promotion campaigns often focus on the benefits of participating in exercise and sport. For example, being physically active for at least 30 minutes on five or more days each week can help you not only to look and feel better, but it can also help reduce your risk of heart disease, cancer, stroke and diabetes. There are obvious health benefits for the individual but also for the nation as a whole, as participation in exercise and sport is a key illness prevention and disease reduction measure, cutting care and treatment costs to the NHS and government in the long run.

Figure 5.1 Benefits of exercise

Case study

Jack is 14 years old. He lives on a small estate on the edge of town with his parents. Jack plays a lot of computer games on his console. He's also a keen keyboard player, practising for a couple of hours each day. Jack is popular at school, partly because he is very funny. He uses his humour to defend himself when people laugh at his size; Jack is seriously overweight. His parents are concerned about this though his mum insists he does not overeat. She believes that lack of exercise has led to his weight problem.

1. What factors might be contributing to Jack's weight gain?

2. Why is Jack's weight likely to lead to health problems if he doesn't do something about it?

3. How might Jack and others benefit from health promotion activities that focus on the value of exercise and participation in sport?

The benefits of safe drinking

Alcohol is a very popular, widely available and accepted part of social life in the United Kingdom. Research shows that 98 per cent of the adult population use alcohol. Many people enjoy a drink and there is usually nothing wrong with that. In small, controlled quantities alcoholic drinks can be part of a pleasurable social occasion. In fact, some types of alcoholic drink, such as red wine, have been shown to be good for health. Studies have shown that people who regularly drink small amounts of alcohol tend to live longer than people who don't drink at all. This is because alcohol protects against the development of **coronary heart disease** – it has an effect on the amount of **cholesterol**, or fat, carried in the bloodstream reducing the likelihood of the formation of the clots which cause heart disease.

Maximum health advantage can be achieved from drinking between one and two units of alcohol a day. There is no additional overall health benefit to be gained from drinking more than two units of alcohol a day. However, there are possible negative effects from doing so.

Health risks associated with alcohol

The health risks associated with alcohol result from consuming it in large quantities, either regularly or in binges. People who frequently drink excess amounts of alcohol have an increased risk of:

- high blood pressure
- coronary heart disease
- liver damage and cirrhosis of the liver
- cancer of the mouth and throat
- psychological and emotional problems, including depression
- obesity.

Key terms

Cholesterol: a fat-like substance that is made by the body and carried in the blood but which also occurs in meat, diary products and some fish

Coronary heart disease: a health problem in which the circulation of blood to the heart is inadequate because of damage to arteries or heart muscle

Alcohol, if consumed in small quantities, can be beneficial for health, but can also be very damaging if consumed in large quantities

Alcohol is also a depressant. This means that it reduces certain brain functions and affects judgement, self-control and co-ordination. This is why alcohol increases the risk of a person becoming involved in fights, domestic violence and accidents. It has been estimated that up to 40,000 deaths per year could be alcohol related. In 1996, 15 per cent of fatal road accidents resulted from people driving whilst under the influence of alcohol.

Peer pressure can make some people feel they should consume excess alcohol

Your assessment criteria:

2A.M1 Discuss how different types of health promotion are used to benefit the health and wellbeing of individuals and the nation, using selected examples

2A.D1 Analyse the benefits of different types of health promotion to individuals and the nation, using selected examples

Investigate

Using the Internet, investigate the health impact of drinking excessive amounts of alcohol. Produce a poster designed to inform 14 to 16 year-old adolescents about the links between alcohol consumption and health problems.

Case study

Jodie started drinking when she was 14 years of age. She used to drink in her local park with some older teenagers and a couple of her friends. Most weekends, Jodie drank a couple of bottles of cider and any vodka that was available. Jodie thought that drinking was fun and that it made her happy. She realised when she was 19 years of age that the opposite was true. Jodie found herself thinking about alcohol at work and college, and would go to the pub for a few drinks at lunch time. Jodie was eventually sacked from her job as a trainee hairdresser for coming to work smelling of alcohol. After making a promise to her mum and dad, Jodie hasn't drunk any alcohol for three months. Jodie's GP (family doctor) also told her about the physical effects that long-term alcohol abuse and binge drinking could have on her health.

1. Suggest some reasons why young teenagers like Jodie start drinking alcohol.

2. Identify four effects of long-term alcohol abuse or binge drinking on physical health.

3. What are the benefits, to Jodie and to wider society, of sticking to the recommended safe limits for alcohol consumption if she does start drinking alcohol again in the future?

The benefits of quitting smoking

Despite it being legal for people aged 18 or over to buy and smoke tobacco, cigarettes have got a very bad reputation with health professionals. This is because smoking cigarettes, or any other kind of tobacco product, has no health benefits at all. Instead, smoking cigarettes directly damages your physical health. This is one of the most important pieces of health promotion information that health professionals regularly give to people. Their advice is always to 'stop smoking' – you should be told this if you smoke cigarettes. People who fail to take note of this warning run a considerable risk of causing themselves long-term health damage, and possibly dying as a direct result of their smoking habit.

The health problems associated with smoking tobacco include an increased risk of developing:

- coronary heart disease

- stroke

- high blood pressure

- bronchitis

- lung cancer

- other cancers, such as cancer of the larynx, kidney and bladder.

Investigate

Use library sources or the Internet to find out about the connections between smoking and these diseases.

Smoking cigarettes is harmful to health because the nicotine, carbon monoxide and tar contained in cigarette smoke circulate deep into the body. Nicotine is a powerful, fast-acting and addictive drug. Smokers absorb it into their bloodstream and feel an effect in their brains seven to eight minutes later. Some smokers say this is 'calming'. However, the physical effects of smoking also include an increase in heart rate and blood pressure, and changes in appetite. The high concentration of carbon monoxide in cigarette smoke reduces the oxygen supply to the smoker's body and can cause fat deposits to form on the walls of the arteries. This leads to hardening of the arteries and to circulatory problems, causing smokers to develop coronary heart disease. Cigarette tar contains many substances known to cause cancer. It damages the cilia (small hairs) lining the lungs which help to protect them from dirt and infection. Because these lung protectors get damaged, smokers are more likely than non-smokers to get throat and chest infections. About 70 per cent of the tar in a cigarette is deposited in the lungs when cigarette smoke is inhaled.

The use of tobacco is now less widespread and less socially acceptable than it was even 20 years ago. Health promotion advice and campaigns, such as National No-Smoking Day, have significantly reduced levels of smoking in the population as a whole. However, in 2007, 28 per cent of manual workers and 13 per cent of non-manual workers in the UK were still smokers and there were over 43,000 smoking-related deaths from cancer in 2010 (Cancer Research UK, 2012).

Smoking prevalence: 1992–2010

Prevalence of cigarette smoking by socio-economic group, adults aged 16 and over, Great Britain

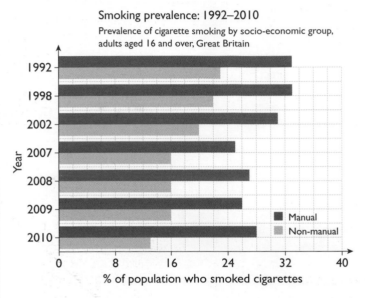

Source: Cancer Research UK (2012)

Figure 5.2 Smoking statistics

Investigate

What does the data produced by Cancer Research UK show about trends in smoking in Great Britain?

Teenage girls are one of the few social groups who are more likely to smoke now than in the past. Tobacco use is, therefore, still a major cause of preventable disease and early death in the United Kingdom. The health benefits of quitting smoking are considerable for individuals who do smoke. Government and local health care providers also benefit as the financial burden of providing health care services for those with smoking-induced diseases is also reduced.

Targeting selected health risks

Focusing on a health risk

Health promotion activities typically identify and focus on lifestyle choices or behaviours that increase an individual's risk of disease and illness or which reduce quality of life. For example, individual health risk advice and wider health promotion campaigns may focus on:

- substance misuse and binge drinking

- immunisation

- safe sex

- unhealthy eating

- smoking

- road safety

- (lack of) handwashing

- participation in sport and exercise.

All of these issues are associated with risks to health and wellbeing if they are not dealt with appropriately. The health promotion challenge is to find a way of giving individuals, communities or members of the wider population well-researched information on a health risk in a format that appeals to them and is easy to understand.

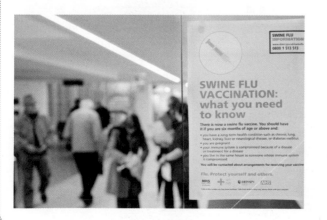

Your assessment criteria:

1B.3 Identify the main effects of the chosen health risk on individuals

1B.4 Produce materials for a health-promotion activity, with guidance

2B.P3 Describe the chosen health risk and its main effects on individuals, using research findings from different sources

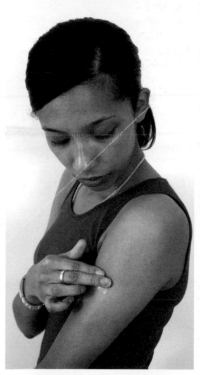

Immunisation is an important way of preventing the spread of a variety of infectious diseases

Investigating a chosen health risk

A health promotion campaign should be based on thorough knowledge and understanding of a health risk. Potential sources of information on a topic include:

- websites
- books
- newspapers and magazines
- leaflets
- journals
- DVDs and TV programmes
- Department of Health publications
- health professionals with practical knowledge of an issue or care area
- service users with personal experience of a particular health problem or issue.

Obtaining and summarising background information can be time-consuming but is a necessary first step in planning health promotion activities. This stage of the process should focus on identifying the links between a lifestyle choice or behaviour and the likely short, medium and long-term health consequences for people who expose themselves to the risk.

Gathering data on a health risk

Government agencies, such as the Department of Health, the Office for National Statistics and the National Health Service, as well as private and independent sector organisations, produce data on health topics that can be used to develop understanding of health risks. Reports and studies on health risks tend to focus on population-level data, summarising this in the form of statistics.

These statistics can give health promotion workers a good understanding of the general trends and patterns of health and illness experience in relation to a health risk, but can also seem impersonal and distant from everyday life. Case studies that describe the experiences of people who have been affected by health risk factors can be an alternative and more accessible source of information on a topic. For example, an individual's account of their experience of substance misuse and the negative impact it had on their own family and work life can be a useful way of grabbing the attention of people who would take little notice of statistics.

? Reflect

Which health risk would you be most interested in researching? Identify two or three possible topics and then reflect on which one interests you most.

 Investigate

Where could you begin looking for information on your chosen health risk? Make a list of possible sources and begin exploring one or two of them. Ask your tutor for advice if you are short of ideas.

The data that is gathered in order to understand a health topic should be:

- produced by a reputable source

- reliable and credible

- as recent as possible

- directly relevant to and informative about the health risks associated with the lifestyle choice or behaviour.

Summarising key aspects of the data, making a record of where the data was found (who produced and published it) is also important. This is because being able to quote from and reference sources of background data adds to the credibility of health promotion activities, making people feel more confident that the information, advice or guidance is reliable.

People who have experience of particular health problems can sometimes use their expertise to advise, guide and inform others

Identifying and creating health promotion materials

Health promotion campaigns can make use of a variety of communication methods and materials to deliver health messages or information. These include:

- posters

- leaflets

- games and role plays

- presentations (talks and lectures)

- wall displays

- seminars and workshops

- information films and videos

- information packs

- television and radio campaigns.

? | Reflect

What kinds of materials would be most appropriate and effective in communicating health messages on your chosen topic?

The materials or delivery methods used to communicate specific health messages must appeal to and be effective in reaching the intended audience. The types of materials or methods used must also be:

- capable of achieving the overall aims of the health promotion activity (see Table 5.2)

- an appropriate way of describing the health risk and of providing health advice

- cost effective (TV adverts are very expensive; wall displays are not, for example)

- relatively easy for the person carrying out the health promotion activity to create and use.

Table 5.2 Aims and methods in health promotion

Health promotion aim	Appropriate method or material
Raising awareness of health issues	• Talks, displays or presentations • Group work • Mass media • Poster and leaflet campaigns
Improving knowledge or providing information	• Presentations • Games • Wall displays • Posters and leaflets • Mass media
Empowering people by improving self-awareness, self-esteem and decision-making abilities	• Group work and role play • Social skills training • Assertiveness training • Counselling
Changing attitudes, behaviour and the lifestyles	• Games • Skills training • Self-help groups • Presentations

Your assessment criteria:

1B.4 Produce materials for a health-promotion activity, with guidance

2B.P4 Produce appropriate materials for a health-promotion activity, describing the health risk and health advice

2B.M3 Produce materials for a health-promotion activity tailored to a target group, describing the health risk and health advice

 Investigate

Visit places in your local area where you would expect to find health promotion information. These might include your GP surgery, local library, a sports centre or a youth club. Identify examples of health promotion material on display. Write a brief report describing the information that was available, explaining who it was aimed at and what the health messages were. You could also say whether you think the material (and the way it was presented) was effective, and what other information could be displayed or provided to promote health improvement.

Health promotion leaflets and booklets are often displayed in health centres, libraries and sports centres

Table 5.3 identifies a number of different types of health promotion materials and outlines some of their strengths and limitations.

Table 5.3 Strengths and limitations of health promotion materials

Material	Strengths	Limitations
Leaflets	• Can be read in own time • Easy and cheap to make • Can summarise a lot of information	• Can be too general • Require good reading skills • Easy to ignore or lose
Videos / DVDs	• Can show real-life situations • Easy to use and to engage with • Can be seen by lots of people	• Requires specialist equipment • Can become outdated very quickly • Viewers may not think about content
Posters	• Easy way to raise awareness of an issue • Can give basic information to a lot of people • Easy and cheap to produce	• Can deteriorate • People don't or can't read them, or learn to ignore them • Need to be displayed very publicly
Websites	• Provide lots of information to many people • Can be easily updated • Can be viewed in own time • Can be eye-catching and interactive	• Requires computer skills and Internet access • Not suitable for all age groups • Need to be able to find it on the Internet

AFFECTED BY CANCER? WE CAN HELP YOU

WE ARE MACMILLAN. CANCER SUPPORT

Macmillan Support Line
0808 808 00 00
www.macmillan.org.uk

 Investigate

Television adverts and website-based health promotion campaigns aim to deliver health messages in distinctive ways. Some do this in a subtle way; others do it in a very strong and sometimes shocking way. They try to persuade the person reading or watching health messages either to do something or to think about something.

1. *Make a list of the features you believe are important in making health messages memorable or persuasive.*

2. *What is your favourite or most memorable health promotion campaign? Identify it and describe the features you like and which you think made it distinctive.*

Targeting a population group

Health promotion campaigns tend to target specific groups in the population. The groups in the community that are identified as being in need of specific advice, guidance or information on health topics are known as **target groups**. The health promotion message and the methods used to communicate it must appeal to members of the target group. Health promotion campaigns have been targeted at:

- children
- adolescents
- employees
- members of sports or social clubs
- pregnant women
- cigarette smokers
- people who are obese
- people who have an alcohol problem
- people who misuse drugs and other substances
- the homeless
- travellers
- pre-retirement groups.

Each of these groups faces, and needs to be aware of, a range of health risks. The health messages and the methods or materials used to deliver them must be suitable for the particular target group. Different messages and health promotion materials would be needed to promote healthy lifestyles to children and adolescents, for example.

Evaluating a health promotion strategy

In order to ensure that health promotion activities are effective, health care practitioners and agencies running health promotion campaigns generally undertake an evaluation. The purpose of an evaluation is to assess the outcomes of a health promotion activity and to check if the original aims and objectives have been met. An evaluation will generally try to measure the outcome ('How many people stopped smoking?', 'Are members of the group less likely to binge drink?') and also the effectiveness of the methods used ('Was the questionnaire easy to follow or too complicated?'). Methods of evaluation include:

Your assessment criteria:

 2B.M3 Produce materials for a health-promotion activity tailored to a target group, describing the health risk and health advice

 Key term

Target group: section of the population identified as being the focus for health advice, guidance or information

Discuss

Choose any one of the following topics to develop a health message targeted at children:

- dental health
- balanced diet
- smoking
- exercise
- personal safety.

- Identify a message suitable for promoting good health and wellbeing to a group of children aged between seven and nine years.

- Identify two health promotion methods or types of material that could be used to get this message across to these children. Explain why you think the methods or materials would be appropriate and effective.

- before and after questioning of participants using questionnaires, interviews, discussions or written tests

- observation of changes in attitudes and behaviours

- changes in demand for health information

- records of changes in health status, for example weight, blood pressure changes.

The aim of an evaluation is always to gain feedback from the target audience. By acting on the feedback received, health promoters will be able to improve subsequent campaigns.

Your assessment criteria:

2B.D2 Evaluate the strategies used to address the chosen health risk, using research findings

2B.D3 Make recommendations for how the health-promotion materials could be adapted for a different target group

Assessment checklist

To achieve level 1, my portfolio of evidence must show that I can:

Assessment criteria	Description	✓
1A.1	State what is meant by health promotion, identifying the purpose and aim(s) of one health-promotion activity	
1A.2	Outline how health promotion is used to benefit individuals	
1B.3	Identify the main effects of the chosen health risk on individuals	
1B.4	Produce materials for a health-promotion activity, with guidance	

To achieve a pass grade, my portfolio of evidence must show that I can:

Assessment criteria	Description	✓
2A.P1	Describe health promotion and the purpose and aims of three different health-promotion activities	
2A.P2	Describe how different types of health promotion are used to benefit the health and wellbeing of individuals and the nation	
2B.P3	Describe the chosen health risk and its main effects on individuals, using research findings from different sources	
2B.P4	Produce appropriate materials for a health-promotion activity, describing the health risk and health advice	

To achieve a merit grade, my portfolio of evidence must show that I can:

Assessment criteria	Description	✓
2A.M1	Discuss how different types of health promotion are used to benefit the health and wellbeing of individuals and the nation, using selected examples	☐
2B.M2	Explain how the chosen health risk affects individuals and how these effects can be addressed through health promotion, using research findings from different types of sources	☐
2B.M3	Produce materials for a health-promotion activity tailored to a target group, describing the health risk and health advice	☐

To achieve a distinction grade, my portfolio of evidence must show that I can:

Assessment criteria	Description	✓
2A.D1	Analyse the benefits of different types of health promotion to individuals and the nation, using selected examples	☐
2B.D2	Evaluate the strategies used to address the chosen health risk, using research findings	☐
2B.D3	Make recommendations for how the health-promotion materials could be adapted for a different target group	☐

6 | The impact of nutrition on health and wellbeing

Learning aim A:
Explore the effects of balanced and unbalanced diets on the health and wellbeing of individuals

▶ Topic A.1 Dietary intake and food groups

▶ Topic A.2 Long-term effects of balanced and unbalanced diets

Learning Outcome B: Understand the specific nutritional needs and preferences of individuals

▶ Topic B.1 Factors influencing the diet of individuals and their associated dietary needs

▶ Topic B.2 Nutritional variation during life stage development

▶ Topic B.3 Considerations for nutritional planning

Dietary intake and food groups

Introduction to this chapter

A good understanding of diet can help an individual to maintain or improve their personal health. Health and social care workers can use their knowledge of nutrition to promote the health of the individuals for whom they care. The dietary needs of individuals change as they move through different life stages. However, people of all ages require a balanced diet.

This chapter introduces you to the dietary needs of people who use care services, and to the components of a balanced diet. It also considers the effects of an unbalanced diet. You will investigate and examine the dietary needs of people who use care services and produce some diet plans to meet these needs.

This topic focuses on the way a balanced diet provides the basis for good health and development.

Your assessment criteria:

1A.1 Identify components of a balanced diet, giving examples of each

2A.P1 Describe the components of a balanced diet and their functions, sources and effects

Key terms

Fibre: the indigestible portion of plant-based food, also known as roughage

Macronutrients: nutrients required in relatively large amounts to enable the body to function

Micronutrients: nutrients required by the human body in small amounts only

Nutrients: naturally occurring chemical substances found in the food we eat

Nutrients for health, growth and development

Food is essential for life and plays a very important role in an individual's physical health, growth and development. The food we eat should be nutritious if it is going to be beneficial to our physical health. This means it should contain a variety of **nutrients**. There are five basic nutrients which help the body in different ways:

1. carbohydrates provide the body with energy

2. fats also provide the body with energy

3. proteins provide the chemical substances needed to build (grow) and repair body cells and tissues

4. vitamins help to regulate the chemical reactions that continuously take place in our bodies

5. minerals are needed for control of body function, and to build and repair certain tissues.

? | Reflect

Can you identify at least two sources of each nutrient shown in Table 6.1 in the food that you have eaten over the last two days? Are any of the nutrients missing from your diet?

Carbohydrates, proteins and fats are referred to as macronutrients because the human body requires a lot of them to function. Vitamins and minerals are referred to as micronutrients as they are needed in much smaller amounts.

As well as eating food that contains a balance of these five nutrients, people also need fibre and water in their diet. Although these are not counted as nutrients they are vital for physical health. Table 6.1 provides more information on the sources and functions of nutrients.

 Investigate

Using the Internet, find out the names of vitamins A, C, B1, B2, B3, B6 B12 and vitamin E. Identify a source of food containing each of these vitamins and find out what role the vitamin plays in the body. Present your findings in a table.

Table 6.1 Sources of essential nutrients

Nutrient	Food source	Function
Carbohydrates – the three types of carbohydrate are simple (sugars), complex (starch) and non-starch polysaccharides (fibre).	Sugar sources – milk, fruit and fruit juice, and sugar-based products (e.g biscuits, cakes, chocolate) Starch sources – potatoes, yams, cereals Fibre sources – fruit and vegetables, and food made from bran	Sugars and starch are good energy sources. Fibre helps gut function and prevents constipation.
Proteins – these are the only source of essential amino acids for human beings. Essential amino acids play a vital role in many of the chemical processes that occur in the body.	Animal protein sources – meat, fish, milk, cheese and eggs Plant protein sources – peas, beans, cereals and seeds	Proteins are essential for the growth and repair of body tissues and are a source of energy. They also supply essential amino acids.
Fats and oils – saturated fats found in animal and dairy products are less healthy fats and can cause heart disease. Unsaturated fats are found in olive oil and have a beneficial effect on the heart. Polyunsaturated fats are found in fish and soya oil and also have health benefits.	Animal and dairy sources – meat, butter, cheese Plant sources – vegetable and nut oils Fish sources – mackerel, tuna and other oily fish	Fats and oils are a source of energy and warmth for the body.
Vitamins: A, B, C, D, E and K	Fruit and vegetables	Vitamins are needed to maintain various body functions, including eyesight, healthy skin and gums, bone strength and blood clotting, for example.
Minerals: calcium, sodium, iron and potassium	Minerals can be obtained from vegetables, meat, dairy products and salt	Like vitamins, minerals are needed to support various body functions.

Balancing your diet

A healthy intake of food contains suitable amounts of each of the five basic nutrients; this is known as a **balanced diet**. A person who consumes a balanced diet will obtain sufficient nourishment to enable their body to grow and function properly. Consuming a balanced diet reduces the risk of diet-related conditions, such as heart disease, strokes and diabetes, and **malnutrition**. A balanced diet will also provide sufficient energy for the person to meet their activity needs. The amount and type of foods that are healthy for a person to eat varies for each individual and changes over the course of their life.

The balance of good health

The food pyramid in Figure 6.1 shows the main five food groups – and the proportion of each food type – that make up a balanced diet.

You will see from the food pyramid that a balanced diet is based on starchy, carbohydrate foods. These are the main source of energy in an individual's diet. Fruit and vegetables make up the next 'layer' of the pyramid. They are a key source of vitamins and minerals, as well as fibre, in the diet. Protein foods can come from animal or vegetable sources but should be eaten in only moderate amounts. Sugars and fats are at the top of the food pyramid because they should be eaten least often and should form only a very small part of a person's diet. Sugary and fatty foods provide calories (energy) but tend to have very little other nutritional value.

Your assessment criteria:

1A.1 Identify components of a balanced diet, giving examples of each

2A.P1 Describe the components of a balanced diet and their functions, sources and effects

Key terms

Balanced diet: a diet that contains adequate amounts of all the nutrients needed for growth and activity

Malnutrition: inadequate nutrition caused by over- or under-eating, or a diet that lacks nutrients

How to eat a balanced, healthy diet

- Enjoy a variety of different foods.

- Eat the right amount to be a healthy weight.

- Consume plenty of foods rich in starch and fibre, such as bread, cereals, potatoes.

- Eat plenty of fruit and vegetables.

- Consume moderate amounts of meat and fish.

- Eat moderate amounts of milk and dairy products.

- Consume small amounts of fatty and sugary foods.

- Drink plenty of water.

Figure 6.1 Components of a balanced diet

Dietary reference values

One way of working out how much an individual needs to eat to have a balanced, healthy diet is to refer to **Dietary Reference Values** (DRVs). The Department of Health produces a table of DRVs that provides guidance on the amount of energy or the amount of an individual nutrient that different age groups need for good health. There are three different values for each nutrient:

- *Reference Nutrient Intake* (RNI) – this is the amount of a nutrient that is sufficient for almost every member of a defined group of people. The RNI is higher than most people's needs.

- *Estimated Average Requirement* (EAR) – this is an estimate of the *average* need for food energy or a nutrient for a defined group of people. Some members of the group will need more than this average while others will need less.

- *Lower Reference Nutrient Intake* (LRNI) – this is the amount of a nutrient that is sufficient for a small number of individuals in a group of people. These people will have the lowest nutrient needs.

DRVs provide some guidance on the daily intake of each nutrient and can be used as the basis for the recommendations and diet-related treatment plans of dieticians, doctors and other practitioners who are promoting healthy eating and a balanced diet.

| Age | EARs in MJ/d (kcal/d) | |
	Males	Females
0–3 months	2.28 (545)	2.16 (515)
4–6 months	2.89 (690)	2.69 (645)
7–9 months	3.44 (825)	3.20 (765)
10–12 months	3.85 (920)	3.61 (865)
1–3 years	5.15 (1230)	4.86 (1165)
4–6 years	7.16 (1715)	6.46 (1545)
7–10 years	8.24 (1970)	7.28 (1740)
11–14 years	9.27 (2220)	7.72 (1845)
15–18 years	11.51 (2755)	8.83 (2110)
19–50 years	10.60 (2550)	8.10 (1940)
51–59 years	10.60 (2550)	8.00 (1900)
60–64 years	9.93 (2380)	7.99 (1900)
65–74 years	9.71 (2330)	7.96 (1900)
75+ years	8.77 (2100)	7.61 (1810)
Pregnancy		+0.80 (200)
Source: Committee on Medical Aspects of Food and Nutrition Policy (COMA), 2002		

Figure 6.2 Estimated average requirements of males and females at different ages

Key term

Dietary Reference Values: *statistics produced by the Department of Health which recommend nutritional intake for different sections of the UK population*

Reflect

How do you decide what is 'enough' to eat? Do you count calories or pay attention to the fat, sugar and salt content of the foods you eat?

Investigate

Look at how the amount of EAR calories changes through the life course. At what age are both males and females recommended to consume most calories?

Energy balance

An individual's diet should have an energy balance. Some foods provide large amounts of energy per gram of the food while others do not. An individual who balances the types of food they consume should be able to achieve a good energy balance from their diet.

Nutrient deficiencies and malnutrition

A diet that contains a sufficient amount and variety of food lays the foundations for good health. In general terms, no food is unhealthy in itself. However, unbalanced and insufficient diets can be the cause of health problems associated with nutritional **deficiencies**.

People who eat too much (over-nutrition) or too little food (under-nutrition), or who consume a diet that does not provide them with enough nutrients or energy to meet their needs will become malnourished. Eating too much food is linked to **obesity**, heart disease and dental health problems, and is associated with developed western societies. Eating too little food deprives the body of essential nutrients and can lead to health problems like kwashiorkor, iron-deficiency and ultimately to starvation (see page 144–5). Under-nutrition is rare in the UK but is more common in less developed countries where there are significant food shortages.

Case study

Marina is a 21-year-old student teacher. She has been overweight since her early teens. Marina is reluctant to talk about her size but admits that she is 'too heavy'. Marina doesn't cook for herself, eats a lot of take-away food and ready meals, and consumes cans of fizzy drink throughout the day. Though she doesn't drink alcohol every night, Marina consumes almost twice the weekly recommended number of units of alcohol for a woman. Marina's knowledge of nutrition is poor. She doesn't really know or understand anything about her nutritional needs or the nutrients in her food. Marina says she just enjoys eating and chooses food that she knows she will enjoy.

Marina is now 25 kg overweight and is aware she is developing some health problems. Her feet are always cold and often bluish in colour. She becomes breathless if she has to walk any distance, tires quickly if she has to lift things and says she often has aches and pains in her ankles, knees and shoulders.

1. What is wrong with Martina's dietary intake at the moment?

2. What does Marina need to do in order to eat a balanced diet?

3. How will eating a balanced diet help Marina to improve her health?

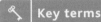

Your assessment criteria:

1A.2   Identify three effects of an unbalanced diet on the health and wellbeing of individuals

2A.P2   Describe the effects of an unbalanced diet on the health and wellbeing of individuals, giving examples of their causes

Key terms

Deficiency: a lack of something

Obesity: a medical condition in which there is an excess of body fat and a body mass index (BMI) of 30+

Eating a healthy diet can become an issue for both males and females who have body image issues

Long-term effects of balanced and unbalanced diets

Diet and long-term health

A balanced diet is a healthy diet because it helps to maintain and improve an individual's general health. Reasons for balancing your diet and some of the positive health effects of this have been outlined on page 140. As well as reducing the risk of developing long-term health problems, a balanced diet can also have a positive impact on a person's health by, for example:

- increasing the person's immunity to infections

- giving the person greater energy levels and increased concentration

- enabling faster healing of skin, tissues and mucus membranes.

Diet and ill-health

The links between an unbalanced diet and ill-health are widely known. Diets that are high in sugar, saturated fats and salt can lead to long-term health problems, for example. Malnutrition is the term given to an inadequate or unbalanced diet. This covers both over-nutrition and under-nutrition.

Over-nutrition

Over-nutrition occurs when a person consumes too much food. A person who overeats may also be consuming a diet that contains an inappropriate balance of nutrients. This is likely to be the case if the individual consumes a diet that is high in saturated fats, salt and sugar.

Your assessment criteria:

1A.2 Identify three effects of an unbalanced diet on the health and wellbeing of individuals

2A.P2 Describe the effects of an unbalanced diet on the health and wellbeing of individuals, giving examples of their causes

2A.M1 Compare the effects of balanced and unbalanced diets on the health and wellbeing of two individuals

2A.D1 Assess the long-term effects of a balanced and unbalanced diet on the health and wellbeing of individuals

? | Reflect

Do you avoid or restrict your consumption of any foods because they are associated with ill-health or because they affect your appearance?

A range of health problems can occur as a result of over-nutrition. These include:

- obesity – excess food that can't be used as energy is converted into body fat

- coronary heart disease – excess **saturated fat** in the diet increases **cholesterol** levels which can lead to **atheroma plaques** in the arteries; narrowing of the arteries leads to heart disease and blockage leads to heart attacks

- type 2 diabetes – excess glucose (sugar) is present in the blood because the person's body can't produce enough **insulin** to convert it into energy. High levels of blood glucose damage blood vessels, nerves and organs. This form of diabetes is closely linked to obesity.

Under-nutrition

Under-nutrition is caused by not eating enough food or by eating a diet that contains an inappropriate balance of essential nutrients. Under-nutrition is much more common in less developed countries where food is scarce. However, babies, older people and those with medical conditions that affect their ability to absorb nutrients or who starve themselves (such as in the condition anorexia nervosa) may be undernourished.

This child's swollen stomach is the result of under-nutrition rather than eating too much

Kwashiorkor and marasmus are health problems that result from under-nutrition. They are usually experienced by children in less developed countries. Marasmus results from a diet that has insufficient energy and protein to meet the child's needs. Marasmus leads to loss of muscle and body fat, infection, dehydration and circulatory disorders. Kwashiorkor is a similar condition to marasmus, also resulting from a diet that contains insufficient protein. The effects are slow growth, tiredness, oedema, diarrhoea and a swollen stomach. Oedema is the medical term for swollen or puffy parts of the body caused by fluid retention.

Nutrient deficiencies

Nutrient deficiencies are a form of under-nutrition. They occur when a person's long-term diet lacks some important nutrients. For example, people who don't eat fruit or vegetables may develop health problems because of the lack of vitamins and minerals in their diet. Table 6.2 identifies examples of conditions that result from specific nutrient deficiencies.

 Investigate

How can kwashiorkor be treated? Using books or the Internet, investigate how different types of food need to be given in a controlled way to children suffering from kwashiorkor.

Table 6.2 The effect of nutritional deficiencies on health

Condition	Deficiency	Effect on health
Anaemia	Iron	Lack of iron limits the ability of the blood to carry oxygen and other nutrients around the body. Anaemia results in tiredness, weakness and breathlessness.
Rickets	Calcium and vitamin D	Rickets is a disease of infancy and childhood that affects the skeletal system. A lack of calcium and vitamin D results in a softening of the bones, leading to fractures, deformity and muscle weakness.
Night blindness	Vitamin A	This condition prevents sufferers from seeing in dim light or when it is dark. Lack of vitamin A (found in carrots, and other fruit and vegetables) affects rod function in the eye.
Beriberi	Thiamine (vitamin B1)	Beriberi is a disease of the nervous system caused by a lack of thiamine in the diet. Thiamine is found in unrefined cereals, fresh fruit, fresh meat and fresh vegetables. Thiamine is needed to breakdown energy molecules such as glucose and is also present in nerve cells. Symptoms include weight loss, severe tiredness, pain in the limbs, irregular heart rate and oedema.
Scurvy	Vitamin C	This condition is caused by insufficient vitamin C in the diet. Vitamin C is found in fruit and vegetables and is needed for healthy skin and gums, and wound healing. The symptoms of scurvy include spongy, bleeding gums (and loose teeth), bleeding under the skin and general weakness.
Lethargy, apathy, muscle weakness	Vitamin E	Lack of vitamin E can lead to problems with physical co-ordination, damage to eyesight and anaemia.
Impaired blood clotting	Vitamin K	Lack of vitamin K usually occurs because the body can't absorb this vitamin from food, or as a result of long-term use of antibiotics. People with vitamin K deficiency are more likely to experience bleeding (gums, nose bleeds and heavy menstrual bleeding) and bruising. It can also lead to osteoporosis and hip fractures in the long-term.

Tooth decay doesn't result directly from a nutrient deficiency. It is caused by acid that dissolves the enamel surface of the teeth, exposing the inner dentine which then decays. The acid is produced by bacteria that feed on sugar in the mouth.

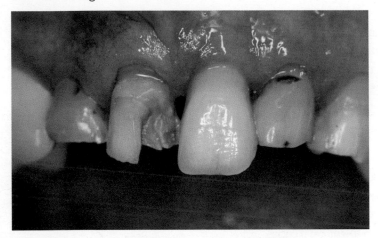

Tooth decay is closely linked to a high sugar intake

? | Reflect

Think about what you do to protect your dental health. Do you brush and floss your teeth, and visit the dentist regularly?

Case study

Andre is 15 years of age. He is already 30 kg overweight for a boy of his height. Andre's doctor is concerned about the effects of Andre's weight on his health. He has warned Andre that he must lose weight and exercise more in order to reduce the risk of developing type 2 diabetes and heart disease. Andre doesn't take these warnings seriously. He's never heard of anyone getting diabetes from eating pizza and chips! He also thinks that heart disease is something that older people get because they haven't looked after themselves properly.

1. Produce a leaflet that identifies the links between diet, obesity and type 2 diabetes. It should be aimed at 15-year-old boys like Andre.

2. How would you explain the causes of heart disease to a 15-year-old boy like Andre? Suggest how you would go about this.

3. Plan a healthy lunch for Andre that is low in fat, salt and sugar but which you think he would enjoy eating.

Factors influencing the diet of individuals and their associated dietary needs

Influences on diet

Who decides on your diet? Many adolescents would say that they have a lot of individual choice and can make their own decisions about the food and drink they consume. However, parents and other care providers often play a very significant part in choosing the diet of infants, children and adolescents. Adults and older people are typically seen as being able to make their own, entirely free choices. A closer look at people's dietary choices suggests that they are influenced and guided by a range of different factors, including religion and **culture**, **social class** background and, increasingly, the **media**.

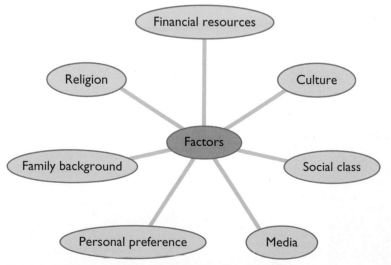

Figure 6.3 Examples of factors influencing the diet of individuals

Your assessment criteria:

1B.3 Identify the specific dietary needs of an individual

2B.P3 Describe the specific dietary needs of two individuals at different life stages

2B.M2 Explain the factors influencing the dietary choices of two individuals with specific dietary needs at different life stages

2B.D2 Discuss how factors influence the dietary choices of two individuals with specific dietary needs at different life stages

🔑 Key terms

Culture: the shared beliefs, values, language customs and traditions (way of life) of a group of people

media: methods of communication (television, radio, Internet, newspapers) used to reach a mass audience

Social class: a group of people with the same economic, social and educational status and resources

? Reflect

What kind of choices do you make about your own dietary intake? What factors influence your diet?

Culture

Food has a big significance for many people who see it as being more than 'fuel' to meet their energy needs. The food that people choose to eat often gives them a sense of identity and provides a link to their culture. People from the same cultural background tend to eat the same types of food. They also share ideas about what tastes good and how food should be prepared and cooked. Many national and cultural celebrations are marked by special feasts or the preparation of particular significant foods.

Religion

Some religions set out dietary restrictions for their followers. These usually prevent people from consuming certain foods because they are thought to be 'unclean' or because they are from a **sacred** source. Many religious beliefs about food also had an important health and safety function in the past when food preparation and preservation techniques were more basic. The lack of mechanisms to refrigerate or preserve foods led to the development of rituals, such as draining the blood from slaughtered animals and the avoidance of foods that spoil easily (eggs, meat, dairy products). Avoidance of over-eating (gluttony), stimulants (especially alcohol) and eating a vegetarian diet were also incorporated into some religious beliefs as ways of promoting healthier, 'purer' lives for followers. In a similar way, fasting is seen as a way to purify or improve the body and attract the approval of God, Allah or Buddha. Pregnant or nursing mothers, people who have chronic illnesses or who are acutely unwell and those who are frail or disabled are not usually expected to fast.

Your assessment criteria:

1B.3 Identify the specific dietary needs of an individual

2B.P3 Describe the specific dietary needs of two individuals at different life stages

 Key term

Sacred: believed to be holy or having a special religious significance

 Investigate

Using the Internet, library sources and people you know, carry out an investigation into the types of food and kind of diet consumed by people from a different cultural background to your own. You could focus on Indian, Turkish, Caribbean, Chinese, Bengali or Mediterranean diets, for example.

Table 6.3 Religious beliefs and food

Religion	Restrictions	Rationale	Feasting and fasting
Buddhism	Refrain from eating meat; most eat a vegetarian diet, some eat fish No beef products	Natural foods from the earth are considered most pure	Birth, enlightenment and death of Buddha
Hinduism	Most eat a vegetarian diet but some eat restricted amounts of meat and fish Cows are sacred, so no beef, but milk, yoghurt and butter are seen as 'pure'	Cow is sacred and can't be eaten Fasting promotes spiritual growth	On major Hindu holidays and days that have personal meaning
Islam	Food must be *Halal* (permitted) No pork or birds of prey (*Haram*) Avoid over-indulgence and stimulants (especially alcohol)	Failure to eat properly minimises spiritual awareness Fasting cleanses evil elements	Regular fasting but especially during Ramadan (ninth month of Islamic year) when fasting is from sunrise until sunset
Judaism	Food must be *Kosher* (correct) No pork or shellfish Meat and dairy products must be prepared and eaten separately	Land animals without cloven hooves seen as unclean Kosher process based on the Torah (religious scripture)	Fasting practised during Yom Kippur and other festivals
Roman Catholicism (Christianity)	Meat restricted on certain days	Restrictions mark religious festivals in a symbolic way	Feasting at Easter and Christmas Fasting during Lent
Protestantism (Christianity)	Few restrictions on food choices or fasting observed	Gluttony and drunkenness are 'sins' to be controlled	

Moral choices – vegetarianism and veganism

Some people choose to avoid certain foods, such as meat and fish, because of non-religious but ethically-based beliefs and values. This includes, for example, vegetarians and vegans.

People who have a vegetarian diet don't eat meat or fish, though most will eat eggs and dairy products. Vegetarians can still get all the nutrients they need from a varied vegetarian diet. This should include sources of plant protein such as cereals, beans, eggs and cheese. Vegans, who eat no animal products at all, can get all of their essential nutrients

Investigate

Investigate the food practices and festivals of Islam or Judaism. Produce a leaflet or poster that could be used to inform health, social care or early years workers about the food preferences, restrictions and 'rules' of followers of the religion you choose.

provided their dietary intake is sufficiently varied. For example, they can get protein from nuts and pulses and can avoid vitamin and mineral deficiencies by using supplements from non-animal sources – such as yeast extract for vitamin B12.

Environment

The place, or environment, where a person lives affects their access to food and their ability to locate and store sufficient food to meet their particular needs. This may sound odd in an age of national supermarket chains and in a country such as the UK where there is an abundance of food. In less developed countries, however, people from the same part of the country tend to eat the same foods, harvest and pick the same produce and cook the same kinds of meals. In the UK, most people go to the shops to buy their food rather than grow it themselves. Despite this, not everyone has the same access to high quality, fresh food or even to a good range of shops. Minority communities and low-income groups living in socially deprived parts of UK towns and cities are more likely to live in 'food deserts' where they have little or no opportunity to buy fresh food because local shops don't sell it. For practical and financial reasons, people living in areas like this tend to make use of the fast food outlets and processed convenience foods that are available to them.

Availability of food

The vast majority of the UK population have access to sufficient food. This is both a positive thing because it means under-nutrition and starvation are very rare in the UK, but is also a problem for those people who over-consume. In less developed countries where there is insufficient food to feed the whole population, people may have diets that provide them with too few nutrients. This can lead to conditions and illnesses such as kwashiorkor and marasmus (see page 145) and, in severe cases, to starvation. The abundance of food in developed countries such as the UK plays a significant part in the growing obesity problem within the population. Knowing how much to eat and when to stop eating can become a problem when there seems to be a limitless supply of food.

Your assessment criteria:

1B.3 Identify the specific dietary needs of an individual

2B.P3 Describe the specific dietary needs of two individuals at different life stages

Key term

Food desert: an area or place where people experience problems in obtaining healthy food

 ### Discuss

In a small group or with a class colleague, discuss the quality of the food shops in your local area. Do you live in a 'food desert' or is it possible to buy a range of fresh as well as packaged and frozen foods?

Diseases and illness related to under-nutrition are more common in less developed countries

Socio-economic factors

A person's social class, income level, their family upbringing and food preferences, peer group pressure and media influences are referred to as socio-economic factors that influence dietary intake.

Social class

A social class consists of people who have generally similar economic, social and educational status. In general terms people often make a distinction between working class, middle class and upper class groups. The attitudes and values that people have, their income and the lifestyle choices they make about issues such as diet are sometimes seen an indicator of a person's social class status. Knowledge of food, understanding about dietary issues and simply being able to afford some types of food but not others are all linked to social class. Evidence from research studies such as the National Food Survey (ONS, 2008) indicate that people in the higher, more well off social classes tend to eat healthier food whilst poorer people in the lower social classes are more likely to eat food that has a higher fat and sugar content.

The media

'The media' is a general term given to several different sources of information, including newspapers, magazines, television, radio and the Internet. Information about diet – from recipes and cookery programmes to news stories about food scares and diet-related health problems such as obesity – appear frequently in the media. The media can have a huge impact on an individual's knowledge about food, diet and health, as well as on their attitudes towards their own diet. People may choose certain foods because they are being strongly advertised and seem popular in the media. Alternatively, news stories about diet-related

 Key term

Socio-economic factors: non-biological influences, such as relationships, lifestyle (socio) and money-related (economic) factors, which influence an individual's living circumstances, personal development and experiences

 Investigate

In a small group, carry out a survey of print (newspaper and magazine) and television media to identify examples of food-related articles, programmes or advertisements. Try to decide:

- who the food-related information is targeted at

- what kinds of food-related 'messages' are being communicated

- whether food is being discussed in a positive healthy way or in a more negative unhealthy way

- what you think the impact of the media might be on people who read the material.

research or food scares can cause people to change their diets to avoid certain foods. Though we might like to think that we are making free and well informed choices about what we eat and drink, the media play a very important role in persuading us to eat or drink specific food products.

Fast food products are heavily advertised in Western societies like the UK

Peer pressure

Peer pressure is the term given to the way an individual can be influenced by their **peer group** to change their attitudes, values or behaviour in order to be accepted into the group. It is a factor that can influence the dietary choices of people in all life stages but is perhaps strongest during childhood, adolescence and early adulthood. During these life stages individuals often want to find ways of 'fitting in' and making friends, so are wary of being too different from others. One consequence can be that peer pressure leads to unhealthy dietary choices. Adolescents, for example, may show a preference for fast food (perceived to be 'cool') rather than a healthy balanced diet.

Family and personal preferences

Everybody learns something about food from the food 'rules' and preferences of their family, as part of their primary socialisation during infancy and childhood. Many of our food preferences and attitudes towards what and how we eat are established in early childhood. Personal preferences do have a big effect on what food we choose to buy and consume in every life stage. Personal preferences about diet may be modified by the beliefs a person goes on to develop about issues such as killing animals, eating meat or by health concerns relating to diet.

Income and food costs

An individual's ability to buy a sufficient amount of good quality food for a balanced diet is linked to factors such as social class and

⚲ Key term

Peer group: *a group of people of about the same age and status*

? Reflect

Can you think of any instances where you have experienced peer pressure to choose or try particular foods? Were you under pressure to eat healthier or less healthy food?

geographical location that you have already learnt about. Equally as important are food costs in relation to a person's income. People who are in the higher social classes and who live in affluent areas with plenty of local facilities tend to have more money and better access to healthy food. People who live on low incomes in more deprived areas are less likely to be able to afford and have less access to the healthier foods that will provide them with a balanced, nutritious diet.

Case study

Leila is 35 years of age. She is the mother of two children, aged 5 and 10. They all moved to the Seaborn Estate two years ago when they were re-housed by the local council. Leila now regrets moving from her small flat in a busy, inner city area. Her biggest complaint is that there are few facilities and no 'proper shops' on the estate where she lives. The nearest shop selling fresh fruit and vegetables is a bus ride or two-mile walk away. Leila has got into the habit of doing much of her shopping at a small local convenience store on the estate. This sells tins, ready meals and processed foods in packets, but no fresh food. She is also a regular customer at the local take-away as her children love pizzas and burger and chips. Leila is frustrated with the problems she has obtaining healthy food. She is convinced that the diet her family consumes is less healthy since they moved house.

1. What factor(s) have the greatest influence on the type of diet Leila and her children consume?

2. How does the concept of a 'food desert' help to explain Leila's food choices?

3. Suggest two things Leila could do to improve the quality of her family's diet.

Illness

A person's appetite and dietary intake can change as a result of illness, or of the treatment they receive for that illness. Some physical illnesses and mental health problems reduce a person's appetite due to pain, tiredness or feeling sick. Medication and other treatments for physical illness and mental health problems may suppress or increase a person's appetite. Similarly, people who become very conscious about their weight or appearance can develop eating disorders such as anorexia nervosa and bulimia nervosa. For many people, the consequences of illness are short-term disruptions to their normal eating pattern and dietary intake. For others, appetite and food intake can be long-term health issues.

? | Reflect

Think about the last time that you were unwell. Did your condition affect your appetite or what you ate and drank?

Underlying health conditions

A number of health conditions have a direct effect on an individuals dietary needs leading to specific nutritional needs. These conditions include food allergies, lactose intolerance, coeliac disease, diabetes, irritable bowel syndrome and Crohn's disease, for example.

Food allergies

A food allergy is a type of intolerance to food where there is evidence of an **immunological reaction**. The number of people in the population with a diagnosed food allergy is very low. However, many more people have psychological aversions to different foods which are not true allergies but which tend to be reported as such.

Examples of food allergies include:

- wheat or gluten intolerance (coeliac disease)

- lactose intolerance

- peanut allergy.

Allergy tests can be used to identify people's food allergies or intolerances

Food allergies can be diagnosed by skin tests using an extract of the food containing the alleged allergen. However, skin tests often report 'false positive' results and many more people believe themselves to have food allergies than is the case. Where a person does have a food allergy, the usual treatment is to exclude the food from the person's diet. It is important to ensure that this does not lead to the loss of important sources of nutrients from the diet.

Your assessment criteria:

1B.3 Identify the specific dietary needs of an individual

2B.P3 Describe the specific dietary needs of two individuals at different life stages

Key term

Immunological reaction: a protective response from an individual's immune system (in this case, to certain types of food)

Reflect

Do you or any members of your family have food allergies? What impact does this have or your (or their) health and wellbeing?

Lactose intolerance

Lactose is a sugar found in milk and milk products. Some people are unable to digest lactose and suffer digestive symptoms such as:

- flatulence (wind)

- bloating

- diarrhoea

- abdominal pain (cramps).

These symptoms are caused by undigested lactose passing into the colon. Lactose intolerance can be inherited or can result from gastroenteritis or other conditions of the digestive system. People who have severe lactose intolerance require a diet without milk or milk-based products. Those with mild lactose intolerance can usually tolerate milk taken with (or in) meals and have fewer symptoms if they consume fermented rather than fresh dairy products; most people with lactose intolerance can eat yoghurt and cheese because the lactose has been modified or is virtually non-existent in these products. Because milk and milk products are important sources of essential nutrients, such as calcium and riboflavin, avoidance of dairy products is not advisable without good reason. If milk and milk products are excluded it is sensible to make other changes to the diet to compensate.

People who have lactose intolerance tend to avoid consuming milk or milk-based drinks

Case study

Alice is one year old. Her mum Claire initially breast-fed her and then gave Alice some formula milk for a few months. Alice often brings her milk back up and doesn't seem to like drinking it. Claire is now concerned that Alice might have a 'milk allergy'.

1. Why is milk an important part of a child's diet?

2. What is the correct term for the 'milk allergy' that Claire is referring to?

3. if Alice does have a problem tolerating milk, what other foods could she be given to ensure she obtains the nutrients she needs?

Gluten and wheat intolerance

Gluten is made when liquid meets non-soluble protein in flour. It is the rubbery, chewing gum-textured material that gives kneaded dough its elasticity and which enables bread made from wheat flours to rise. Wheat plays a very important part in a nutritious diet for most people. It is found in bread, cakes, pasta, some breakfast cereals and as an additive in a wide range of other products including soups, sauces and sausages. Wheat is **fortified** in the United Kingdom with iron, niacin and thiamine. However, some people avoid gluten and wheat products because they have a diagnosis of coeliac disease or wheat allergy, or because they believe themselves to be allergic to wheat.

Coeliac disease is the main form of wheat intolerance. Gluten in the diet triggers symptoms of the disease such as general tiredness, diarrhoea, weight loss, constipation, stomach bloating and wind. People with coeliac disease must follow a gluten-free diet. Fresh meat, fish, cheese, eggs, milk, fruit and vegetables are all gluten free. However, because wheat is a widespread additive in food products, people with coeliac disease are likely to need the advice of a dietician to ensure their diet avoids gluten while also including sufficient nutrients.

Type 2 diabetes

Type 2 diabetes is a condition in which the amount of glucose in the blood is too high. Dietary factors play a part in the development of diabetes and are also important in controlling it. Eating a healthy, balanced diet and maintaining a healthy weight are important strategies for delaying the onset of or controlling type 2 diabetes.

People with diabetes should eat a diet that is:

• low in saturated fat

• low in salt

• high in fresh fruit and vegetables

• high in starchy (complex carbohydrate) foods such as bread, rice and pasta.

🔧 **Key term**

Fortified: food that has been enriched or strengthened in some way

📋 **Investigate**

Go to the NHS Choices website (http://www.nhs.uk) to find out more about coeliac disease, Type 2 diabetes, Irritable Bowel Syndrome and Crohn's disease.

Irritable Bowel Syndrome

This is a common condition of the digestive system that causes stomach cramps, bloating, diarrhoea and constipation. Making changes to diet and lifestyle often relieves these symptoms. For example, avoiding foods containing insoluble fibre, such as wholegrain bread, bran, cereals, nuts and seeds and restricting tea, coffee and alcohol intake is thought to help. The exact causes of irritable bowl syndrome are unclear but they it can be triggered by stress, low immunity and problems with a person's gut or digestive muscles.

Crohn's Disease

This is a long-term condition that causes inflammation of the lining of the digestive system. The symptoms include diarrhoea, abdominal pain, fatigue and weight loss. The symptoms of Crohn's disease can go away (remission) and then return. The exact cause of this disorder is unknown but it has been linked to genetic inheritance, problems with the immune system, infection, smoking and environmental factors. There is currently no cure. People with Crohn's disease usually need to take medication to relieve symptoms and may require surgery to deal with the physical changes that can occur in parts of their digestive system. Sufferers are recommended to avoid dairy products, fatty and spicy foods.

Investigate

Go to Crohn's and Colitis UK, the national society for Crohn's disease and colitis, to find out more about the causes and impact of these conditions on sufferers.

Case study

Gillian, aged 35, gets painful stomach cramps, bloating and constipation every few months. Her symptoms are making her feel quite unwell, tired and unhappy. Gillian has tried, on and off, to reduce the amount of wheat in her diet and rarely eats bread as she thinks this has something to do with her problems. Her GP has referred her to a local hospital for a 'biopsy'. He also told her that he thinks she may have coeliac disease. Gillian is quite upset as the doctor said this is incurable and that she will have to make big changes to her diet.

1. What kind of 'big changes' would you expect Gillian to make to her diet if she does have coeliac disease?

2. Describe how an investigation is carried out to diagnose coeliac disease.

3. Plan an appetising and nutritious gluten-free lunch and evening meal for Gillian.

Nutritional variation during life stage development

Your assessment criteria:

1B.4 Create, with guidance, a nutritional plan for a selected individual

2B.P4 Create a nutritional plan for two individuals with different specific nutritional needs

Dietary needs at different life stages

An individual's dietary needs change as they grow and develop, moving through different life stages. An infant's food needs are very different to those of an adolescent or an older person, for example.

The type, amount and range of foods that a person eats should vary according to their life stage, the kind of environment they live in and the lifestyle they lead. Table 6.4 (Page 163) sets out the recommended daily amounts of food, expressed in terms of **kilocalories**, that males and females need as they age.

Infancy (0–2 years)

Nutrition is very important in the early years of life. Babies and infants need the right types of food to help them grow and develop normally, and to prevent them from developing certain illnesses. Breast milk contains all the nutrients that a young baby needs. The first milk from a mother's breast is **colostrum**. This protein-rich liquid contains antibodies that protect the baby against infection. Colostrum is produced for two or three days, after which time the breast starts to **lactate** (produce milk).

Formula milk is an alternative to breast milk. It is produced as liquid and powdered milk. Formula milk is different to cows' milk which doesn't contain the right balance of nutrients for a human baby. Different formula milks are available to suit an infant's stage of feeding. Infants gradually move to mixed feeding, changing from milk to solid foods, from about six months old as they are weaned.

Key terms

Colostrum: *thick, yellow breast milk that is rich in protein, minerals and antibodies*

Kilocalories: *The energy value in food equal to 1000 calories*

Lactate: *to produce milk*

Investigate

Weaning foods can be prepared at home by sieving, liquidising or mashing a variety of fruits, vegetables or dairy products. Identify three examples of each of these types of food that are suitable for weaning a baby on to solid food.

Early childhood (3–8 years)

Children need the right types of food to promote their physical growth and to provide 'fuel' or energy for their high level of physical activity. High energy and growth foods like bread, potatoes, milk, cheese, meat, fish, fruit and vegetables can support growth and development during this life stage. Sugar-rich sweets and high-fat snacks appeal to many children but are best avoided as they don't provide nutrients and can cause weight and other health problems.

Case study

Lewis is an active, healthy eight-year-old boy. His favourite foods are ice cream, chips and chicken. Lewis always asks for one of these every day and would really like to eat them all the time. Lewis' mum tries to give him a varied diet but is struggling to get Lewis to eat fresh fruit and vegetables. Lewis says he doesn't like vegetables and that his friends all eat crisps at break times not fruit. Lewis often complains that he is feeling hungry and seems to want to eat most of the time. Despite this, his mum has recently discovered that Lewis throws away the fruit she gives him to take to school as a snack. Lewis's mum has told him that his health will suffer if he doesn't eat fresh fruit and vegetables, and that eating a lot of crisps and sweets is bad for him. This doesn't seem to have made any difference to the way he thinks about food.

1. Why do you think that Lewis might often feel hungry?

2. What would you say or do to explain to Lewis the importance of eating fruit and vegetables?

3. What might be the health consequences of eating too many sweets and crisps during childhood?

? Reflect

What kinds of foods would you include in a lunch box for an active growing child? You choice should support growth and development, and meet the child's high energy needs.

Adolescence (9–18 years)

Adolescents experience a growth spurt during puberty. As a result they have very high energy needs – which result in big appetites. It is important for adolescents to choose healthy, nutritious foods to meet their growth and energy needs. However, because many adolescents have a lot of choice over their dietary intake, foods and drinks that are high in fat and sugar can become a significant feature of some teenagers' diets. High fat and sugar-laden snacks can add a significant amount of calories to a person's diet while providing very few nutrients. Diet-related obesity, diabetes and problems related to nutritional deficiency can result from a poor diet during this life stage. Eating a balanced diet throughout adolescence is much better for health and development than bouts of dieting to overcome weight gain.

Early to middle adulthood (19–65 years)

A healthy diet for an adult should include plenty of complex carbohydrates (bread, potatoes, pasta, rice), moderate amounts of meat or fish and plenty of fruit and vegetables. The amount of food an adult needs to eat is likely to vary and is affected by an individual's:

- gender
- body size
- height
- weight
- the environment (for example, whether they live in a cold or a warm country)
- the amount of physical activity the individual does in their daily life.

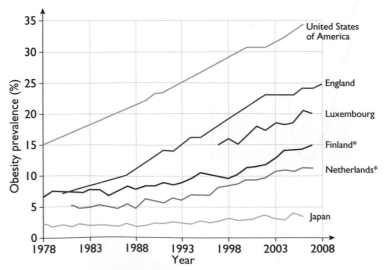

Source: OECD, accessed at www.noo.org.uk 24 September 2012
*Self reported data (prevalence rates for other countries are based on measured data)

Figure 6.4 Statistics on obesity and dieting

Parents need to make healthy dietary choices for their children during childhood and early adolescence

Investigate

What does Figure 6.4 say about the prevalence of obesity in England?

An adult who is very active will burn more energy (calories) than a person who lives a **sedentary** life. Obesity as a result of over-eating is an increasing problem in the UK adult population. Heart disease, strokes and some cancers are all linked to consuming too much food, particularly foods that are high in saturated fat, salt and sugar. People who consume a lot of processed food, especially take-aways and ready-meals, increase their risk of developing diet-related health problems. Consuming alcohol, particularly more than the recommended limits, also adds calories and may contribute to weight gain during adulthood.

Women who are pregnant or breastfeeding need to ensure that their diet is very nutritious in order to provide nourishment for themselves and their growing baby (see Table 6.4) on page 163. A woman who is pregnant or breastfeeding should consume a diet that contains sufficient energy, protein, iron, calcium, folate and vitamins C and D. It is also important to avoid certain foods that may contain substances that can adversely affect the development of the baby.

Old age (65 years+)

An individual's nutritional needs generally decline during old age. This is because physical changes, such as weight loss and reduced activity level, mean the older person uses less energy. However, eating less can also lead to nutritional deficiencies if a person's diet is not sufficient or balanced. Older people can become malnourished if their diet becomes deficient in any of the main nutrients. A lack of iron and vitamins and minerals (and eating convenience foods that are high in salt, fat or sugar) can cause or make worse health problems.

Key term

Sedentary: a type of lifestyle with a lack of physical activity

Physical work like this needs to be fuelled by a nutritious diet

Considerations for nutritional planning

Individual nutritional needs

Every individual needs food in sufficient quantities to survive; it is a basic and fundamental human need. A lack of nutritious food over a period of time can adversely affect health and physical performance. The amount of nutritious food needed varies from person to person. It depends on:

- age
- gender
- body size
- height
- weight
- the physical and climatic conditions, for example, whether it is a cold or a warm country
- whether the person is living an active life or one that is not physically active (a sedentary life).

Individuals in different life stages have different nutritional requirements (Table 6.4). For example:

- Babies and infants need suitable nutrition in adequate quantities to enable them to grow and develop normally and to prevent certain minor illnesses.
- Young children need greater amounts of some nutrients than their size would indicate, because they are growing.
- Adolescents need adequate nutrients in quantities that maintain their growth and sustain their physical activities.
- Pregnant women need extra energy and increased amounts of certain nutrients to nourish themselves and their baby.
- Older women might need to take extra supplements of oestrogens and do regular exercise to prevent osteoporosis, a painful arthritic condition which affects the larger and weight-bearing bones in the body.
- People who are exposed to cold weather must have additional nutrients because the body uses more energy to stay at the same temperature.
- Men need more calories to keep their tissues healthy as their bodies have a greater percentage of muscle tissue than women's bodies.

Some groups of people also have special diets. These require them to leave out or include specific food groups to meet their personal values or special physical needs.

Your assessment criteria:

1B.4 Create, with guidance, a nutritional plan for a selected individual

2B.P4 Create a nutritional plan for two individuals with different specific nutritional needs

2B.M3 Compare nutritional plans for two individuals with different nutritional needs

? Reflect

How can a woman adjust her diet when she is pregnant?

✎ Key term

Osteoporosis: a bone disease that leads to an increased risk of fracture

Vegetarians do not eat meat or fish. They can still obtain all their nutrients from a diet containing no meat. Their proteins can be obtained from cereals, beans, eggs and cheese. Vegans, who eat no animal products at all, can obtain all the essential nutrients if their vegetarian diet is sufficiently varied. Pregnant or nursing mothers must eat and drink sensibly in order to provide adequate nutrition and fluids for themselves and for their children. People with conditions such as lactose intolerance, irritable bowel syndrome, coeliac disease, Crohn's disease or food allergies may also have specific dietary requirements to maintain their health.

Table 6.4 Recommended daily amounts (kilocalories) throughout the lifespan

Age range	Males (kilocalories)	Females (kilocalories)
0–3 months (formula fed)	545	515
4–6 months	690	645
7–9 months	825	765
10–12 months	920	865
1–3 years	1230	1165
4–6 years	1715	1545
7–10 years	1970	1740
11–14 years	2220	1845
15–18 years	2755	2110
19–59 years	2550	1940
60–64 years	2380	1900
65–74 years	2330	1900
75+ years	2100	1810
Pregnant		+200*
Lactating:		
1 month		+450
2 months		+530
3 months		+570
4–6 months		+480
6+ months		+240

*= last three months only

Source: DEFRA (1995) *Manual of Nutrition*, 10th edition

Investigate

Look at Table 6.4 and identify the recommended daily kilocalories for:

- *a 7–10-year-old boy*
- *a 25-year-old woman*
- *a 40-year-old man.*

Assessment checklist

To achieve level 1, my portfolio of evidence must show that I can:

Assessment criteria	Description	✓
1A.1	Identify components of a balanced diet, giving examples of each	☐
1A.2	Identify three effects of an unbalanced diet on the health and wellbeing of individuals	☐
1B.3	Identify the specific dietary needs of an individual	☐
1B.4	Create, with guidance, a nutritional plan for a selected individual	☐

To achieve a pass grade, my portfolio of evidence must show that I can:

Assessment criteria	Description	✓
2A.P1	Describe the components of a balanced diet and their functions, sources and effects	☐
2A.P2	Describe the effects of an unbalanced diet on the health and wellbeing of individuals, giving examples of their causes	☐
2B.P3	Describe the specific dietary needs of two individuals at different life stages	☐
2B.P4	Create a nutritional plan for two individuals with different specific nutritional needs	☐

To achieve a merit grade, my portfolio of evidence must show that I can:

Assessment criteria	Description	✓
2A.M1	Compare the effects of balanced and unbalanced diets on the health and wellbeing of two individuals	☐
2B.M2	Explain the factors influencing the dietary choices of two individuals with specific dietary needs at different life stages	☐
2B.M3	Compare nutritional plans for two individuals with different nutritional needs	☐

To achieve a distinction grade, my portfolio of evidence must show that I can:

Assessment criteria	Description	✓
2A.D1	Assess the long-terms effects of a balanced and unbalanced diet on the health and wellbeing of individuals	☐
2B.D2	Discuss how factors influence the dietary choices of two individuals with specific dietary needs at different life stages	☐

7 | Equality and diversity in health and social care

Learning aim A
Understand the importance of non-discriminatory practice in health and social care

▶ Topic A.1 Discriminatory and non-discriminatory practice in health and social care

▶ Topic A.2 Impact of discriminatory and non-discriminatory practice in health and social care

**Learning aim B
Explore how health and social care practices can promote equality and diversity**

▶ Topic B.1 Factors that may affect the care needs of individuals

▶ Topic B.2 How adapting services to meet the diverse needs of service users promotes equality and diversity in health and social care

Discriminatory and non-discriminatory practice in health and social care

Introduction to this chapter

The United Kingdom is a country with a growing and increasingly diverse population. Health and social care workers need to understand cultural diversity because it affects individuals' rights and the quality of care services they experience. This unit introduces you to the diversity of individuals in UK society and shows how an understanding of diversity helps to promote equality of opportunity for people who use care services. You will also gain an overview of equality and rights laws, and the responsibilities of care organisations and their employees.

Your assessment criteria:

1A.1 Define non-discriminatory practice in health and social care, using two examples

2A.P1 Describe non-discriminatory and discriminatory practice in health and social care, using examples

This topic will help you to understand the term 'discrimination' and explains how health and social care workers use non-discriminatory care practices to avoid treating some people unfairly.

Diversity

Health and social care workers work with colleagues, service users and other adults from a wide range of social, cultural, religious, language and ethnic backgrounds. They work with men and women, people with different types of ability and disability, individuals who speak different languages and who have different cultural traditions, as well as people who could be described as middle class, working class, as 'black', 'white' or of mixed **heritage**. All health and social care workers should show respect for **diversity** and be able to work with people from a wide variety of backgrounds.

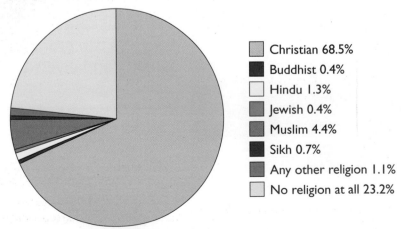

Christian 68.5%
Buddhist 0.4%
Hindu 1.3%
Jewish 0.4%
Muslim 4.4%
Sikh 0.7%
Any other religion 1.1%
No religion at all 23.2%

Source of data: Integrated Household Survey April 2010 to March 2011 Experimental Statistics, Office for National Statistics 2011

Figure 7.1 Religious diversity in the UK

🔑 Key terms

Diversity: *the range of differences (social, cultural, language, ethnic, ability and disability) within a population*

Heritage: *the origins, traditions or background that a person inherits from their family*

❓ Reflect

Think about the different forms of diversity within your local population. Are there different ethnic communities, groups of people who speak languages other than English or different religious communities, for example?

Equality

You will probably know from your own personal experiences, and perhaps from being a service user yourself, that people who need health and social care services want to be treated equally and fairly. However, this doesn't always mean that all service users should be treated *the same*. **Equality** in health and social care settings is about giving each person the appropriate opportunities to receive care and treatment, to have choices and to make decisions to the best of their ability and in line with their own interests. Valuing and treating each service user as an individual is a very important first step in promoting this kind of **equality of opportunity**.

Discrimination and discriminatory practice

Unfair discrimination can result from the way people respond to social differences. All people are different but sometimes some people are treated less favourably, or even with hostility, because they are members of minority groups, for example. Discrimination can be:

- direct – when a person is treated less favourably because they are a woman, black or disabled, for example

- indirect – when everyone is treated in a similar way but this disadvantages certain people or groups.

Treating black people less favourably than white people when they apply for jobs, or not appointing a woman to a post because she may become pregnant are examples of unfair discrimination. Unfair discrimination may be based on:

- ethnicity – racism

- gender – sexism

- disability – disablism

- sexuality – homophobia

- religion – sectarianism.

People can be discriminated against because of stereotyping, labelling and **prejudice**.

 Your assessment criteria:

2A.P1 Describe non-discriminatory and discriminatory practice in health and social care, using examples

 Key terms

Equality: treating a person fairly or in a way that ensures they are not disadvantaged

Equality of opportunity: a situation in which everyone has an equal chance

Inclusive services like this one provide equality of opportunity for service users

Key term

Prejudice: a strongly held negative belief or attitude relating to particular group of people

Prejudice

Prejudices are sets of negative, critical or hostile ideas about a person or a group of people. They are prejudgements that are usually based on false or inadequate information and which are damaging to the person or group to whom they are applied. Prejudices can become fixed or very difficult to change. They are closely connected to **stereotypes**. When people act on their prejudices, they discriminate unfairly against people.

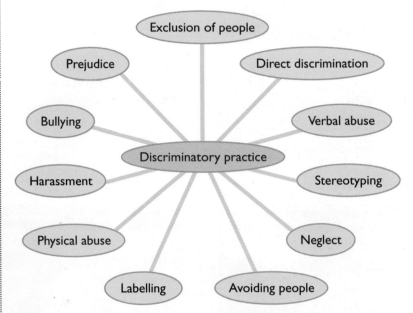

Figure 7.2 Forms of discriminatory practice

An individual might express their prejudice towards others by:

- using hostile language

- not sitting next to certain people

- avoiding working with another individual or giving them less time than they need to receive appropriate care or support

- not touching another person

- having negative body language towards certain people.

These discriminatory behaviours devalue and disrespect people. They can also lead to unfair and unequal treatment or discrimination. Sometimes discriminatory behaviours are unthinking and thoughtless, rather than deliberate and calculated. However, there are times when health and social care workers do deliberately discriminate against others – this is always unacceptable and should be reported.

Your assessment criteria:

2A.P1 Describe non-discriminatory and discriminatory practice in health and social care, using examples

Key term

Stereotype: *a simplified and often negative way of talking or thinking about an individual or group of people*

Reflect

How might discriminatory behaviours like these affect the emotional wellbeing of a person who experiences them?

Case study

In January 2009, a reporter from the BBC programme *Inside Out West* carried out an investigation into racial discrimination by lettings and employment agencies. Thirty agencies that supplied temporary workers were contacted by the programme. Each was asked whether they could provide candidates for a receptionist post. The researcher telephoned each agency to ask whether they could advertise the post to 'white only' workers. These are a selection of the replies.

Agency: 'That's fine. You are not allowed to say it but, no, we certainly hear what you say. That's not a problem.'

Agency: 'We'll ignore it and pretend you didn't say it but listen to what you said, if you see what I mean.'

Agency: 'It's difficult with the accent over the phone isn't it? I understand that, yeah, shouldn't really say that but taken on board.'

Agency: 'OK. You are not supposed to tell me that but I will forget you did (laughter) but bear it in mind.'

Researcher: 'Just send through white.'

Agency: 'Yep – Normal people.'

Even though this is unlawful, 25 of the 30 agencies agreed to provide 'white only' candidates.

1. What kind of prejudice is being exposed by the researcher?

2. How should the agency staff respond to the researcher's request for 'white only' job candidates?

3. Why is it wrong to favour one ethnic group over another when trying to fill a job vacancy?

Stereotyping

Stereotyping involves making assumptions about 'types' of people and applying them to individuals. Stereotypes don't take individual differences into account and can be crude caricatures of people (for example, 'all male nurses are gay' or 'all feminists are man-haters'). When people make stereotypical assumptions about others, inappropriate and discriminatory treatment can occur.

Health and social care workers should acknowledge individual differences because these are important to each person's identity (who we believe we are), and because it helps us to avoid clumsy and insensitive stereotyping. Remember, people are not 'all the same'.

? Reflect

1. Complete these stereotypical views that some people hold:

   • 'All men are ...'

   • 'All teenagers are ...'

   • 'All gay people are ...'

   • 'All black people are ...'

   • 'All single mothers are ...'

2. Can you think of reasons why each of the stereotypes you have produced is not actually true?

Labelling

'Labelling' involves summing up a person in a single label or term, such as 'schizophrenic', 'aggressive' or 'stupid'. Labels are usually negative and damaging; they stop us from seeing the person as a whole person. Labels can also be very difficult to shift; no other information about the person seems to matter when a strong label is applied to them. This is damaging because it strips away the person's individuality and dignity, and exposes them to insensitivity and unfair discrimination. Labelling can also lead to a self-fulfilling prophecy, if the person who is labelled conforms to the expectations or predictions of the label.

Refusal of medical treatment

Denial of medical treatment on non-clinical grounds is often the result of unfair discrimination. For example, some groups of people, such as those who are homeless, travellers, as well as those with drug or alcohol problems, find it more difficult to access the health and social care services they need. This can be due to prejudices held by health or social care workers who feel that members of these groups don't deserve treatment (if their problems are 'self-inflicted') or that contact should be avoided in general. Similarly, organisations with assessment and access policies that discourage or prevent minority racial or religious groups from accessing services are setting up indirect discriminatory barriers. In other cases, health or social care workers may make decisions about an older person's suitability for treatment or care that are based on age-related prejudices.

Offering inappropriate treatment or care

Care or treatment that fails to acknowledge and recognise an individual's beliefs, wishes or preferences can be inappropriate and may be abusive to the person. For example, insisting that a Muslim woman receives personal care from a male member of staff would constitute inappropriate care. Similarly, health or social care workers who are task-focused and determined to 'get the job done' run the risk of providing care that is impersonal, inappropriate and contrary to an individual's particular needs. It is always best to work in a person-centred way that is sensitive to every individual's needs, wishes and preferences.

Giving less time than needed

Health and social care workers who are rushed and impatient tend to focus on the task they are trying to perform as quickly as possible, rather than on the person whose needs they should be meeting. This can lead to people feeling their needs don't matter, that they are not being valued and that the health or social care worker doesn't really care.

Your assessment criteria:

1A.1 Define non-discriminatory practice in health and social care, using two examples

2A.P1 Describe non-discriminatory and discriminatory practice in health and social care, using examples

Investigate

Find out what the Liverpool Care Pathway involves and identify the reasons why it has become a controversial approach to providing care for older people nearing the end of their life.

Good care is person-centred and should not be rushed just to 'get the job done'

Health and social care workers are often under a lot of pressure to provide care for a number of individuals in a short space of time. However, despite these pressures they must always ensure that they give each individual sufficient time – or draw their manager's attention to the difficulties they face in meeting each individual's needs without additional help.

Non-discriminatory practice in health and social care

Health and social care workers must value and treat fairly and equally each person who needs care or support, every colleague and every relative or visitor. This means developing ways of working that:

- value diversity in society and promote equality of opportunity

- recognise the particular needs of people from diverse backgrounds, including those who come from minority religious and cultural backgrounds

- adapt care to meet the diverse needs of different individuals.

Promoting equality of opportunity and fair treatment

Care organisations try to promote equality of opportunity as a way of preventing discriminatory practice. Care organisations must have relevant policies and procedures in place to achieve this. Health and social care workers should also be aware of the ways in which discrimination occurs and what their responsibilities are in challenging and preventing it. Other ways of promoting non-discriminatory practice include:

- using varied materials to portray positive images of diversity – visual displays should avoid stereotypes and celebrate diversity and difference, for example

- organising diverse activities that celebrate different religious festivals and promote understanding of different religious beliefs and cultures

- using books and toys that avoid stereotypical images of men and women, ethnic groups and other social differences

- providing appropriate health and social care to meet the needs of individuals

- adapting care to meet the diverse needs of different individuals

- providing equality of access to health and social care services.

Visual displays in care settings should reflect the diversity of service users

173

Individual workers' responsibilities

Induction training and policies usually tell workers about their responsibilities towards equal opportunities. Basically, health and social care workers must respect and meet the individual needs of each service user. They need to:

- think about how best to communicate to meet each individual's language needs

- consider how they can avoid and challenge prejudice

- avoid stereotyping and labelling others

- challenge incidents of unfair discrimination.

Institutional responsibilities

Care organisations and institutions must have equal opportunities policies and training, and appropriate supervision of staff. They should ensure that their policies, procedures and codes of practice are strong enough to protect individual rights.

Working with colleagues

Working with colleagues in a care setting should be a supportive and enjoyable experience. However, this is not always the case as tensions can arise in the workplace. Direct and indirect discrimination can occur and should always be challenged. This is difficult to do, but a care worker who witnesses discrimination by a colleague should report this to their employer or manager.

Working with service users

Health and social care workers need to find ways of promoting positive, non-discriminatory practice. Strategies for doing so include:

- encouraging people who use care services to make choices, and accepting their decisions, wishes and preferences

- finding out about the preferences of service users when providing care

- facilitating religious worship and the expression of personal identity and beliefs

- ensuring that the food offered to an individual meets their religious and dietary needs

- finding out about and meeting the individual's particular needs when providing care or support.

Your assessment criteria:

2A.M1 Explain the importance of legislation and codes of practice in promoting non-discriminatory practice in health and social care, using examples

2A.D1 Assess the impact of discriminatory practice for health and social care workers, with reference to selected examples

Impact of discriminatory and non-discriminatory practice in health and social care

The effects of discrimination

If you have ever been bullied, treated differently or unfairly in comparison to others, you will have some idea about what it feels like to experience discrimination. You may have felt upset or distressed when this happened to you. Perhaps you put the experience behind you and have forgotten about it. But imagine what it must feel like to be discriminated against regularly or to feel like this happens to you all of the time.

Emotional and psychological effects

Discrimination can have a negative effect on an individual's self-image and sense of self-worth. If discrimination is an isolated event, or if it is dealt with quickly, the person may be affected only temporarily. If the discrimination happens over a long period, a person's confidence and self-esteem can be damaged permanently.

People can feel disempowered and devalued by unfair discrimination. As well as reducing work, education and lifestyle opportunities, unfair discrimination can lead to depression, negative behaviours (such as criminality and aggression) and long-term health problems.

Social effects

People who experience prejudice and discrimination often experience forms of social stigma. This means they are marked out in a negative way as different and as of lesser value than other people. This can lead to social exclusion – individuals are denied access to resources and opportunities in education, employment and care services, for example.

Disabled people, people with mental health problems, older people and members of black and minority ethnic groups are known to experience stigma and social exclusion. These people tend to live in poverty, lacking the income and social influence to change their poor standard of living and circumstances.

Your assessment criteria:

1A.2 Identify how one code of practice or piece of legislation promotes non-discriminatory practice in health and social care

2A.P2 Describe how codes of practice and legislation promote non-discriminatory practice in health and social care

2A.M1 Explain the importance of legislation and codes of practice in promoting non-discriminatory practice in health and social care, using examples

2A.D1 Assess the impact of discriminatory practice for health and social care workers, with reference to selected examples

Key terms

Social exclusion: *a process that results in certain social groups being pushed to the margins of society (because of poverty or discrimination) where they are unable to participate fully in society*

Social stigma: *social disapproval of personal characteristics, behaviours (lifestyles) or beliefs that are felt to be unacceptable or 'abnormal'*

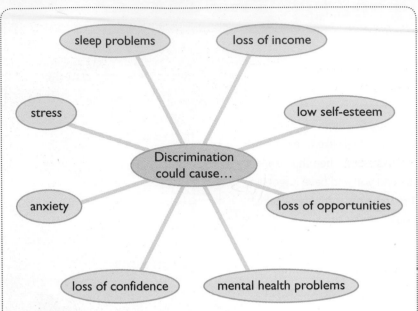

Figure 7.3 Some effects of discrimination

Your assessment criteria:

1A.2 Identify how one code of practice or piece of legislation promotes non-discriminatory practice in health and social care

2A.P2 Describe how codes of practice and legislation promote non-discriminatory practice in health and social care

2A.M1 Explain the importance of legislation and codes of practice in promoting non-discriminatory practice in health and social care, using examples

2A.D1 Assess the impact of discriminatory practice for health and social care workers, with reference to selected examples

Legislation and discrimination

People in the United Kingdom are free to live their lives in the way they wish – provided they don't break the law. **Legislation**, or written laws, protects the rights of individuals and imposes responsibilities to promote equal opportunities on employers and employees in care settings.

Equality and anti-discrimination laws

The main laws promoting equality and protecting people against discrimination are:

- The European Convention on Human Rights and Fundamental Freedoms
- The Mental Health Act (1983) and (2007)
- The Convention on the Rights of the Child (1989)
- The Children Act (2004)
- The Race Relations (Amendment) Act (2000)
- The Disability Discrimination Act (2005)
- The Human Rights Act (1998)
- The Data Protection Act (1998).

These laws influence the rights of individuals and standards of quality in care provision. Every health and social care organisation needs to have **policies** and **procedures** that put these laws into action.

> **Key term**
>
> *Legislation: written laws also known as Statutes and Acts of Parliament*

> **Investigate**
>
> *Use the Internet to find out which of these laws are now covered by the Equality Act 2010.*

> **Key terms**
>
> *Policy: a plan of action*
>
> *Procedure: a way of doing something*

The European Convention on Human Rights and Fundamental Freedoms

This Convention established the European Court of Human Rights and provides the basis for the Human Rights Act (1998). It gives every individual the *right*:

* to life

* not to be tortured, punished or to receive degrading treatment

* not to be enslaved

* to freedom and a fair trial

* to freedom of thought, religion and expression

* to marry and join organisations

* not to be discriminated against.

The Mental Health Act (1983) and (2007)

The 2007 piece of legislation updated the Mental Health Act (1983), which was the main piece of law affecting the treatment of adults experiencing serious mental disorders in England and Wales. The Mental Health Act (2007) seeks to safeguard the interests of adults who are vulnerable because of their mental health problems by ensuring that they can be monitored in the community by care practitioners and admitted to hospital if they don't comply with treatment. The Mental Health Acts (1983) and (2007) also protect the rights of people who use mental health services in a number of ways. Both Acts give individuals the right to appeal against their detention in hospital and give them some rights to refuse treatment. The 2007 Act gives individuals detained in hospital the right to refuse certain treatments, such as electroconvulsive therapy, and ensures that a person can only be detained in hospital if appropriate treatment is available for them.

The Convention on the Rights of the Child (1989)

This legislation introduced rights for children and young people under 18 years of age. It is based around the principles that:

* decisions about a child should be based on what is in the child's best interests

* children should not be discriminated against

* children should be free to express themselves

* children have the right to survive and develop.

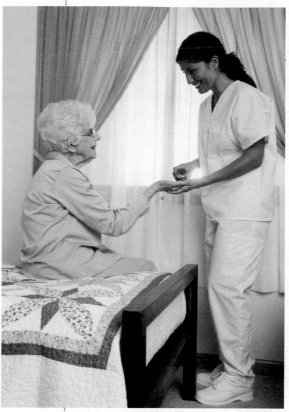

Your assessment criteria:

1A.2 Identify how one code of practice or piece of legislation promotes non-discriminatory practice in health and social care

2A.P2 Describe how codes of practice and legislation promote non-discriminatory practice in health and social care

? | Reflect

What are the pros and cons of people having a right to refuse treatment for mental illness? Would you want to be able to say 'no' to medication or other forms of treatment if you became mentally unwell?

The Children Act (2004)

This piece of legislation updated the Children Act (1989) following an inquiry into the death of Victoria Climbié in 2000. The Children Act (1989) established that health and social care workers should see the needs of the child as **paramount** when making any decisions that affect a child's welfare. Under the 1989 Act local authorities are required to provide services that meet the needs of children identified as being 'at risk'. The goal of the Children Act (2004) is to improve the lives of all children who receive informal or professional care. It covers all services that children might use, such as schools, day care and children's homes, as well as health care services. The Children Act (2004) now requires care services to work collaboratively so that they form a protective team around the child.

The Children Act (2004) resulted from a report called *Every Child Matters* that led to significant changes in the way services for children and young people are provided in the UK. The aims of *Every Child Matters* (www.everychildmatters.gov.uk) are that all children should:

- be healthy
- stay safe
- enjoy and achieve
- make a positive contribution
- achieve economic wellbeing.

The ongoing *Every Child Matters* programme of children's service development ensures that safeguarding remains the key priority for everyone who is part of the children's workforce. People who work with children, young people and vulnerable adults now have to have their backgrounds checked by the Criminal Records Bureau (CRB) to ensure they are suitable to be working with vulnerable people. In 2009, a Vetting and

A range of legislation now exists to safeguard the rights and interests of children, particularly those seen as being at risk of harm or neglect

🔑 **Key term**

Paramount: *most important*

📋 **Investigate**

Using the Internet, investigate the case of Victoria Climbié and try to identify why her death led to changes in the way that services for children operate and are organised in the United Kingdom. Produce a short summary or magazine article of your findings.

Case study

Beverley, aged 15, suffered neglect and abuse at the hands of her mother and step-father for six years before the local authority and police became aware of the situation. From the age of nine, when her mother remarried, Beverley was forbidden to play with her two half-brothers. She was also locked in her room at night, given little to eat and made to do all the household chores.

Beverley was deliberately excluded from family life by her parents. They made her use an outside toilet, stopped her having any books in her room and starved her of love and affection, even though she could see her siblings being hugged and cuddled. Because she was shabbily dressed, underweight and often unkempt, Beverley was bullied at school. Beverley was frightened of her mother who didn't want to be near her, shouted at and hit her, and always made her stay at home on family days out. Beverley eventually told a teacher at school what her life was like at home. A doctor who examined her said that she was underweight, had eyesight and teeth problems, and had suffered emotional abuse and neglect. Beverley and her half-brothers were removed from the family home by social workers. Her parents admitted charges of cruelty and neglect, and were given community sentences.

1. In what ways was Beverley subjected to ill-treatment?
2. Identify examples of legislation that could be used to protect Beverley and promote her rights.
3. How did care practitioners intervene to safeguard Beverley's interests and wellbeing?

Barring Scheme that is administered by the **Independent Safeguarding Authority** and the Criminal Records Bureau requires all adults who work with children to register. Equivalent agencies called Disclosure Scotland and Access Northern Ireland operate in other parts of the UK.

The Race Relations (Amendment) Act (2000)

The Race Relations Act (1976) made racial discrimination unlawful. The Act defined racial discrimination as 'less favourable treatment on racial grounds'. The Race Relations (Amendment) Act (2000) extended and strengthened the 1976 law by making racial discrimination by public authorities, such as the Police, NHS and local authorities, for example, unlawful. The Race Relations Acts of 1976 and 2000 aim to eradicate racial discrimination and to promote equal opportunities for members of all ethnic groups.

The Disability Discrimination Act (2005)

This Act safeguards the rights of disabled people by making unlawful 'less favourable treatment' of disabled people in employment, the provision of goods and services, education and transport. The aim of the Act is to ensure that disabled people receive equal opportunities and that employers, traders, transport and education providers make 'reasonable adjustments' to their premises and services to allow access. The Equality Act (2010) aims to simplify the law against all types of discrimination (see Chapter 8).

 Key term

Independent Safeguarding Authority – an organisation created to prevent unsuitable people from working with children and vulnerable adults (www.isa-gov.org.uk/)

 Investigate

Use the Equality and Human Rights Commission website (www. equalityhumanrights.com) to find out about the rights of disabled people and those with mental health problems.

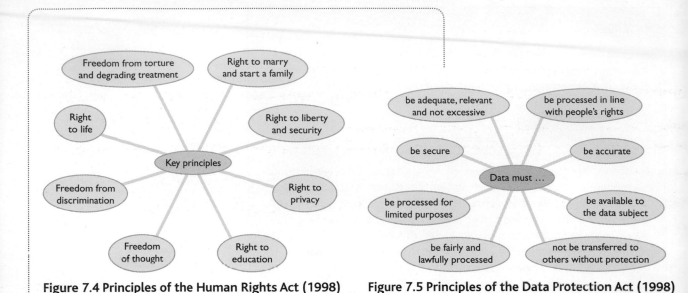

Figure 7.4 Principles of the Human Rights Act (1998)

Figure 7.5 Principles of the Data Protection Act (1998)

The Human Rights Act (1998)

The Human Rights Act (1998) is the most recent addition to equality law in the United Kingdom. It is important in relation to care environments because it entitles people resident in the United Kingdom to seek redress for infringements of their human rights by a 'public authority'. A 'public authority' is an organisation that has a public function or which operates in a public sphere. As such, the legislation covers all kinds of care homes, hospitals and social services departments, for example.

The Data Protection Act (1998)

The most important law on confidentiality of information is the Data Protection Act (1998). This sets out rules for the processing of personal information. The eight main principles of the Act are illustrated in Figure 7.5.

The Data Protection Act (1998) says that information which can be used to identify a particular patient or service user must be protected and should not be revealed to people who don't actually need to know about it. This can mean that certain people in a care organisation need to know about *some* of the information held on a particular person, but don't need to know *all* of the details. In such cases they should only be provided with access to the part of the information relevant to their work or particular needs.

Your assessment criteria:

1A.2 Identify how one code of practice or piece of legislation promotes non-discriminatory practice in health and social care

2A.P2 Describe how codes of practice and legislation promote non-discriminatory practice in health and social care

? | Reflect

What effect do you think that a breach of confidentiality might have on the relationship between a service user and a health or social care worker?

Case study

Francine is 30 years old. She came to the United Kingdom as a refugee from West Africa three years ago. Francine is working in a care home and has managed to make some friends. Until a few months ago, Francine was settled, happy with her lifestyle and had been getting over the traumatic experiences that made her leave her own country.

Francine was admitting a new resident to the care home when the resident's husband accused her of deliberately not listing his wife's jewellery or money. Francine politely explained that the deputy manager was doing this but received a volley of abuse that really shocked her. The resident's husband has since made several complaints about Francine and has written a letter stating that he doesn't want her to play any part in meeting his wife's care needs. Francine tried to speak with him to reassure him but was angrily told to 'keep your dirty black hands off my wife'.

1. What kind of prejudice is affecting the way that Francine is being treated by the resident's husband?

2. Identify two pieces of legislation that protect Francine from unfair discrimination.

Codes of practice

The standards of practice that health and social care workers have to meet are set by their **regulatory bodies,** by the government and by their employer's policies and procedures. Health and social care workers and their employers have a variety of responsibilities to meet the law and national minimum standards of care provision.

Codes of practice provide guidance and rules on ways of behaving and standards of practice. They identify what a care worker should do in specific situations. Codes of practice reflect standards of good practice in care settings. The Nursing and Midwifery Council produces a code of practice for nurses and midwives, while the General Social Care Council (England), the Care Council for Wales, the Scottish Social Services Council and the Northern Ireland Social Care Council each produce a code of practice for social care and social workers in their region. Health and social care workers who breach the code of practice of their regulatory body are liable to be disciplined and may even be barred from working in their profession.

Workplace policies and procedures

A policy is a set of guidelines or rules that tells health and social care workers how to do things in a certain way in a particular care setting. Policies usually include a range of procedures that are designed to put the policy into practice. Procedures set out how tasks, such as giving an injection or medication, should be performed. Such procedures ensure consistent, safe and effective standards of care practice.

Key terms

Code of practice: a document setting out standards for practice

Regulatory body: an independent organisation that regulates (controls and directs) the practice of health or social care workers

Regulatory bodies
Nursing and Midwifery Council (NMC)
General Medical Council (GMC)
Health and Care Professions Council (HCPC)

Figure 7.6 Regulatory bodies for health and social care workers in the UK

Factors that may affect the care needs of individuals

Respect, choice and care needs

People who use health and social care services are entitled to expect they will be treated equally and fairly, regardless of their personal characteristics or cultural background. Health and social care organisations and individual workers need to understand social and cultural diversity and have to find ways of promoting equality of opportunity and fair treatment for all.

Basic care needs of service users

Health, social care and early years services are designed to meet the physical, intellectual, emotional and social (PIES) needs of different client groups. A client group is a group of service users who, because they are in the same life stage, have a similar range of **basic needs**. Table 7.1 identifies the physical, intellectual, emotional and social needs that all human beings must meet to:

- be physically healthy (Physical needs)

- develop their knowledge, skills and abilities (Intellectual needs)

- develop communication skills and personal relationships (Social needs)

- feel secure and have good mental health (Emotional needs).

Table 7.1 Examples of PIES needs

Type of need	Examples of need
Physical needs	A balanced diet and sufficient fluids Warmth and shelter Exercise, sleep and rest Good hygiene Protection from harm, illness and injury
Intellectual needs	Interesting and purposeful activities Learning opportunities Mental challenges and new experiences
Emotional needs	Love, support and care A sense of safety and security Self-confidence and self-esteem Opportunities to express feelings
Social needs	Attachment to a trusted carer Relationships such as friendships, work relationships, and intimate and sexual relationships A sense of identity and belonging within a community

Your assessment criteria:

1B.3 Identify the different needs of individuals in relation to health and social care provision

2B.P3 Describe the different needs of service users in health and social care, with reference to examples

Key term

Basic needs: the physical, intellectual, emotional and social requirements for health and wellbeing

? Reflect

Find a diagram of Maslow's hierarchy of needs and reflect on the way PIES is linked to this.

An individual's PIES needs change throughout the life course

A person's physical, intellectual, emotional and social needs are affected by their:

- stage of development (life stage)
- health status
- abilities and disabilities
- social and cultural background.

For example, a healthy infant is almost completely dependent on others (their parents or carers usually) to meet all of their PIES needs. By contrast, a physically and mentally healthy adult is generally able to meet their needs without much assistance from others. If a person experiences ill-health or development problems, they will have specific care needs. It is also important to take an individual's social and cultural background (Figure 7.7) into account when assessing and meeting their care needs, as a range of factors can affect the appropriateness and quality of care provided.

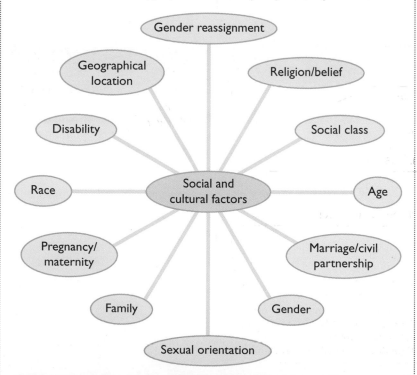

Figure 7.7 Social and cultural factors affecting care needs

 Discuss

In a small group or with a class colleague, discuss how two or three of these social and cultural factors could affect a person's care needs.

Gender, sexual orientation and care needs

A person's gender can affect their expectations of the way they would like to be treated by health and social care workers. In particular, an individual may prefer to receive in-patient hospital care in a same-sex ward or to be examined and treated by a care worker who is the same sex– particularly if intimate or personal care is required. A person's gender should be taken into account when you think about how best to provide privacy and protect their dignity in a care setting. Respecting individual choices and beliefs also extends to sexual orientation. A person's sexual orientation may be gay, lesbian, heterosexual or bisexual. People who identify themselves as gay/lesbian or bisexual may have experienced prejudice (**homophobia**) and unfair discrimination because of their sexuality. It is very important that individuals are given respect and are not denied fair and equal treatment in a care setting because of their sexual orientation.

Age and care needs

The UK population consists of a number of different age groupings. Infants, children, adolescents, adults and older people are examples of age groupings. In situations where an age group is stereotyped or treated in a negative way, **ageism** may occur. Showing respect and communicating appropriately with individuals of all ages is essential in health and social care work. It is important, for example, to find out how an older person wishes to be addressed (by their first name or more formally as 'Mr' or 'Mrs', for example). Similarly, the use of appropriate language is important when dealing with colleagues, as well as clients. It is best to avoid using slang or jargon – people may not understand you and may think that you are being disrespectful, rather than friendly or informal.

Disability and care needs

A disability is a condition or problem that limits a person's mobility, hearing, vision, speech or mental function. A person may be born with a disabling condition or problem, or may acquire their disability as the result of an accident, illness or some form of trauma. Some people have more than one disability.

The care needs of disabled people are extremely varied. It is important to assess each individual and provide care that meets their particular needs. A disabled person may be treated unfairly or less favourably than an able

Your assessment criteria:

1B.3 Identify the different needs of individuals in relation to health and social care provision

2B.P3 Describe the different needs of service users in health and social care, with reference to examples

Key terms

Ageism: *unfair discrimination because of prejudice relating to an individual's age or age group*

Homophobia: *prejudice and unfair discrimination against people who are gay, lesbian or bisexual*

A person's gender should be taken into account when planning and providing care

bodied person because of deliberate prejudice against disabled people or because others don't understand their particular needs. Prejudice against disabled people is known as disablism. Where people act on their disablist prejudices, disability discrimination may occur.

'Race', ethnicity and care needs

An individual may be classified as belonging to a particular ethnic group because of their place of birth, background or skin colour, for example. People also identify themselves with particular ethnic groups when they say they are 'black', 'white', 'Bengali' or 'Scottish', for example. Prejudice and unfair treatment in relation to a person's ethnicity is known as racial discrimination. Care organisations should always take the cultural and language needs of non-white ethnic groups into account when organising and providing services. Ensuring equality of access to services, appropriate language support and being sensitive to the cultural needs (relating to diet, faith and privacy, for example) of individuals from different racial, or ethnic, backgrounds are key aspects.

Religion, belief and care needs

Some people have a particular religious faith because their family follows that religion and this becomes part of their socialisation. Other people acquire religious beliefs later in life. Religion can have a big influence on an individual's lifestyle. Some people base their everyday life around prayer and religious 'rules' for living. Others have no religion at all and live a completely secular life. However, religion does tend to cause strong feelings (for and against) and can lead to discrimination because a person belongs to, or doesn't belong to, a particular faith community. Health and social care workers need to value the religious and other beliefs that are an important part of service user's lives. They can do this, for example, by:

- developing knowledge and awareness of the faiths, lifestyles and practices of people from a range of backgrounds (for example, Christianity, Islam, Judaism, Hinduism and Buddhism)

- understanding and respecting secular beliefs such as humanism and atheism

- organising and taking part in activities and events that celebrate religious holy days, festivals and traditions

- providing appropriate facilities for worship and making links with local religious leaders (such as priests, imams, rabbis and ministers).

Key term

Secular: *non-religious*

Reflect

What do you know about the different religious faiths that people have in the UK? How would you find out more about a particular religion if you were asked to care for somebody whose faith was important to them?

A person's beliefs may have a direct impact on their preferences for care and on how they wish their body or organs to be treated in the event of their death.

Family, marriage and civil partnership

There is a range of different family structures in the United Kingdom. These include nuclear families, extended families, lone-parent families, blended families and foster families. In some families parents are married, while in others they cohabit and remain unmarried. A family's response to an individual's need for care may or may not be supportive. It is always important to find out whether (and, if so, how) an individual wishes their family to be involved in their care. Health and social care workers should never make assumptions or judgements or hold prejudices about a person's family background.

Pregnancy, maternity and care needs

A woman who is pregnant or who has recently delivered a baby is likely to have a number of specific care needs. Before birth, the woman should be supported to create a birth plan – identifying how she would like to give birth and who she would like to provide support as her birthing partner. Acknowledging these support needs will contribute to the woman's emotional wellbeing. Similarly advice, guidance and practical support with post-natal (following birth) care and breastfeeding are also important ways of promoting the physical and emotional wellbeing of a new mother and baby.

A woman's care and support needs are different before and after giving birth

Geographical location and care needs

Health and social care services can be difficult to access if they are located several miles from where an individual lives. Location can be a particular problem for people who live in rural (country) areas; the problem is made even worse for people who rely on public transport. Sometimes people have to travel very long distances to obtain specialist health care. As a result, geographical location of services may act as a barrier for access to care. Health and social care facilities that are difficult to get to are unlikely to be used by people who do not have easy access to their own transport.

 Discuss

How does the geographical location of your home affect your access to care services. Discuss the benefits and disadvantages of this in a small group or with a class colleague.

How adapting services to meet the diverse needs of service users promotes equality and diversity in health and social care

Personalising care and support

Health and social care services need to be able to meet the diverse needs of people within the UK population. Providing a 'one-size-fits-all' approach is insensitive to the varying needs of different client groups and to the particular needs of diverse individuals. An individual's care needs are likely to be affected by their stage of development, as well as by a range of social and cultural factors.

Infants' care needs

Infants have a wide range of care needs because they are vulnerable and dependent on others for their survival and development. A summary of the care needs of infants who are healthy and developing normally is presented in Table 7.2 below.

Your assessment criteria:

1B.4 Identify ways that health and social care provision can be adapted to meet the diverse needs of a selected individual

2B.P4 Describe how health and social care provision can be adapted to meet the diverse needs of different individuals, with reference to examples

Key term

Attachment relationship: a relationship based on a close emotional bond between two people (for example, parent and child)

Table 7.2 The care needs of infants

Care needs	Purpose of care	Ways of meeting care needs
Physical care	Provision of basic physical care and protection	• Assistance with feeding • Being washed and cleaned regularly • Having nappies changed • Being dressed • Receiving vaccinations to prevent infections • Having physical health monitored • Having personal safety monitored and safeguarded
Intellectual stimulation	Development of basic thinking and language skills	• Stimulating toys and books to play with • Being read stories or rhymes, and sung to • Encouragement to babble and make sounds
Emotional support	Establishing basic attachment relationship	• Consistent, emotionally-responsive relationship with a parent or carer • Reassuring, soothing and comforting response when upset
Social support	Development of relationship and interaction skills	• Attachment relationship with a parent or carer • Regular contact with parents or other carers • Opportunities and encouragement to play

An infant who has physical health or developmental problems is likely to require specialist assistance from health and early years practitioners to meet their specific care needs. Examples of these are outlined in Figure 7.8.

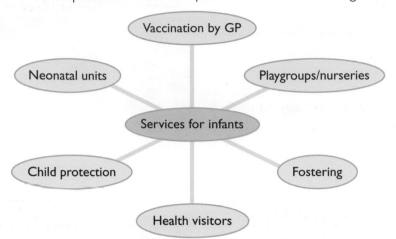

Figure 7.8 Additional care needs and services for infants

Your assessment criteria:

1B.4 Identify ways that health and social care provision can be adapted to meet the diverse needs of a selected individual

2B.P4 Describe how health and social care provision can be adapted to meet the diverse needs of different individuals, with reference to examples

Children's care needs

Children are more physically robust than infants, and have a range of physical skills that enable them to be more independent. As a result of their physical, intellectual, emotional and social development, an individual's care needs change throughout childhood. The care needs of a five-year-old child are likely to be very different to those of a nine-year-old child because of this ongoing development. Care in childhood focuses on encouraging development and increasing a child's capabilities.

An individual's care needs change significantly as they move from infancy into childhood

A child may have additional or **specific care needs** because they experience:

- problems with their physical or mental health

- difficulties with learning, behaviour or relationships with others

- social or financial problems affecting their family.

A range of health, educational and social care services are provided to meet the specific or additional care needs of children. Examples of these are outlined in Figure 7.9 on page 190.

 Key term

Specific care needs: *care needs resulting from particular defined health, development or social support problems*

Table 7.3 Care needs of children

Care needs	Purpose of care	Ways of meeting care needs
Physical care	Provision of physical care and protection to enable further development to occur	• Encouragement to eat a balanced diet • Provision of warmth and shelter • Help and encouragement to wash and dress • Opportunities and encouragement to exercise and develop physical skills • Regular rest and sleep • Protection from harm
Intellectual stimulation	Stimulation and support of intellectual abilities to develop knowledge, understanding and skills	• Play opportunities • Educational support and encouragement to learn basic reading, writing and numeracy skills • Books to read, television to watch, music to listen to • Friends and adults to learn from and talk to
Emotional support	Building self-confidence, emotional security and self-esteem	• Supportive parents or carers to provide love and affection • Respect and being valued by parents, friends and other adults • Opportunities to have fun, feel happy and express own feelings • Encouragement and positive feedback from parents, teachers and others which boosts self-esteem
Social support	Supporting development of social skills and relationships	• Help and support to develop friendships with other children and safe relationships with adults outside of the family • Opportunities to play and learn alongside other children • Opportunities to experience a range of social activities and events • Development of basic organisational skills to deal with everyday activities

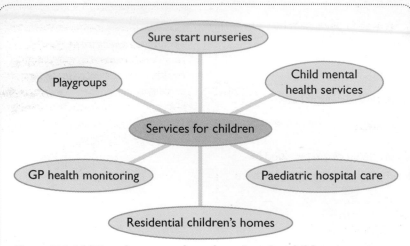

Figure 7.9 Additional care needs and services for children

Your assessment criteria:

1B.4 Identify ways that health and social care provision can be adapted to meet the diverse needs of a selected individual

2B.P4 Describe how health and social care provision can be adapted to meet the diverse needs of different individuals, with reference to examples

Adolescents' care needs

Care in adolescence focuses less on directly meeting basic needs and more on providing opportunities, encouragement and support, so that the individual can gradually take on the responsibility of meeting their own needs independently.

Table 7.4 Care needs of adolescents

Care needs	Purpose of care	Ways of meeting care needs
Physical care	Maintenance of good physical health and wellbeing to support growth and development through puberty	• Encouragement to eat a balanced diet • Shelter, physical security and warmth • Encouragement and facilities to ensure good personal hygiene • Opportunities and encouragement to be physically active and to exercise
Intellectual stimulation	Stimulation and extension of intellectual skills and abilities	• Education and learning opportunities • Opportunities to work and train in areas of interest • Stimulating books, music, television • Opportunities to talk and explore ideas and beliefs with others
Emotional support	Provision of supportive relationships to enable development of personal identity, self-confidence and self-esteem	• Supportive relationships with parents or carers to provide love and affection • Friendships that are supportive and stimulating • Respect and feeling of being valued as a capable person by parents, friends and other adults • Opportunities to have fun, feel happy and express own feelings • Encouragement and positive feedback from parents, teachers and others which boosts self-esteem
Social support	To promote sense of belonging and social inclusion	• Active and supportive circle of friends • Opportunities to socialise with others • Opportunities to take part in leisure activities and meet new people

As in childhood, an adolescent may develop additional or specific care needs because they experience:

- problems with their physical or mental health

- difficulties with their learning, behaviour or relationships with others

- social or financial problems affecting their family.

A range of health, educational and social care services are provided to meet the specific or additional care needs of adolescents. Examples of these are outlined in Figure 7.10 below.

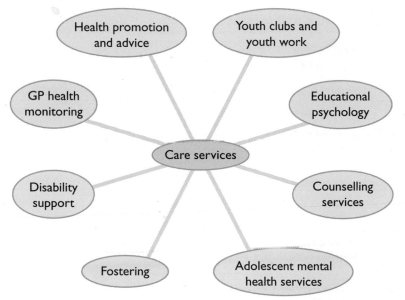

Figure 7.10 Additional care needs and services for adolescents

Adults' care needs

Adults have largely completed their physical growth and have developed many of the skills, abilities and attributes that they will make use of throughout the rest of their life. As a result, an adult's care needs tend to focus on maintaining and refining the different aspects of their health and wellbeing.

An adult may develop additional or specific care needs because they experience:

- problems with their physical or mental health

- difficulties in their personal or work relationships

- social or financial problems.

> **? Reflect**
>
> *How do you think the parents of an older adolescent (16–17 years) could encourage and enable them to be more independent, while also providing an appropriate level of support and assistance?*

Table 7.5 Care needs of adults

Care needs	Purpose of care	Ways of meeting care needs
Physical care	To maintain physical health and wellbeing, and minimise effects of ill-health	• A balanced diet and adequate fluids • A warm, safe place to live • Good hygiene • Opportunities to exercise • Sleep and rest • Access to health facilities
Intellectual stimulation	To provide a focus for using and developing intellectual abilities	• Stimulating work or other occupation • Stimulating relationships with others • Access to books, television, music, etc. • Learning opportunities and educational guidance and support
Emotional support	To achieve and maintain fulfilling and stable personal relationships, positive self-esteem and personal identity	• Love and support from close relationships (partner, family, children) • Respect from and feeling valued by others • A sense of personal identity • Independence and opportunities to make own decisions • Stable and fulfilling personal relationships
Social acceptance and involvement	To establish and maintain a social network and an active social life	• An active and supportive circle of friends • Opportunities to take part in social activities • Opportunities to enjoy leisure activities

Older peoples' care needs

Later adulthood is the final stage in an individual's life. It is also a stage in which an individual's care needs are likely to increase. Many older people are very healthy and live active, enjoyable lives. However, the loss of physical and sensory abilities, and the reduction in a person's social network as they retire from work and see less of old friends, are features of many older people's lives. As a result, the care needs of older people tend to focus on using support, services and adaptations to maximise independence, maintain an active lifestyle and minimise the effects of illness and ageing.

Exercise and social activity are important for older people

Key term

Balanced diet: *a diet that contains adequate amounts of all the necessary nutrients required for healthy growth and activity*

Table 7.6 Care needs of older people

Care needs	Purpose of care	Ways of meeting care needs
Physical care	To maximise physical health and wellbeing, and minimise ill-health and disabling effects of ageing	• Housing that provides warmth, shelter and safety • A balanced diet and adequate fluids • Provision of mobility support and assistance • Glasses, hearing aids, other prostheses • Opportunities to be physically active and to exercise • Access to health facilities
Intellectual stimulation	To maintain and use intellectual capabilities in ways that are stimulating and interesting	• Learning opportunities • Stimulating activities and hobbies • New experiences • Opportunities for reminiscence • Books, television, magazines and newspapers • Conversation
Emotional support	Maintenance of supportive relationships, self-esteem and strong personal identity	• Supportive and loving relationships with partners, friends and family members • Being treated with respect and dignity by others • Being given opportunities to make choices and to be independent • Stable relationships
Social support	To maintain social network and active social life	• Contact with friends and relatives • Opportunities to socialise • Participation in leisure activities

Individuals with specific care needs

An individual may have specific care needs because they experience:

• learning difficulties

• physical disabilities

• sensory impairments (hearing, visual)

• mental health problems.

Examples of the different kinds of care services provided for people with specific care needs are outlined in Figure 7.11 below. Because people experience these problems in different ways, their care needs also vary to some extent.

Key term

Prosthesis: *an artificial device used to replace a missing body part, such as a limb or eye*

Investigate

Use the Internet or library resources to investigate the causes and effects on health and wellbeing of one of the specific care need groups you have read about in this topic. Present your findings in the form of a short leaflet or poster.

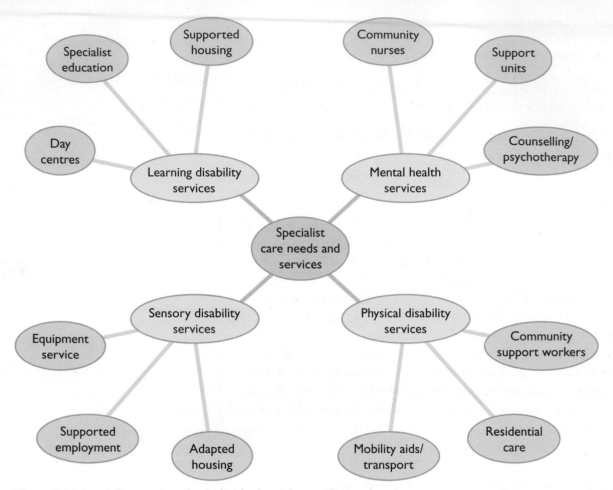

Figure 7.11 Specialist services for individuals with specific needs

Adaptations to services

Diversity and difference within the population, as well as the specific needs and preferences of individuals with disabilities and health conditions, mean that care services have to be adaptable. This can be achieved by:

- providing flexible and easily accessible referral systems

- providing a wide range of physical, cultural, language and other support services

- being responsive to the differing dietary requirements and personal care needs of individuals

- providing suitable prayer facilities and opportunities for people to observe religious rituals

Your assessment criteria:

2B.M2 Explain the benefits of adapting health and social care provision to meet the diverse needs of different individuals, with reference to two selected examples

- using a person-centred approach to care provision that respects individuals' choices and acknowledges their preferences for how care is provided

- involving families and partners in care planning and provision, and offering suitable visiting arrangements

- ensuring staff communicate effectively using appropriate language and offer independent advocacy where this is required.

Benefits of adapting services

Making reasonable and appropriate adaptations to the facilities, services and ways of working in health and social care settings is important in addressing the diverse needs of service users. The benefits of adapting services for individuals are that people are more likely to feel they are being respected, treated equally and not being discriminated against. This, in turn, ensures that an individual's dignity, privacy and sense of security are protected in ways that promote positive care relationships and a greater level of satisfaction with care services. Health and social care workers who offer person-centred care are likely to be sensitive to the need to adapt services for particular individuals. Focusing closely on the needs of the individual helps to improve the overall quality of care and also ensures that everyone, regardless of background or ability, gains access to the care services they require.

Assessing the effectiveness of care provision

The effectiveness of health and social care provision for an individual can be assessed in a number of ways. Care organisations, and health and social care workers, use a number of strategies including:

- evaluating how well an individual's care plan goals have been achieved

- carrying out 'before and after' comparisons to see how much change has occurred in an individual's ability to function, live independently or manage their health problems

- obtaining an individual's own views – and perhaps those of their relatives – on their experiences of care and how this has affected them

- carrying out multidisciplinary reviews where different health and social care workers discuss and evaluate their contributions to care provision and comment on its effectiveness

- reviewing and comparing the experiences of different individuals to assess the strengths and weaknesses of the care and services that are provided.

Your assessment criteria:

2B.D2 Assess the effectiveness of health and social care provision for different individuals with diverse needs, with reference to two selected examples

? | Reflect

Have you ever been asked to complete a questionnaire or to answer a few questions about the effectiveness of care that you have received? If 10 was excellent, how would you rate the quality of the care you receive from your local GP practice?

Assessment checklist

To achieve level 1, my portfolio of evidence must show that I can:

Assessment criteria	Description	✓
1A.1	Define non-discriminatory practice in health and social care, using two examples	☐
1A.2	Identify how one code of practice or piece of legislation promotes non-discriminatory practice in health and social care	☐
1B.3	Identify the different needs of individuals in relation to health and social care provision	☐
1B.4	Identify ways that health and social care provision can be adapted to meet the diverse needs of a selected individual	☐

To achieve a pass grade, my portfolio of evidence must show that I can:

Assessment criteria	Description	✓
2A.P1	Describe non-discriminatory and discriminatory practice in health and social care, using examples	☐
2A.P2	Describe how codes of practice and legislation promote non-discriminatory practice in health and social care	☐
2B.P3	Describe the different needs of service users in health and social care, with reference to examples	☐
2B.P4	Describe how health and social care provision can be adapted to meet the diverse needs of different individuals, with reference to examples	☐

To achieve a merit grade, my portfolio of evidence must show that I can:

Assessment criteria	Description	✓
2A.M1	Explain the importance of legislation and codes of practice in promoting non-discriminatory practice in health and social care, using examples	☐
2B.M2	Explain the benefits of adapting health and social care provision to meet the diverse needs of different individuals, with reference to two selected examples	☐

To achieve a distinction grade, my portfolio of evidence must show that I can:

Assessment criteria	Description	✓
2A.D1	Assess the impact of discriminatory practice for health and social care workers, with reference to selected examples	☐
2B.D2	Assess the effectiveness of health and social care provision for different individuals with diverse needs, with reference to two selected examples	☐

8 | Individual rights in health and social care

Learning aim A
Investigate the rights of individuals using health and social care services

▶ Topic A.1 The rights of individuals using health and social care services

▶ Topic A.2 How care workers can uphold the rights of service users

Learning Aim B
Examine the responsibilities of employers and employees in upholding service users' rights in health and social care

▶ Topic B.1 Responsibilities of employers and employees in ensuring safety

▶ Topic B.2 Responsibilities of employers and employees in ensuring confidentiality

The rights of individuals using health and social care services

Understanding individuals' rights

The United Kingdom is a diverse society. This means that it consists of people with a variety of different backgrounds and characteristics. Health and social care workers need to have a good awareness of diversity as this has an impact on equality and rights issues, and on the way people expect to be treated in health and social care environments. Every individual who uses care services has the right to be respected, to be treated equally and not to be discriminated against. Knowledge of the diverse nature of UK society enables health and social care workers to understand that providing fair and equal treatment is an essential part of good care practice.

Diversity and UK society

The population of the United Kingdom is diverse in many ways (see Figure 8.1). This means that it consists of people with a variety of different backgrounds, characteristics and **cultures**.

Key term

Culture: common values, beliefs and customs, or a way of life

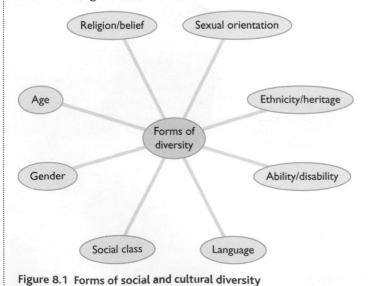

Figure 8.1 Forms of social and cultural diversity

Health and social care workers work with colleagues, service users and other adults from a wide range of social, cultural, language and ethnic backgrounds. They provide care and support for men and women, people with different types of ability and disability, individuals who speak different languages and who have different cultural traditions, as well as people who could be described as middle class, working class, as 'black', 'white' or of mixed **heritage**. The **diversity** of the people who use care services should be viewed in a positive way and as a reflection of differences within wider society. These differences impact on people's needs. As a result, health and social care workers have a responsibility to understand and value difference as a way of meeting people's individual needs.

Promoting equality

Each person who uses UK health and social care services should be treated equally and fairly, regardless of their background. In the United Kingdom, a number of laws make **unfair discrimination** unlawful. These ensure that everyone has the same 'rights' of access to health, social care and early years services, for example. Despite this, **prejudice** and unfair discrimination make it more difficult for some social groups to access and use care services. Challenging prejudice and discrimination, and promoting equality is an important part of the work of care organisations and of health and social care workers. Figure 8.2 identifies a range of rights that all service users have and which should be promoted and respected by health and social care workers.

Figure 8.2 Individuals' rights in health and social care settings

Key terms

Diversity: forms of difference

Heritage: the origins, traditions or background that a person inherits from their family

Prejudice: a strongly held attitude towards a particular group which will often persist even when shown to be unjustified or unfounded

Unfair discrimination: the unjustified and less favourable treatment of a person or a group, usually as a result of prejudice

Investigate

You can find out about the way equalities are promoted in the United Kingdom at the Equalities Commission website (www.equalityhumanrights. com).

The role of legislation

The law, or legislation, plays an important role in giving individuals rights to equality and in protecting them from unfair discrimination. There is a variety of anti-discrimination laws in the United Kingdom including:

- The Human Rights Act (1998, updated 2000)

- The Equality Act (2010)

- The Mental Health Act (1983).

The Human Rights Act (1998, updated 2000)

This law gives every individual a range of rights that must normally be respected by health and social care workers (Figure 8.3). Service users should be kept informed of their rights, including the right to access legal support if required. There are situations in which an individual's human rights can be over-ruled by health or social care workers or by relatives – if the person poses a risk or is incapable of making a decision regarding their own welfare.

Your assessment criteria:

1A.1 Identify the individual rights of service users in health and social care

1A.2 Identify how current and relevant legislation protects the rights of service users, with reference to one example

2A.P2 Describe how current and relevant legislation protects the rights of service users, using examples

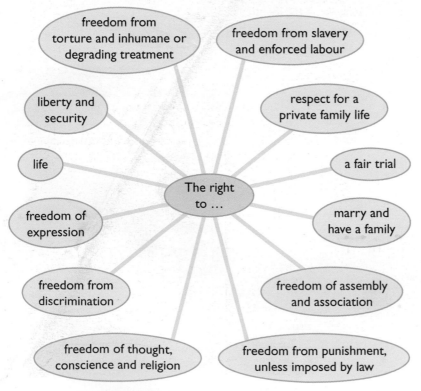

Figure 8.3 **Rights protected by the Human Rights Act (1998, updated 2000)**

The Equality Act (2010)

The Equality Act was introduced in October 2010. It replaced seven other pieces of legislation to provide a simpler anti-discrimination law designed to protect individuals from unfair treatment, and to promote a fair and more equal society. The Equality Act 2010 protects people who use health and social care services from unfair discrimination, harassment and victimisation to ensure that we all have equality of opportunity.

The Mental Health Act (1983)

The Mental Health Act (1983) applies to England and Wales. It focuses on the care and treatment of people with diagnosed mental disorders. Under this Act, a person may be admitted to hospital or to a 'place of safety' in order to receive care or treatment, even though they may disagree. The Act also provides a right of appeal against compulsory admission and protection relating to treatment for mental disorders.

Investigate

What does your local NHS Trust, Primary Care Trust or local authority say about equal opportunities for people who use their services? Use the Internet to locate the organisation's website and search for information on equal opportunities. Compare your findings with those of your class colleagues.

Your assessment criteria:

2A.M1 Explain ways in which service users' individual rights can be upheld in health and social care, using selected examples

Promoting and protecting service users' rights

Health and social care workers owe a duty of care to each person they care for or support. This means that they must put the individual's needs and rights first when they are planning or providing care. Health and social care workers try to promote and protect the rights of services users through:

- anti-discriminatory practices
- ensuring privacy
- using a person-centred approach
- showing empathy
- being honest.

> **? | Reflect**
>
> *What does it mean to 'show empathy'? Can you think of a time when you have empathised with another person? Why is it important to be able to do this in health and social care practice?*

Anti-discriminatory practice

Promoting equal opportunities and challenging unfair discrimination is part of the role of all health and social care workers. These workers often provide services for people who experience health and social problems that are triggered or made worse by poverty, unemployment and unequal access to society's resources.

Promoting equality in the care setting means that health and social care workers need to address their own prejudices and should tackle any unfair discrimination that they see. The best way of putting equal opportunities principles into action is through **anti-discriminatory practice**. This means developing ways of working that:

- recognise the needs of people from diverse backgrounds, including those who come from minority religious and cultural backgrounds

- actively challenge the unfair discrimination that people have experienced

- counteract the effects of any unfair discrimination on people.

Health and social care workers who use an anti-discriminatory approach to practice:

- use non-discriminatory language (non-sexist, non-racist, non-disablist words and phrases)

- become self-aware, tolerant of difference and are prepared to change their ideas about people

- view service users as diverse and different, and of equal value regardless of their physical, mental or cultural characteristics

- accept individuals' physical, social and cultural differences as a positive and interesting feature of care work, rather than as a problem.

 Key term

Anti-discriminatory practice:
an approach to care practice that challenges instances of prejudice and unfair discrimination and which aims to counter their negative effects

 Discuss

In a small group or with a class colleague identify reasons why each of the people in the picture opposite may experience unfair discrimination because of prejudice.

Case study

Abdullah is 32 years old. He came to the United Kingdom as a refugee and suffered a brain injury as a result of being attacked in the street by two men. The attack on Abdullah was treated as a hate crime because the two men shouted racial abuse before assaulting him. Abdullah now lives with his sister who is his main carer. He attends a day centre where he has made some friends. Abdullah has slowly had to relearn how to wash, dress and feed himself, and requires help and support to adapt to new people and changes in his routine. He is often frightened of strangers and has to be taken to and from the day centre by his sister. Abdullah is not able to make decisions for himself or live independently at the moment.

1. What kind of prejudice led to the attack on Abdullah?

2. Identify two pieces of legislation that protect Abdullah from unfair discrimination.

3. Explain why it is important for health and social care workers to relate to Abdullah in a non-discriminatory way.

Your assessment criteria:

2A.M1 Explain ways in which service users' individual rights can be upheld in health and social care, using selected examples

Ensuring privacy during personal care

An individual should always have privacy when personal care is being provided. For example, an individual should not be exposed to the view of others when they are being dressed, undressed, taken to the toilet or being helped to wash. Health and social care workers can take simple practical precautions, such as closing doors, keeping curtains drawn and not leaving individuals partially undressed. It is also important to respect an individual's right to privacy in their room. Knocking before entering and checking that you may come in is much more respectful than simply throwing the door open; carrying out tasks without asking or sitting on a person's bed or chair without asking permission is also disrespectful.

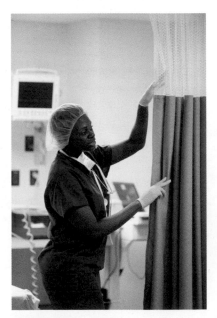

Health care workers should always respect an individual's right to privacy and dignity when delivering care or treatment

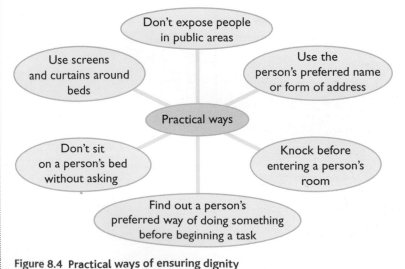

Figure 8.4 **Practical ways of ensuring dignity**

Showing respect for their dignity and privacy is a very important way of showing a person that you value them as an individual. It also shows that you acknowledge the individual's rights, whatever their needs, problems or personal difficulties.

Using a person-centred approach

The *person* with health or social care needs should always be the main focus of a care worker's attention and efforts. Person-centred approaches to practice can improve standards of care by focusing on the needs, characteristics, wishes and preferences of each individual, not just on their illness, disability or social problem. Health and social care workers who adopt a person-centred approach try to:

- understand different types of human need (physical, intellectual, emotional, social and spiritual, for example) and the way the person experiences them

- learn how to establish and maintain supportive relationships

- put the individual at the centre of their care practice and planning.

Person-centred approaches to health and social care challenge traditional task-centred approaches where care workers focus on 'getting the job done' as efficiently as possible. The task-centred approach can lead to impersonal treatment that fails to meet a person's real needs. Involving Individuals in the planning and delivery of their care and support is a way of acknowledging an individual's rights and emphasises that health and social care workers should work in partnership, doing things *with* rather than *for* or *to*, the individual wherever this is possible.

Person-centred care requires good communication and relationship-building skills

> **? | Reflect**
>
> *Is taking all residents to the toilet before breakfast an example of a person-centred or task-centred approach to care?*

Showing empathy

Health and social care workers who are able to empathise have the ability to understand other people's feelings. Empathy involves putting yourself in the place of the other person and trying to appreciate how they see and experience the world. People who are able to empathise don't make guesses or assumptions about what the other person is really thinking or feeling; instead they pay careful attention to the other person's verbal and non-verbal communication, listen actively and use empathy-building statements to check what the other person is thinking and feeling. For example, comments such as, 'it sounds as though you are unhappy about that' or, 'you seem to find the idea of surgery quite frightening' indicate that the care worker appreciates the individual's feelings and viewpoint. Saying, 'you seem to be ...' or, 'it sounds as though ...' also leaves room for the individual to correct any misinterpretation or misunderstanding on the part of the care worker. Being able to empathise improves a health or social care worker's ability to:

- establish and maintain relationships

- communicate effectively with others

- respect and acknowledge individual's rights.

Being honest

Being genuine and truthful with individuals receiving care or support is very important, even when answering difficult questions and giving answers that may be upsetting. Individuals who are receiving health and social care services are often at a point in their lives where they may be feeling very vulnerable and insecure. As a result, they need to be able to trust the people who provide care and support. Care relationships should be based on trust and honesty, with the care worker always safeguarding and promoting the rights of each individual.

Your assessment criteria:

2A.M1 Explain ways in which service users' individual rights can be upheld in health and social care, using selected examples

Care workers can form close, supportive relationships with service users but must always maintain professional boundaries

---

? | **Reflect**

Would you always want care workers to be honest with you about the state of your health or are there some things that you would rather not know?

Benefits of upholding service users' rights

Health and social care workers should always try to uphold the rights of service users. Ensuring that service users' rights are respected:

- shows that health or social care workers value all individuals

- is a way of avoiding discriminatory practice

- ensures that care is person-centred and recognises each individual's needs

- is an effective way of engaging and involving service users in their own care

- ensures that health and social care workers are practising within the legal and regulatory framework of care

- minimises conflict with service users.

Upholding service users' rights is an important aspect of good practice for health and social care workers. However, there are some situations where this is difficult or even impossible.

Difficulties of upholding service users' rights

Upholding service users' rights may be difficult or impossible because:

- a service user's wishes (to take part in dangerous sports, to go out for a long walk when unwell or to continue smoking cigarettes in hospital, for example) may not be compatible with their health or safeguarding needs

- a health or social care worker may need to implement a law (such as the Mental Health Act) under which a person is being detained or treated in hospital against their will

- the service user lacks the mental ability to make judgements or decisions about what is in their best interests (because of dementia, learning disability or brain injury, for example).

In situations in which it is difficult or even impossible to uphold a service user's rights, a health or social care worker needs to be able to justify their decisions or actions. It isn't easy to find a balance between upholding rights and minimising risks. The best interests of the individual service user should always be the main factor that guides the health or social care worker in making a decision.

Your assessment criteria:

2A.D1 Assess the benefits and potential difficulties of upholding service users' rights in health and social care, using selected examples

 Investigate

Find out how dementia can affect an individual's judgement and their ability maintain their own safety.

Safeguarding and safety responsibilities

Many people who use care services are at a vulnerable point in their lives and put a lot of trust in health and social care workers to provide them with the protection, help and support that they need. Some groups of service users, including children, older people, disabled people and people with mental health problems are vulnerable to exploitation and abuse by others. Some people who use care services may also find it difficult to follow the basic health and safety precautions that would protect them from the dangers of everyday life, as well as from abuse or exploitation. This can be a result of the problems that they have, such as learning disabilities or memory problems, or because unscrupulous people can influence them easily. As a result, many people who need care face a greater risk of harm or abuse (physical, emotional or sexual abuse, for example). To safeguard individuals from danger and harm, health and social care workers should:

- be aware of any signs or indicators of abuse or exploitation

- ensure that their own health and hygiene does not pose a threat to the health and safety of others, and that they manage their personal safety at work

- follow the infection control, moving and handling, accident and waste disposal procedures set out in their employer's health and safety policies

- make use of any **risk assessments** that have been carried out to minimise health and safety hazards

- respond appropriately to security risks in the workplace

- report health and safety and security issues to relevant people.

Risk assessment

By law, care organisations are required to carry out formal risk assessments of their care settings. Risk assessment aims to identify potential risks to the health, safety and security of health and social care workers, individuals who use care services and visitors to a care setting.

Health and social care workers have a duty of care to safeguard and protect from harm the people they care for and support. However, it is also important not to be too protective or overly restrictive. People who use services should be supported to take part in activities that involve some element of risk, for example. Health and social care workers have to achieve a balance between providing a safe and stimulating environment for individuals, and minimising health and safety hazards and risks within it.

Your assessment criteria:

1B.2 Identify how an employee can plan to maximise the safety of service users.

2B.P2 Describe how an employee can plan to maximise the safety of service users

 Key term

Risk assessment: the process of evaluating the likelihood of a hazard actually causing harm

? Reflect

What potential health and safety hazards may exist in a busy care setting, such as a nursing home for older people? Think about aspects of the environment that may be hazardous to older people with physical and sensory impairments, for example.

Risk assessment recognises that care activities, equipment and the care setting itself can be hazardous, but that steps can be taken to minimise (or remove altogether) the level of risk. The ultimate aim of a risk assessment is to ensure that people use care settings without coming to any harm. The Health and Safety Executive has identified five stages of a risk assessment. These stages and their purpose are identified in Table 8.1.

Table 8.1 The five stages of risk assessment

Stage	Key questions	Purpose
1: Identifying the risk	• What are the hazards?	• To identify all hazards that could cause a risk
2: Estimating the risk	• Who is at risk?	• To evaluate the risk of hazards causing harm
3: Controlling the risk	• What needs to be done? • Who needs to do it?	• To identify risk control measures, and responsibilities for reducing or removing the risk
4: Monitoring risk control measures	• Are the risk control measures being implemented?	• To monitor the implementation and effectiveness of risk control measures
5: Reassess the risk	• Is risk controlled? • Can the risk be reduced still further?	• To evaluate the effectiveness of current risk control strategies • To identify new risks or changes to risk levels • To consider new strategies for controlling risk

The Management of Health and Safety at Work Regulations (1999) place a legal duty on employers to carry out risk assessments in order to ensure a safe and healthy workplace. The risk assessments that are produced should clearly identify:

• the potential hazards and risks to the health and safety of employees and others in the workplace

• any preventive and protective measures that are needed to minimise risk and improve health and safety.

Key term

Health and Safety Executive: the government agency responsible for monitoring and enforcing health and safety laws in the workplace

Care workers must try to minimise the risks faced by service users when they choose to participate in outdoor and adventure activities

Many larger care organisations employ people in health and safety officer roles to carry out their risk assessments, and manage health and safety issues generally. In smaller care organisations this might be the responsibility of one or more of the managers or of a senior practitioner.

Risk assessment by health and social care workers

Health and social care workers can also carry out their own ongoing risk assessments in their everyday work. Basically this involves:

- being alert to possible hazards

- understanding the risks associated with each hazard

- reporting any health and safety concerns that are identified.

Risk issues that need to be assessed and addressed by health and social care workers as part of their everyday work include risks associated with:

- moving and handling people and equipment

- hazardous chemicals (such as cleaning fluids, disinfectants and sterilising fluids)

- medicines

- infection control

- personal security.

Your assessment criteria:

1B.2 Identify how an employee can plan to maximise the safety of service users.

2B.P2 Describe how an employee can plan to maximise the safety of service users

2B.M2 Explain why risk assessment is important in health and social care

Discuss

In a small group or with a class colleague, and using a scale of 1–5 (where 5 is very high risk and 1 is very low risk), identify the main hazard in each of the following situations, estimate the risk and then briefly describe how the risk could be minimised.

- *The playgroup kitchen floor has just been washed and is still wet.*

- *A half-full laundry bag of dirty linen has been left at the top of the stairs outside a hospital ward.*

- *In a nursing home, an elderly resident's window has been left wide open to air her room.*

- *The scissors have been left out on the craft-room table at the learning disability day centre.*

- *A workman who is fitting a new security pad to the front door of the nursery has left the door wide open and unattended while he goes to his van for some tools.*

The value of risk assessments

Risk assessment is now a part of all care work and has come to be seen as a vital part of good practice in health and social care. It is much more than a form-filling activity that generates lots of paperwork and takes up the valuable time of health and social care workers! Risk assessment is valuable because it:

- identifies hazards and risks in a care setting in a systematic, clear and ongoing way

- reduces accident and injury levels in health and social care settings and promotes safe care practice

- ensures that care organisations and health and social care practitioners take health and safety and risk management seriously

- draws attention to the needs of vulnerable people, prioritising their safeguarding and protecting the right of everyone in a care setting to a safe, secure environment.

Health and safety procedures

Employers, employees and service users all have health and safety responsibilities in care settings. Employers are responsible for providing:

- a safe and secure work environment

- safe equipment

- information and training about health, safety and security.

Care organisations (employers) must provide a work environment that meets expected health and safety standards. It should be possible for health and social care workers to work safely and for service users to receive safe care.

Employees (health and social care workers) have a responsibility to:

- work safely within the care setting

- monitor their work environment for health and safety problems that may develop

- report and respond appropriately to any health and safety risks.

Both employers and employees have to work within a range of health and safety laws (see Table 8.2 on page 214) in order to provide safe care for service users. People who receive care are expected to behave in a reasonable and safe way in order to protect their own health and safety, as well as that of others. This means that they must follow all health and safety instructions (for example, no smoking) and abide by the health and safety policies of the care setting.

Your assessment criteria:

1B.2 Identify how an employee can plan to maximise the safety of service users.

2B.P2 Describe how an employee can plan to maximise the safety of service users

2B.M2 Explain why risk assessment is important in health and social care

2B.D2 Evaluate the importance of the use of risk assessments in health and social care, using selected examples

Investigate

Go to the Health and Safety Executive's website (www.hse.gov.uk) if you want to find out more about the health and safety responsibilities of employers and employees in the workplace.

The Health and Safety at Work Act (1974)

This is the main piece of health and safety law in the UK. It affects everyone present in a care setting but focuses mainly on employers and employees. Under this Act, health and social care workers share responsibility for health and safety in care settings with the care organisation that employs them. To meet their legal responsibilities, employers must:

- carry out health and safety risk assessments

- develop health and safety procedures, such as fire evacuation procedures

- provide health and safety equipment, such as fire extinguishers, fire blankets and first aid boxes

- ensure that care settings have safety features, such as smoke alarms, fire exits and security fixtures (electronic pads on doors and window guards, for example)

- train their employees to follow health and safety procedures, and to use health and safety equipment and safety features appropriately

- provide a range of health and safety information and warning signs to alert people to safety features, such as fire exits and first aid equipment, and to warn them about prohibited areas and non-smoking regulations, for example.

Your assessment criteria:

1B.2 Identify how an employee can plan to maximise the safety of service users.

2B.P2 Describe how an employee can plan to maximise the safety of service users

 Key terms

Statute: a written piece of legislation, also known as an Act of Parliament

Regulations: written rules that create or limit rights or responsibilities

Table 8.2 A summary of health and social care legislation

Laws and regulations	Effects
The Health and Safety at Work Act 1974	This is the main piece of health and safety law in the UK. It affects both employers and employees. Under this statute, health and social care workers share responsibility for health and safety in care settings with the care organisation that employs them.
Food Safety Act (1990)	This Act states that people working with food must practice good food hygiene in the workplace. Food must be safely stored and prepared, and must not be 'injurious to health'. Local authority environmental health officers enforce this law.
Food Safety (General Food Hygiene Regulations) (1995, 2005,2006)	These regulations require people preparing food in a care setting to identify possible risks surrounding food hygiene and to put controls in place to ensure any risk is reduced. The Food Safety Regulations also specify how premises that provide food should be equipped and organised.
The Manual Handling Operations Regulations 1992 (amended 2002)	These regulations cover all manual handling activities, such as lifting, lowering, pushing, pulling or carrying objects and people. A large proportion of workplace injuries are due to poor manual handling skills. Employers have a duty to assess risks of any activity that involves manual handling. They must put in place measures to reduce or avoid the risk. Employees must follow manual handling procedures and co-operate on all manual handling issues.

Reporting of Injuries, Diseases and Dangerous Occurrences Regulations (1995) (RIDDOR)	These require employers to notify a range of occupational injuries, diseases and dangerous events to the Health and Safety Executive or other relevant authorities.
Data Protection Act (1998)	This Act protects the individual's right to confidentiality (paper and electronic records). An individual has the right to: • know what information is held about them and the right to see and correct this if it is inaccurate • refuse to provide information • have up-to-date and accurate data held about them • have data removed when it is no longer necessary for an organisation to hold it • have the confidentiality of their information protected.
Management of Health and Safety at Work Regulations (1999)	These regulations place a responsibility on employers to train staff in relation to health and safety legislation, fire prevention, and moving and handling issues. They also require employers to carry out risk assessments and to remove or reduce any health and safety hazards identified. Employers must write safe working procedures based on risk assessments carried out.
Care Homes Regulations (2001)	These regulations aim to establish standards of good practice in care homes. Care homes must be registered and inspected by the Care Quality Commission (CQC); the manager of a home must have appropriate leadership and management qualifications and is responsible for health and safety of the home. This includes carrying out risk assessments and informing the CQC of any event that endangers the health and safety or wellbeing of people on the premises.
Control of Substances Hazardous to Health Regulations (2002) (COSHH)	These require employers to assess the risks from hazardous substances and to take appropriate precautions to ensure that hazardous substances are correctly stored and used.
Civil Contingencies Act (2004)	The Act gives guidance on the responsibilities of public services in dealing with major public emergencies and accident hazards. Public services need to anticipate, prepare for, prevent, respond to and recover from major emergencies. Emergencies include extreme weather, terrorist attack, industrial or other major accidents and pandemics (e.g. flu) that undermine the ability of public services to carry out their functions without the power of the law behind them.
Care Minimum Standards	The Care Standards Act (2000) established National Minimum Standards for care services in 2003. Different standards exist for different types of care setting but all have a health and safety focus. Each care setting should: • carry out risk assessment on each individual to ensure health and safety • have procedures and policies about security, abuse and neglect, bullying and complaints, for example. • ensure staff receive health and safety training and that security measures are adequate.

Health and social care workers carry out their legal responsibilities by:

- developing an awareness of health and safety law

- working in ways that follow health and safety guidelines, policies and procedures

- monitoring the care environment for health and safety hazards

- dealing directly with hazards that present a health and safety risk, where it is safe to do so

- reporting health and safety hazards, or the failure of safety systems or procedures to a supervisor or manager.

Control of substances harmful to health

A range of potentially hazardous substances are present in care settings. These include cleaning agents, such as disinfectants and detergents, medicines, art and craft materials (paints, glues and clay, for example) and sterilising fluids. Substances can be hazardous because they are toxic (poisonous), corrosive (burning) or irritant. Hazard symbols (see Figure 8.5) should be printed on bottles, packets and canisters to indicate the kinds of dangers each poses.

The Control of Substances Hazardous to Health (COSHH) Regulations (2002) state that all hazardous substances must be correctly handled and stored to minimise the risks they present. The COSHH file that must be kept in each care setting provides details of:

- the hazardous substances that are present

- where they are stored

- how they should be handled

- how to deal with any spillage or accident involving a hazardous substance.

The COSHH file should provide details about the health and safety risks and effects of each hazardous substance, as well as information on how to deal with them in an emergency.

Reporting and recording accidents and incidents

Health and social care workers are expected to report accidents, incidents, diseases, illnesses and conditions that are infectious or which present a significant risk to health, safety or hygiene. The Reporting of Injuries, Diseases and Dangerous Occurrences Regulations (RIDDOR) 1995 say that, by law, the following situations must be recorded and reported to the Health and Safety Executive:

- death in the workplace

- injuries that lead to three or more days off sick.

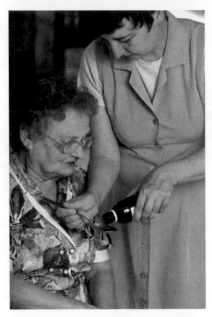

Medication must be safely stored and carefully managed in all care settings

Figure 8.5 Hazard symbols

The following must also be recorded and reported:

- a range of infectious diseases and illnesses, including malaria, tetanus, typhoid, typhus, measles and salmonella.

- environmental problems such as overflowing drains, the presence of hazardous chemicals (including cleaning substances) and gases.

Infection control and use of protective equipment

Health and social care workers should always follow basic infection control procedures. People who use care services are vulnerable to infection because of their poor physical health and can suffer serious complications or additional health problems if they contract an infection. Basic infection control procedures include:

- maintaining good standards of personal hygiene (relating to dress, hair care, footwear and oral hygiene)

- using appropriate personal protective clothing, such as aprons, gloves and masks

- following standard health, safety and hygiene precautions in the workplace

- washing hands regularly and thoroughly.

Case study

Audrey has been a volunteer nursery assistant at the Elim Pre-School Group for two years. She works at the nursery every Tuesday and brings Buster, her Labrador dog. The children like Buster and spend time patting and stroking him. Buster is very placid, used to children and seems to enjoy padding about in the nursery. Buster is usually very obedient and spends a lot of time sleeping. However, following a visit by an environmental health inspector from the local authority, Audrey has been told not to bring Buster to the nursery. She is quite upset about this as she doesn't understand how Buster could be a health and safety risk.

1. Identify reasons why Buster is a health and safety risk at the nursery.

2. Explain how Buster's presence might lead to food hygiene problems at the nursery.

3. Suggest how health and safety risks can be minimised to allow children to touch and play with pets.

Care organisations must comply with a wide range of laws and regulations that are designed to ensure the safety of those who spend time in care settings. These cover issues such as having an easy-to-use complaints procedure, providing adequate toilets, washing facilities and drinking water, and providing first aid facilities and training for staff. Strong health and safety and hygiene standards are designed to safeguard all users of care settings so that hazards are identified and risks minimised.

Responsibilities of employers and employees in ensuring confidentiality

Service users' records must be securely stored and managed in ways that protect confidentiality in all care settings

Handling information in health and social care

Health and social care workers have to record accurately, store and retrieve information about service users and the care they receive on a daily basis. They may, for example, have to take down information provided by other care workers and record it in an individual's notes or personal file. Health and social care workers who have access to people's records have to protect the **confidentiality** of that information so that others don't access the data inappropriately. Where records are kept as paper or manual files, they should:

- be kept in a locked storage cabinet

- only be accessed by people who are authorised to read them

- be filed alphabetically

- only be updated and changed by people who are authorised to do so (new entries should always be signed and dated).

Where records are kept as electronic files:

- access should be password protected to ensure that only authorised people can read them

- all records should be backed-up to ensure they not lost or erased as a result of computer problems.

Your assessment criteria:

1B.3 Identify how the right to confidentiality is protected in health and social care

2B.P3 Describe how the right to confidentiality is protected in health and social care

Key term

Confidentiality: *protecting the privacy of information*

Reflect

Do you password protect your computer or phone so that others can't gain access to the information it contains? How would you feel if you did find somebody looking through the personal information contained on one of these devices?

218

Information about people who use care services must be managed in accordance with the Data Protection Act (1998) and the Freedom of Information Act (2000, updated 2005). The Data Protection Act (1998) protects the individual's right to confidentiality (for both paper and electronic records). An individual has the right to:

- know what information is held about them, and the right to see and correct this if it is inaccurate

- refuse to provide information

- have up-to-date and accurate data held about them

- have data removed when it is no longer necessary for an organisation to hold it

- have the confidentiality of their information protected.

The Freedom of Information Act deals with access to official information held by public organisations, such as local authorities and the NHS. The Act gives members of the public the right to access information held by public authorities and requires public authorities to have a scheme that allows them to publish this information.

The protection of patient-related data is an important issue in care settings

Case study

Andy, aged 44, woke at 10 am, refused breakfast but then ate a banana and yoghurt before he left the drug rehabilitation unit to go to a physiotherapy appointment. He came back half an hour later and rested on his bed until lunch time, missing two of his group sessions. After eating lunch alone in the dining room, Andy went into the lounge and enthusiastically joined in the activities of the music group.

1. Which aspects of Andy's day would you write about in his records?

2. Andy has asked how his records can be 'kept confidential'. Describe what should happen to ensure the confidentiality of his records is protected.

3. What, if anything, could you tell Andy's relatives if they phoned up and asked about his day?

Confidentiality and privacy

Care service users must be able to trust the people who provide their care. If you cannot trust another person with your thoughts, feelings and dignity you are unlikely to develop a strong relationship with them. The care relationship is based on trust – and particularly on the need for health and social care workers to maintain confidentiality whenever possible.

Your assessment criteria:

2B.P3 Describe how the right to confidentiality is protected in health and social care

2B.M3 Explain why the right to confidentiality is protected in health and social care, using examples

219

There are times in care work when it is important to keep confidences to yourself. For example, if a child at the nursery where you do your work placement swore at you, or an elderly resident at a nursing home refused to bathe after wetting herself, you would be breaching confidentiality to reveal these things to your friends. You should never breach confidentiality in situations where service users have a right to privacy or where their comments or behaviour do not cause harm or break the law. If health and social care workers gossip about issues at work, they are betraying the trust of service users and colleagues.

Nursery workers are breaking confidentiality if they repeat to their friends what children at their workplace say, do or have told them

Disclosure of information

Confidentiality is about sharing, transmitting and storing information about individuals in ways that are appropriate to their care needs; it is definitely not about keeping information secret. This means that confidential information can be shared with other care team members, but only if they need to know about it. Beyond this, a care practitioner must consult individual service users and respect their wishes about who should be given access to information about them.

However, there are sometimes situations when it is necessary to disclose information about a service user that has been given in confidence. For example, even if a service user has requested that what they say is kept secret, this can be overridden when:

- what they reveal involves breaking the law or planning to do so

- they say that they intend to harm themselves or another person

- they reveal information that can be used to protect another person from harm.

 Reflect

How do you think you would feel if you overheard the receptionist and a doctor or nurse at your local GP practice talking openly about your health problems, where you live and your personal circumstances? How do you think this might affect your relationship with care workers at your GP practice?

Key term

Disclose information: *reveal or make something known*

If a service user commits an offence that could have been prevented by a care practitioner (who should have disclosed information given to them in confidence), the care practitioner could be brought to court to face charges. As a result, health and social care workers should never promise service users that what they say will be absolutely confidential. They should explain that there are times when they may have to share information with their colleagues and other authorities.

Dealing with tensions between rights and responsibilities

Health and social care workers often have to deal with difficult situations where the rights of a service user clash with the legal or professional responsibilities of the care worker. For example, a GP who is treating a person for a smoking-related illness can only advise them to give up smoking and cannot refuse to treat them if they continue. Similarly, a social worker who is supporting an individual with learning disabilities cannot stop the person trying out independent living, even if this involves some risk. They have to manage the tension between the person's rights, the risks involved and their own professional responsibilities to monitor, support and provide care for the person.

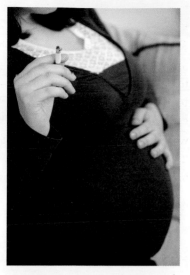

Care workers can advise against smoking whilst pregnant but can't always stop people from doing so

Discuss

Read through the following confidentiality situations. For each scenario, explain:

- *why confidentiality may be important to the client*
- *the dilemma facing the care worker*
- *whether you would break confidentiality and why.*
- *Darren has an appointment with the school nurse for a BCG booster injection. He's worried that it will make him ill. He says that he's just taken some ecstasy and pleads with the nurse not to tell anyone.*
- *Jennifer goes to her GP for contraceptive pills. She asks her GP not to tell her parents. She is 14 years old.*
- *Eileen has terminal cancer. She tells her district nurse that she's had enough of living and is going to end her own life tomorrow. She says it's her choice and asks the district nurse not to interfere.*
- *Yasmin tells her new health visitor that her boyfriend is violent and is beating her. She asks the health visitor not to say anything as she is frightened of what might happen. Yasmin and her boyfriend have a three-month-old baby.*
- *Lee turns up at a hostel for the homeless. He says that he has run away from home because his father has been beating him. He asks the social worker not to contact his family. He is 16 years old.*
- *A man with a stab wound arrives at the hospital casualty department. He won't give his name and asks the nurse not to phone the police. He says that he will leave if she does. He is bleeding heavily.*

Your assessment criteria:

2B.D3 Justify occasions where there is a need for an employee to breach confidentiality, using examples

Assessment checklist

To achieve level 1, my portfolio of evidence must show that I can:

Assessment criteria	Description	✓
1A.1	Identify the individual rights of service users in health and social care	
1A.2	Identify how current and relevant legislation protects the rights of service users, with reference to one example	
1B.2	Identify how an employee can plan to maximise the safety of service users	
1B.3	Identify how the right to confidentiality is protected in health and social care	

To achieve a pass grade, my portfolio of evidence must show that I can:

Assessment criteria	Description	✓
2A.P1	Summarise the individual rights of service users in health and social care	
2A.P2	Describe how current and relevant legislation protects the rights of service users, using examples	
2B.P2	Describe how an employee can plan to maximise the safety of service users	
2B.P3	Describe how the right to confidentiality is protected in health and social care	

To achieve a merit grade, my portfolio of evidence must show that I can:

Assessment criteria	Description	✓
2A.M1	Explain ways in which service users' individual rights can be upheld in health and social care, using selected examples	
2B.M2	Explain why risk assessment is important in health and social care	
2B.M3	Explain why the right to confidentiality is protected in health and social care, using examples	

To achieve a distinction grade, my portfolio of evidence must show that I can:

Assessment criteria	Description	✓
2A.D1	Assess the benefits and potential difficulties of upholding service users' rights in health and social care, using selected examples	
2B.D2	Evaluate the importance of the use of risk assessments in health and social care, using selected examples	
2B.D3	Justify occasions where there is a need for an employee to breach confidentiality, using examples	

9 | Healthy living

Learning aims A: Explore the factors that contribute to healthy and unhealthy lifestyles, and their effects on health and wellbeing

▶ Topic A.1 Defining a healthy lifestyle

▶ Topic A.2 Defining effects of an unhealthy lifestyle

▶ Topic A.3 Factors that contribute to healthy or unhealthy lifestyles and their effects

▶ Topic A.4 Influences on adopting of healthy and unhealthy lifestyles

Learning aims B: Explore ways of improving health and wellbeing

▶ Topic B:1 Ways to improve health and wellbeing

▶ Topic B.2 Types and sources of support available to help promote healthy Lifestyles

▶ Topic B.3 The barriers to achieving a healthy lifestyle

Defining a healthy lifestyle

Introduction to this chapter

An individual's health and wellbeing are strongly influenced by the lifestyle they lead. People who lead healthy lifestyles tend to make beneficial choices about diet, exercise and alcohol consumption. However, others make less healthy lifestyle choices that have negative effects on their health and wellbeing, in both the short and long term. This unit gives you the opportunity to explore what healthy and unhealthy lifestyles involve and the different ways of improving health and wellbeing.

Defining health

What is health? Is it something you're born with, something to do with your body and the way that it works? Or is it more than this? 'Health' is a word that people use all the time but what does it really mean?

The World Health Organisation takes a positive and holistic view when it defines health as: 'a state of complete physical, mental and social wellbeing, not merely the absence of illness or infirmity'. This definition stresses the importance of achieving and maintaining physical fitness and mental stability, for example. It is holistic, or concerned with the whole person, as it focuses on the physical, intellectual, emotional and social effects and benefits of a healthy lifestyle. A person who lives a healthy lifestyle is likely to experience a range of physical, intellectual, emotional and social benefits as a result.

Physical effects and benefits

A healthy lifestyle will have a beneficial or positive influence on a person's physical health and body. For example, a person who achieves and maintains an optimum level of physical health and wellbeing is likely to experience:

- healthy body systems

- a healthy and appropriate weight

- good levels of physical fitness

- high energy levels

- a reduced chance of developing an illness.

 Key terms

Holistic: concerning the whole person

Optimum: the best possible condition or state

Wellbeing: a positive state of physical, intellectual, emotional and social health in which a person feels physically well and psychologically content

World Health Organisation (WHO): an international organisation that provides leadership on global health issues

? Reflect

What do you think 'health' involves? Reflect on your own ideas and the way that you talk about health. Are you healthy? Sometimes? Mostly? Never?

Do you think health involves some specific physical or mental qualities (fitness, correct weight, feeling happy)? Or is health just the absence of illness?

The physical effects of a healthy lifestyle protect an individual against many forms of ill-health, because the body is well maintained, working efficiently and effectively. You can find out more about the physical effects of an unhealthy lifestyle on page 229. The factors that affect an individual's physical health are outlined on pages 232–241.

Intellectual effects and benefits

The intellectual aspects of health and wellbeing impact on an individual's thinking abilities. The intellectual benefits of a healthy lifestyle include:

- improved concentration

- clearer thinking

- improved ability to learn.

A person who lives a healthy lifestyle is likely to be less stressed and less likely to have their intellectual abilities impaired by headaches, hangovers or worries, for example. Getting enough sleep and rest, eating a healthy diet and having supportive relationships all contribute to effective concentration and clear thinking. You can find out more about the intellectual effects of an unhealthy lifestyle on page 230. Factors that affect an individual's intellectual health are outlined on pages 232–241.

Emotional effects and benefits

A person's emotional health and wellbeing Is linked to their 'inner life'– their feelings about themselves and other people. Living a healthy lifestyle is likely to have a positive impact on an individual's emotional wellbeing. For example, the emotional effects of a healthy lifestyle can include:

- greater levels of happiness

- improved mood

- improved self-confidence

- improved self-esteem

- positive self-image

- increased emotional resilience

- improved emotional levels

- reduced stress

- good mental health

- the ability to develop and maintain close intimate and sexual relationships.

 Reflect

Think about the last time when you were unwell. What impact did this have on your emotional wellbeing? Reflect on how illness affected your mood and self-confidence.

 Key term

Resilience: the ability to cope with stress and personal difficulties

A person who makes positive lifestyle choices is likely to feel in control and satisfied with the quality of their life. Being in control, achieving your goals and feeling positive about your life has a beneficial knock-on effect on self-confidence, happiness and overall emotional wellbeing. You can find out more about the emotional effects of an unhealthy lifestyle on page 230. Factors that affect an individual's emotional health are outlined on pages 232–241.

You can find out more about the emotional effects of an unhealthy lifestyle on page 230. Factors that affect an individual's emotional health are outlined on pages 232–241.

Being physically active tends to have a positive effect on a person's mood and emotional wellbeing

Social effects and benefits

The social aspect of health and wellbeing is concerned with the relationships we have with others and the way these contribute to our sense of security; they provide us with a network of support. A person who manages to change their lifestyle from unhealthy to health is likely to experience:

- improved quality of social life

- closer friendships

- extended patterns of social relationships.

Having good friendships, relatives who are loving, and the social skills to form and maintain relationships with others all contribute to social wellbeing. Having an active social life, feeling supported by others and having regular contact with a range of people protects an individual against feelings of loneliness, isolation and low self-esteem. You can find out more about the social effects of an unhealthy lifestyle on page 231. Factors that affect an individual's emotional health are outlined on pages 232–241.

? Reflect

Who provides you with close, supportive relationships? Try to identify how each of your supportive relationships contributes to your sense of wellbeing.

? Reflect

How do your personal relationships and friendships contribute to your health and wellbeing? Think about the way others contribute to your self-esteem, and to your sense of belonging and being cared for.

Defining the effects of an unhealthy lifestyle

The impact of an unhealthy lifestyle

An unhealthy lifestyle can have a significant impact on all aspects of an individual's health and wellbeing. As well as being directly linked to a variety of forms of disease and illness, unhealthy lifestyles can also affect an individual's relationships, emotional life and opportunities in life. A range of lifestyle factors, behaviours and choices increase the risk of an individual becoming ill or unhealthy. These are outlined in more detail on pages 232–241.

Physical effects of an unhealthy lifestyle

The physical effects of an unhealthy lifestyle can impact on an individual's body and their physical functioning. These include an increased risk of experiencing:

- disease and illness
- weight gain or weight loss
- an imbalance in body fat composition
- short-term health problems
- long-term health problems.

To some extent, we all have some influence over whether our lifestyle is healthy or unhealthy. For example, if a person chooses to smoke heavily and drink more units of alcohol than the recommended daily and weekly limits, they are making choices that increase their risk of experiencing both short-term and long-term health problems. In the short term, the person may develop high blood pressure and bronchitis. In the long term, their smoking and excessive drinking could lead to lung, mouth or throat cancer and coronary heart disease. Both of these lifestyle choices (smoking and drinking) are likely to have a negative effect on the individual's health and wellbeing.

? Reflect

List as many words as you can which describe being or feeling 'unhealthy'. Identify the main words that you use when talking with your friends and family about ill-health or being unwell. Are these different to the words you use when talking to your GP or other health care workers?

Key terms

Body fat composition: the location and percentage of fat in the human body

Bronchitis: a respiratory disease in which the mucus membrane in the lungs' bronchial passages becomes inflamed, resulting in a hacking cough that may also be accompanied by breathlessness and phlegm production

...style

...ricting their own
...ectual potential. This is
...ficient sleep, drinks excess
...ors are likely to reduce the
...arly and learn or work effectively.
...n unhealthy lifestyle include:

- red... ...ucation

- negative impa... ...career prospects

- inability to think clearly in... ork, leisure and everyday life situations.

An unhealthy lifestyle may lead to a downward spiral in which the person makes bad decisions based on poor judgement about the health risks and the potential consequences of their behaviour. Not being able to think through or consider situations carefully may also be part of the reason why a person seems to get stuck with an unhealthy lifestyle.

Emotional effects of an unhealthy lifestyle

The reasons some people have unhealthy lifestyles are complex. However, wanting to cheer oneself up, have fun or experience excitement are often reasons given for poor health decisions. For example, a person may say that they eat an unhealthy diet (high in sugar and fat) because they enjoy certain types of food; some people 'comfort eat' to cheer themselves up. Similarly, people who drink excess alcohol are sometimes doing this to 'have a good time' or to 'drown their sorrows'. The problem with these types of lifestyle decisions is that they provide only temporary relief or pleasure. In the longer term, an unhealthy lifestyle is likely to have a negative effect on a person's emotional wellbeing. This might include:

- general feelings of unhappiness and worthlessness

- low **self-esteem**

- negative **self-image**

- feelings of stress and anxiety

- difficulties in developing and maintaining close, intimate and sexual relationships

- psychological dependence.

An unhealthy lifestyle doesn't, in the end, make a person feel good about him or herself. It may, in fact, be a way of coping with or distracting attention from the difficulties and problems that they are experiencing.

? Reflect

Do you know anyone who uses food or alcohol to cheer themselves up, even though they know they are making an unhealthy choice? Why do you think people find it so hard to break these patterns of behaviour?

🔑 Key terms

Self-esteem: *the sense of worth or value that a person attributes to themselves, their skills and abilities*

Self-image: *the way a person views himself or herself*

Defining the effects of an unhealthy lifestyle

The impact of an unhealthy lifestyle

An unhealthy lifestyle can have a significant impact on all aspects of an individual's health and wellbeing. As well as being directly linked to a variety of forms of disease and illness, unhealthy lifestyles can also affect an individual's relationships, emotional life and opportunities in life. A range of lifestyle factors, behaviours and choices increase the risk of an individual becoming ill or unhealthy. These are outlined in more detail on pages 232–241.

Physical effects of an unhealthy lifestyle

The physical effects of an unhealthy lifestyle can impact on an individual's body and their physical functioning. These include an increased risk of experiencing:

- disease and illness

- weight gain or weight loss

- an imbalance in **body fat composition**

- short-term health problems

- long-term health problems.

To some extent, we all have some influence over whether our lifestyle is healthy or unhealthy. For example, if a person chooses to smoke heavily and drink more units of alcohol than the recommended daily and weekly limits, they are making choices that increase their risk of experiencing both short-term and long-term health problems. In the short term, the person may develop high blood pressure and **bronchitis**. In the long term, their smoking and excessive drinking could lead to lung, mouth or throat cancer and coronary heart disease. Both of these lifestyle choices (smoking and drinking) are likely to have a negative effect on the individual's health and wellbeing.

? Reflect

List as many words as you can which describe being or feeling 'unhealthy'. Identify the main words that you use when talking with your friends and family about ill-health or being unwell. Are these different to the words you use when talking to your GP or other health care workers?

🔑 Key terms

Body fat composition: the location and percentage of fat in the human body

Bronchitis: a respiratory disease in which the mucus membrane in the lungs' bronchial passages becomes inflamed, resulting in a hacking cough that may also be accompanied by breathlessness and phlegm production

Intellectual effects of an unhealthy lifestyle

A person who has an unhealthy lifestyle is restricting their own opportunities to develop and fulfil their intellectual potential. This is particularly the case if the person has insufficient sleep, drinks excess alcohol or misuses drugs. All of these factors are likely to reduce the person's ability to concentrate, think clearly and learn or work effectively. As a result, the intellectual effects of an unhealthy lifestyle include:

- reduced potential for success in education

- negative impact on long-term career prospects

- inability to think clearly in work, leisure and everyday life situations.

An unhealthy lifestyle may lead to a downward spiral in which the person makes bad decisions based on poor judgement about the health risks and the potential consequences of their behaviour. Not being able to think through or consider situations carefully may also be part of the reason why a person seems to get stuck with an unhealthy lifestyle.

Emotional effects of an unhealthy lifestyle

The reasons some people have unhealthy lifestyles are complex. However, wanting to cheer oneself up, have fun or experience excitement are often reasons given for poor health decisions. For example, a person may say that they eat an unhealthy diet (high in sugar and fat) because they enjoy certain types of food; some people 'comfort eat' to cheer themselves up. Similarly, people who drink excess alcohol are sometimes doing this to 'have a good time' or to 'drown their sorrows'. The problem with these types of lifestyle decisions is that they provide only temporary relief or pleasure. In the longer term, an unhealthy lifestyle is likely to have a negative effect on a person's emotional wellbeing. This might include:

- general feelings of unhappiness and worthlessness

- low **self-esteem**

- negative **self-image**

- feelings of stress and anxiety

- difficulties in developing and maintaining close, intimate and sexual relationships

- psychological dependence.

An unhealthy lifestyle doesn't, in the end, make a person feel good about him or herself. It may, in fact, be a way of coping with or distracting attention from the difficulties and problems that they are experiencing.

Social effects

An unhealthy lifestyle isn't just damaging to an individual's physical health and wellbeing. An individual's family, friends and even their work colleagues can be affected by the poor judgements and negative health consequences of someone's unhealthy lifestyle. Excessive drinking, lack of sleep, heavy smoking or drug misuse may put pressure on a person's marriage, family relationships or existing friendships. If the person's unhealthy lifestyle also affects their work relationships, they may become **ostracised** by colleagues. The social effects of an unhealthy lifestyle might include:

- loss of friends

- increased pressure on existing friendship groups

- negative impact on family relationships

- decreased levels of involvement in social activities

- social isolation

- increased potential for accidents, injury or criminal record.

Social relationships with partners, family members and friends play an important part in our sense of emotional security and wellbeing. These relationships can be damaged through poor health choices and health behaviours that upset or worry those close to us, or which suggest that we don't care about our loved ones.

Key term

Ostracise: to exclude a person from a group

Investigate

The Al-Anon website (http://www.al-anonuk.org) provides more information on the impact that a person's drinking problems can have on their partner, children and other family members.

Excessive alcohol consumption can lead to a range of physical and mental health problems

Factors that contribute to healthy or unhealthy lifestyles and their effects

Lifestyle factors and personal health

Would you like to be healthy? Most people would answer 'yes' to this question. Research has shown that people say being healthy is just as likely to make them feel happy as winning lots of money. Which would you prefer to have – good health or lots of money? You would have to be very lucky to win lots of money but you can do things that will make you healthier. An individual can make simple choices about health-related issues like personal hygiene, diet and exercise, for example. Your lifestyle choices will have a significant impact on your health and wellbeing.

Diet, nutrition and health

A healthy diet is essential for physical health and wellbeing. The amount and type of food a person requires is affected by the individual's:

- age
- gender
- body size
- height
- weight
- level of physical activity
- environment (for example, whether they live in a cold or a warm country).

A healthy, balanced diet is needed to meet an individual's physical needs for energy and to support their growth and development. The food that we eat has to be nutritious in order to benefit our physical health. This means that it should contain a variety of nutrients. There are five basic nutrients that help the body in different ways:

- carbohydrates and fats provide the body with energy
- proteins provide the chemical substances needed to build and repair body cells and tissues
- vitamins help to regulate the chemical reactions that continuously take place in our bodies
- minerals are needed for control of body functions and to build and repair certain tissues.

? Reflect

What do you do to maintain your health and wellbeing? Think about the activities you do and the lifestyle choices you make to promote and protect your health and wellbeing.

✎ Key term

Balanced diet: a diet containing carbohydrates, fats, protein, vitamins and minerals in appropriate quantities

? Reflect

Is your diet 'balanced' or are there things that you could do to improve what you eat and drink? Think about what you eat and drink during an average week and about ways in which you could improve the nutritional quality of your diet.

As well as eating food that contains a balance of these five nutrients, we also need to consume fibre and water. Although these are not counted as nutrients, they are vital for physical health.

Good nutrition plays an important part in healthy living throughout life. However, an individual's dietary needs change as they grow and develop in different life stages. The type, amount and range of foods that a person eats should vary according to their life stage, the kind of environment they live in and the lifestyle they lead. Table 6.4 (page 163) outlines the recommended daily amounts of food, expressed in kilocalories, that males and females need as they age.

The links between diet, health and ill-health are outlined in more detail in Chapter 6.

Exercise and health

Do you like doing exercise? Some people really enjoy sports, going to the gym or doing strenuous outdoor activities. You might be one of them or you may be one of the large number of people who don't do enough exercise. If you are one of the latter, you should consider doing more exercise because it has many health benefits. For example, exercise:

- keeps the heart healthy

- improves circulation

- helps muscles, joints and bones to remain strong

- improves stamina

- reduces blood pressure

- increases self-esteem and self-confidence

- helps to control and maintain a healthy weight

- makes you feel more energetic

- is a good way of socialising

- helps the body to stay supple and mobile.

Exercise has a positive effect on both physical and mental health, but it is also important not to do too much exercise. People are advised to find a balance between physical activity and rest in order to maintain good physical health and wellbeing. Too much exercise can lead to excessive weight loss and may result in physical damage or chronic injuries to joints or ligaments, for example.

> **Key term**
>
> **Kilocalories:** *the energy value in food equal to 1000 calories*

Regular exercise can bring both physical and psychological benefits

So, what kinds of exercise should you do? The type and level of exercise that an individual can do safely will depend on their age, gender and health status. For example, moderate exercise can be safely undertaken by older and less physically mobile people, including women in the later stages of pregnancy and people with physical disabilities. Younger people who are physically fit can safely undertake more vigorous exercise. Lack of physical exercise can lead to ill-health and conditions such as coronary heart disease, stroke and obesity.

Case study

Troy is 22 years old. He lifts weights at a body-building gym five nights each week. He wants to enter body-building competitions soon. Troy recently went to stay with his parents for a holiday. He had put on 3 stone in weight and has a much more muscular body compared to when they last saw him. Troy told his mum he needs to eat 4500 calories a day to maintain his current size and shape. His mum is concerned that his current calorie intake and weight will have a negative effect on his health.

1. Does Troy's BMI score suggest a healthy or an unhealthy weight?

2. Identify two factors that are likely to have led to Troy's current BMI score.

3. Explain why Troy's BMI score may give a misleading impression of his health and fitness.

Work environment

The physical activity and exertion involved in some kinds of work can have a positive effect on a person's health and fitness. For example, gardeners, builders and fitness instructors do lots of physical exercise in the course of their daily work. Other jobs such as nursing and retail work may not be quite as physically strenuous but still demand a lot of physical activity. Work that is mentally demanding can stimulate a person's intellectual (thinking) development and be a big motivating factor in their life. Work can also be an important source of self-esteem and status. Health and social care workers, for example, often choose their area of work because they want to be useful and make a difference to other people's lives. In this way work has a positive impact on their emotional wellbeing.

Even though work can be good for health and wellbeing, too much work can leave a person feeling stressed and tired. A healthy lifestyle involves a balance between work and non-work time. Leisure time, including having hobbies, enjoying a social life and simply relaxing, is part of a healthy life.

 Discuss

In a small group or with a class colleague, share ideas about your work–life balance. What is a healthy work–life balance for people of your age and in your position in life? Are there things that you could do to improve your current work–life balance?

Alcohol consumption

Alcohol is very popular and widely available; it is an accepted part of social life in the United Kingdom. Some types of alcoholic drink, such as red wine, have also been shown to be good for health. This is because alcohol in moderation protects against the development of coronary heart disease. It also has an effect on the amount of cholesterol, or fat, carried in the bloodstream, making it less likely that the clots which cause heart disease will form. Maximum health advantage can be achieved from drinking between one and two units of alcohol a day. There is no additional overall health benefit to be gained from drinking more than two units of alcohol a day. However, there are possible negative effects from doing so.

The health risks associated with alcohol result from consuming it in large quantities, either regularly or in binges. People who frequently drink excess amounts of alcohol have an increased risk of:

- high blood pressure

- coronary heart disease

- liver damage and cirrhosis of the liver

- cancer of the mouth and throat

- psychological and emotional problems, including depression

- obesity.

Reflect

What types of leisure and recreational activities do you include in your school–life balance? How do these activities contribute to your health and wellbeing?

Key term

Cholesterol: *a fatty substance needed by the body and carried in the blood*

Investigate

Using the Internet or reference books, research the risks associated with binge drinking of alcohol. Create a diagram or table to illustrate these.

Health professionals recommend safe limits of alcohol consumption. These recommended limits are based on 'pub measures'. People who buy alcohol from an off-licence or supermarket to consume elsewhere usually pour themselves larger measures of wines and spirits or consume stronger beer than is sold in licensed premises.

Table 9.1 Recommended units of alcohol

Recommended maximum alcohol limits	Men	Women
units/day	3–4	2–3
per day (g)	24–32g	16–24g
units/week	21	14
per week (g)	168g	112g
number of alcohol-free days per week	2	2

A unit of alcohol is 8g or 10 millilitres of alcohol. A unit is roughly equivalent to half a pint of ordinary strength beer lager, or cider (3–4% alcohol by volume), or a small pub measure (25 ml) of spirits (40% alcohol by volume), or a standard pub measure (50 ml) of fortified wine such as sherry or port (20% alcohol by volume).

Investigate

Using the Internet, investigate the health impact of drinking excessive amounts of alcohol. Produce a poster designed to inform 14–16 year old adolescents about the links between alcohol consumption and health problems.

Case study

Jonas recently turned 18 years old. He celebrated with a group of friends by going out to a pub (and then a nightclub). Overall, he drank 11 pints of beer during the evening. He vomited a couple of times on the way home and had to be helped into bed by his dad. The next morning Jonas said he felt okay though he had a headache.

1. How many units of alcohol did Jonas consume on his birthday?

2. Identify two reasons why binge drinking like this poses a risk to an individual's health and wellbeing.

3. Describe three ways in which drinking excessive amounts of alcohol over a long period can have a negative effect on a person's health or development.

Smoking

Smoking cigarettes, or tobacco in any form, has no health benefits at all. Instead, smoking directly damages an individual's physical health. This is one of the most important pieces of information that health professionals regularly give out to people. Their advice is always to stop smoking. People who don't stop smoking run a high risk of long-term health damage, possibly dying as a direct result of their smoking habit.

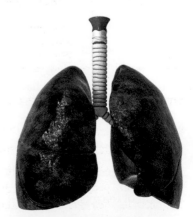

Smoking cigarettes can cause irreversible damage to a person's respiratory system

The health problems associated with smoking tobacco include:

- coronary heart disease

- stroke

- high blood pressure

- bronchitis

- lung cancer

- other cancers, such as cancer of the larynx, kidney and bladder.

Smoking is harmful to health because smoke containing dangerous chemicals is inhaled circulate deep into the body. These substances include nicotine, carbon monoxide and tar.

Table 9.2 Chemicals in cigarette smoke

Chemical	Effects on the body
Nicotine	• Powerful, fast-acting and addictive • Absorbed into bloodstream • Increases heart rate and blood pressure • Causes changes in appetite
Tar	• Damages the cilia (small hairs) lining the lungs that help to protect from dirt and infection • Damage to cilia results in more infections and smoker's cough • Causes mouth, throat and lung cancers when left as a deposit in the body
Carbon monoxide	• A poisonous gas • Reduces the amount of oxygen carried from a smoker's lungs to the tissues • Changes in the blood can cause fat deposits to form on the walls of the arteries, 'hardening' of the arteries and coronary heart disease

Smoking during pregnancy

Smoking reduces the ability of the blood to carry oxygen to all parts of the body. This is particularly important during pregnancy, as it affects the flow of blood to the placenta, which feeds the foetus. Women who smoke during pregnancy have a greater risk of suffering a miscarriage. They also tend to give birth to premature or underweight babies who are more prone to respiratory infections and breathing problems. The risk of cot death is also increased in these babies.

Key term

Placenta: an organ rooted in the lining of the womb that links the baby's blood supply to the mother's blood supply, carrying oxygen and food to the unborn baby

Women who smoke during their pregnancies are more likely to have low birth-weight babies than women who do not

Drug misuse

Drugs are chemical substances that affect the body's chemistry and functioning. Drugs are widely used, and also widely misused, in the United Kingdom. They can be obtained through:

- a doctor's prescription if they are for medical treatment

- 'over the counter', by purchasing them in a chemist, supermarket or other shop (these drugs include medicines and legal substances such as alcohol and tobacco)

- illegally buying 'street', recreational and medicinal drugs.

All sections of the population are affected by drug misuse, but young people are the most likely to risk their health in this way. There are many complex reasons for this.

Drug misuse carries a very high risk of damage to health. This damage might be sudden and catastrophic (people die from drug overdoses) or it can occur over a longer period of time as a result of drug addiction and dependency. Either way, drug misuse is something to avoid if you wish to live a long and healthy life.

Any drug, whether it is legal or illegal, can cause harm if it is misused. For example, while medicines are used to treat disease and illness, they can also have physical and psychological side-effects. The doctor who prescribes them will know about these possible effects and will take care to monitor the patient. To limit side effects, the doctor will prescribe only the dose required. People may misuse prescription drugs by taking more than their doctor prescribes, or they may take medicine not prescribed for them. People who do either of these things run the risk of experiencing harmful and even fatal side-effects.

Some drugs cause people to become psychologically dependent on them if they are taken over a long period of time. This applies to medicinal drugs, as well as to illegal 'street' and recreational drugs. Long-term users often suffer very unpleasant side-effects (withdrawal symptoms) when they try to stop taking these drugs.

Non-prescription drugs are usually illegal. Alcohol, cigarettes and medicines bought from chemists or supermarkets are the exceptions. People who use recreational drugs such as heroin, cocaine, marijuana and ecstasy are usually trying to experience the short-term feelings of mental pleasure and relaxation, or stimulation and physical energy that these different drugs often give. However, in the longer term all recreational drugs present major risks to the user's health. They usually have damaging effects on physical health, as well as on social, psychological and financial wellbeing.

238

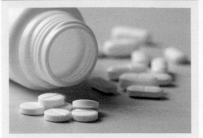

Safe and unsafe sex

Everybody has sexual needs. People have sex for a variety of reasons. These include having babies, having orgasms and expressing sexual needs and feelings. Sex isn't terrible, dirty or dangerous. However, choosing to be sexually active does have consequences. These consequences may affect both physical health and emotional wellbeing. The main health risk of sexual activity is from **sexually transmitted infections**.

There are at least thirty different types of sexually transmitted infection. Each year they affect about one million men and women in the United Kingdom. A person can become infected with a sexually transmitted infection after a single act of unprotected sex with an infected person. Young sexually active people are most at risk of catching sexually transmitted infections. Using a condom during sex is the best way to avoid catching a sexually transmitted infection.

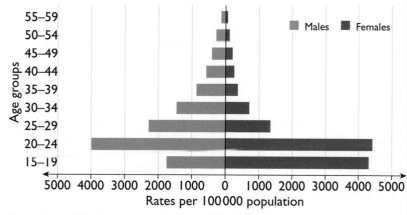

Rates of acute STIs by age group and gender, 2011, England
Source: Health Protection Agency, 2012

Figure 9.1 STI statistics

HIV and AIDS

The human immunodeficiency virus (HIV) is a relatively new and challenging sexually transmitted infection. It is the virus that causes acquired immune deficiency syndrome (AIDS). If the virus, a simple living organism, gets into the bloodstream it attacks and destroys the body's natural defence mechanisms. HIV can be transmitted through three different routes:

- sexual intercourse (anal or vaginal)

- contaminated blood transfusion

- drug misusers sharing non-sterile needles.

 Key term

Sexually transmitted infections: infections which are primarily transmitted through sexual activity that involves contact with bodily fluids

 Investigate

Use medical reference books or a website such as www.teenagehealthfreak.com or www.surgerydoor.co.uk to find out more about the causes, symptoms and consequences of a range of sexually transmitted infections.

 Investigate

Which age group has the highest rate of sexually transmitted infection, according to the data in Figure 9.1?

AVERT, an HIV and Aids charity, reported that around 91,500 people were living with HIV in the UK at the end of 2010. A quarter of these people were unaware of their infection. In 2011, there were 5594 new diagnoses of HIV. As of December 2011, there have been 27,361 diagnoses of AIDS in the UK, and 20,335 people living with HIV have died (not necessarily of causes relating to HIV and AIDS).

Personal hygiene

Good personal hygiene contributes to the maintenance of physical health, as well as to social and emotional wellbeing. Being clean helps to keep the human body in good condition because it prevents the growth of bacteria, viruses and fungi that live on and feed off unclean skin. A person who fails to maintain good personal hygiene may develop skin conditions such as sores and rashes. The body conditions that help bacteria and fungi to grow are:

• moisture from sweat

• warmth from body heat

• food from dead cells and the waste products in sweat.

The areas of the body that need most cleaning are those where sweat is excreted – under the arms, the groin area, the feet, the scalp and hair. Failure to take a daily bath, shower or wash and to clean your teeth, results in a build up of bacteria, dirt and odour. Personal hygiene problems may also have a negative effect on a person's relationships and social life. This is likely to lead to the person feeling rejected and isolated and having low self-esteem.

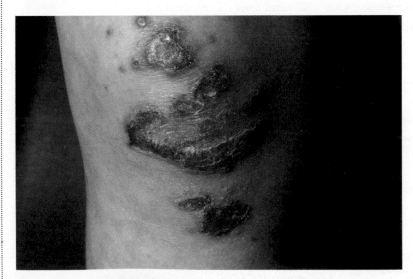

Poor personal hygiene can lead to skin infections and slow down the process of wound healing

✎ | Key term

Excreted: discharged from or pushed out of the body

Sleep patterns

A person who wants to be healthy should take rest and sleep seriously; not everyone does. Some people work too much and feel tired all the time – this isn't healthy. People should have enough rest and sleep every day to maintain their health and wellbeing. The amount of rest and sleep an individual needs will depend on their life stage and physical needs. For example, a four-year-old child sleeps for an average of 10 to 14 hours a night, while a 10-year-old needs nine to 12 hours. Most adults sleep between seven to eight and a half hours every night; others require as few as four or five hours. Most people find that they need slightly less sleep as they grow older.

People who don't get enough sleep lose energy and become irritable. After two days without sleep, concentration becomes difficult. Other effects of sleep loss include:

- mistakes in routine tasks

- slips of attention

- dozing off for a few seconds or more

- falling asleep completely

- difficulty seeing and hearing clearly

- confusion.

Many car accidents are caused by people falling asleep whilst driving and losing control of their vehicle.

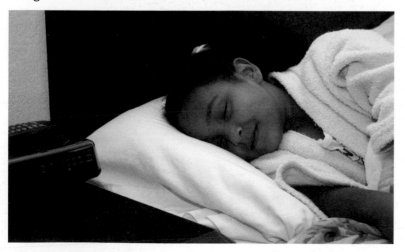

A regular sleep pattern is needed to maintain both physical and mental health

? | **Reflect**

How much sleep do you need to maintain your health and wellbeing? Can you remember a time when your sleep was disrupted, irregular or insufficient? How did this affect your ability to function normally?

Influences on adopting healthy and unhealthy lifestyles

External influences and lifestyle choices

An individual's **lifestyle**, including their attitudes, the choices they make and their behaviour, has an important influence on their health and wellbeing. The lifestyles of healthy people are usually different to the lifestyles of people whose health choices and behaviour lead to ill-health and premature death. Health and social care workers recognise that lifestyle is something that an individual can control and change. However, there are other physical, social and environmental factors that are outside a person's control but which still impact on their health and wellbeing.

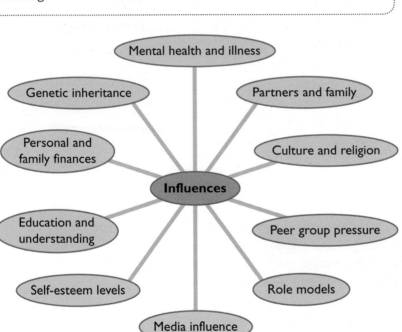

Figure 9.2 Lifestyle influences

- Mental health and illness
- Genetic inheritance
- Partners and family
- Personal and family finances
- Culture and religion
- **Influences**
- Education and understanding
- Peer group pressure
- Self-esteem levels
- Role models
- Media influence

Parents who exercise regularly provide a good example of healthy living for their children

Genetic inheritance

The genes that we inherit from our parents are the biological instructions or codes that tell our bodies how to grow and our cells how to work. As well as playing a very important role in our physical growth and appearance, the genes that we inherit may also make us more vulnerable, or predisposed, to certain diseases and conditions. For example, some people inherit one or more genes that are defective or faulty. These faulty genes can, but don't always, result in a disease or condition that is damaging to health and wellbeing.

Medical researchers and scientists have also discovered that a range of more common health problems and **predispositions** have a genetic component to them, including:

- eye disorders (such as glaucoma)
- high blood pressure
- heart conditions
- high cholesterol
- **haemophilia**.

There is little scientific evidence to suggest that a person's genes predispose them to make particular health choices – such as to drink excessive alcohol, use drugs or smoke cigarettes. However, a person who has inherited a health problem or who is aware that there is a family history of a condition such as heart disease may make informed lifestyle choices. A person with a family history – perhaps based on genetic predisposition – of heart disease or breast cancer has extra motivation to eat a balanced diet and exercise regularly, for example. Despite this kind of knowledge, people don't always do what is best for their health. A person may still make apparently unhealthy choices because they make false assumptions, such as 'it won't happen to me' or 'look at Uncle Norman who has smoked all of his long life without becoming unwell'.

Partners and family

Usually, people are closest emotionally to their partners and to members of their immediate family. This puts partners and family members in a powerful position to influence an individual's lifestyle. A supportive home environment where partners and family members have positive attitudes to health and wellbeing and model appropriate health behaviours makes making healthy choices easier – especially for children and young people. Partners and family members can influence others to adopt healthy lifestyles by:

- supporting individuals to develop a strong sense of identity and self-esteem, so they can resist pressure to make unhealthy choices such as to use drugs, have unprotected sex or consume excess alcohol
- providing healthy food and lifestyle choices, and information
- encouraging and supporting physical activity
- enabling discussion of lifestyle options, including the benefits and disadvantages of making different choices
- setting clear boundaries regarding drug and alcohol use, relationships and diet, for example.

Key terms

Haemophilia: a group of hereditary disorders that impair the body's blood clotting ability

Predispositions: being inclined or more likely to experience something

Investigate

Use research sources such as your school or college library or the Internet to find out about the causes and effect on health and wellbeing of one or more of the following inherited conditions:

- Huntington's disease
- Cystic fibrosis
- Down's syndrome
- Klinefelter's syndrome
- Turner's syndrome.

Culture and religion

A person's cultural background and their religious beliefs have a very strong influence on their chosen lifestyle and the associated health effects. We all learn from and are influenced by the culture into which we are born. Part of this involves learning about aspects of life such as diet, exercise, drug use, alcohol consumption and ways of relating to people. A person's cultural background provides them with basic ideas about what is 'normal' and appropriate behaviour. We are often not aware that culture is influencing our health choices until we experience a different culture with different beliefs about health behaviour. As the UK is a multicultural society, it is important to learn about and understand how different cultures affect the varying lifestyles, health and wellbeing of people who use care services.

Religion can influence lifestyle choices and health behaviour directly and indirectly. Holding religious beliefs can have a positive effect on both physical and mental health, for example. A person's religious faith also influences their choice of friends, their way of making judgements about what is right and wrong, and their way of coping with difficulties in life. Research has also shown that religious participants are less likely to smoke, use drugs or consume alcohol than people who are not religious. As a result religious beliefs do seem to influence lifestyle choices that affect health and wellbeing.

Peer groups

A person's choice of friends and their social interactions influence their health beliefs and behaviours. Peer groups encourage or expect certain behaviours and disapprove of others. Members of peer groups are under pressure to 'fit in' with these expectations. Individuals who want to be accepted by their peers often engage in the group's approved or expected behaviours. Early adolescence is a time when peer groups have an important influence on the decisions young people make with regard to sexual behaviour and the use of tobacco, alcohol and other drugs. Some people have the ability to resist peer group pressure and don't engage in behaviours that are a risk to health or wellbeing. Peer teaching and support are very effective in influencing healthy lifestyle choices during adolescence.

Role models

People often copy the behaviours of those they see as role models. Role models can be parents, as well as media personalities, sports stars, fashion models, older siblings, teachers, community leaders or other relatives, for example. As role models, these people can have a powerful effect on the health-related attitudes and behaviours of those who admire and want to be like them. It is well known, for example, that children whose parents

Key term

Culture: the values, ideas, beliefs and shared way of life within a particular group that is learnt and passed on through socialisation processes

Investigate

How can a person's religious beliefs affect their diet? Identify examples of the way different religious faiths directly and indirectly influence the food practices and dietary choices of their followers.

Key terms

Peer group: typically a group of friends of approximately the same age who see themselves and are seen by others as belonging together in some way

Role model: a person who serves as an example or whose behaviour is copied

smoke, drink to excess and use drugs are more likely to adopt these habits than children whose parents model a more positive lifestyle.

Media influences

Advertising, movies, television programmes, magazines, newspapers, the Internet and music bombard us with messages about lifestyle. These different **media** sometimes glamorise smoking, drug use, fast food and sexual behaviour. As such, people obtain information from the media about lifestyle options and are sometimes persuaded into behaviours or lifestyle choices that have a negative impact on their health and wellbeing. It is important that children and young people understand the media and develop the ability to be critical of media messages that are selling unhealthy lifestyle choices.

Self-esteem, mental health and illness

A person's self-esteem refers to the way they value themselves. Self-esteem develops partly from the way we compare ourselves with other people, as well as from how we believe others see us. People who compare themselves negatively with others, thinking they are not as good, as attractive or as capable, for example, are more likely to have low self-esteem. Similarly, people who feel unloved and who are criticised or rejected by parents, partners or other people they care about are also likely to experience low self-esteem. This can sometimes develop into mental health problems, particularly linked to depression, anxiety or self-harming behaviour.

Some people cope with this rejection by making unhealthy choices relating to drug or alcohol use, smoking or poor diet as a way of finding comfort and blotting out their problems. However, where an individual is living an unhealthy lifestyle because of low self-esteem or mental health problems, appropriate support and treatment can enable them to make positive changes to their lifestyle that also improve their mental health.

Education and understanding

A person's level of education and their ability to understand information about health benefits and risks may affect their lifestyle choices related to diet, smoking, drug and alcohol use, exercise and sexual relationships for example. Children, individuals with learning difficulties, people with a lack of education or those with other forms of intellectual impairment are less able to make positive and safe lifestyle choices. This doesn't mean that brighter, more highly educated people always live healthy lifestyles! Education and ability to understand simply provide people with the tools to examine their lifestyle options – some apparently bright people will still make choices that result in an unhealthy lifestyle.

Key term

Media: forms of mass communication

Investigate

You can find out more about issues relating to self-esteem and mental health and illness at the Mental Health Foundation website (http:// www.mentalhealth.org.uk/).

Ways to improve health and wellbeing

Lifestyle improvements

Have you ever set yourself the goal of 'being healthier' or 'getting fit'? A common time to do this is just after Christmas (when people often feel they have had too much to eat or drink) or a few months before going on holiday. We have probably all wanted to improve our health and wellbeing at one time or another. For example, you may have been on a diet in order to lose weight, tried to give up smoking, taken up a sport or joined a gym to get fit. The good news is that it is often possible to improve your health and wellbeing by making lifestyle changes.

Figure 9.3 identifies a range of areas that a person could focus on to improve their health and wellbeing. The majority of adults should have some control over their habits, behaviour or lifestyle in relation to each of these areas.

Figure 9.3 Areas for potential health improvement

Reflect

If you wanted to improve your own health and wellbeing, which two of the areas given in Figure 9.3 would you choose to focus on? Think about the extent to which you are able to make choices and change your habits or behaviour in these two areas.

Improving health and wellbeing

Health improvement planning should begin with thorough and honest health assessment. This involves collecting basic health-related information and also measuring physical **health indicators**. Table 9.3 (opposite) identifies the kinds of lifestyle topics that a health care worker might ask about and shows the physical measures they may use as part of a basic health assessment.

Key term

Health indicators: *measurable aspects of the body (such as weight and height) or the way the body works (such as blood pressure) that can be used to assess a person's physical health status*

Table 9.3 Information needed for health improvement planning

Lifestyle information
Dietary intake
Amount of sleep
Units of alcohol consumed
Exercise pattern
Use of cigarettes or drugs
Physical measures
Height
Weight
Pulse (before and after exercise)
Blood pressure
Cholesterol level
Blood glucose level
Body mass index (BMI)
Hip/waist ratio

The information collected by the health care worker provides a baseline from which to improve health and wellbeing. The information obtained, combined with the physical measures data, enables the health care worker to identify some of the factors (such as lack of exercise, poor diet) that may be contributing to a health problem (such as obesity) and also provides a basis for setting realistic improvement targets.

Before any health improvement targets are identified, it is important to compare the individual's physical health measures to those expected for someone of their age and physical characteristics. This shows whether any of the person's physical health indicators (blood pressure, for example) may be a cause for concern. The information obtained also helps to focus the person on improving their physical health and wellbeing.

Investigate

Talk to somebody who helps others to get fit – such as a PE teacher, a fitness trainer or a fitness class teacher. Find out how they assess fitness, how they set targets and the methods they use to motivate people to improve their physical fitness.

Key terms

Baseline: *the starting point*

Obesity: *a very overweight state, usually defined as a body mass index of 30 or more.*

Target: *a goal or thing to be achieved*

Case study

Trevor (17), Leila (19), Paula (44) and Sue (62) all work in a nursing home for older people. They have recently volunteered to take part in a health improvement programme being run by the local health centre. Each member of the group has agreed to have their physical health measured and to provide some basic lifestyle information. This will help the health centre staff to assess their current state of health and develop a health improvement plan for each individual. The health measurements that have been recorded are provided overleaf.

Table 9.4

Measure	Trevor	Leila	Paula	Sue
Height	6' 1" (1.85 m)	5' 8" (1.72 m)	5' 4" (1.63 m)	5' 2" (1.57 m)
Weight	13.5 stones (85.7 kg)	7.0 stones (44.5 kg)	14 stones (88.9 kg)	8.5 stones 54.0 kg)
Resting pulse (beats per minute)	80	65	125	87
Blood pressure	120/80	90/65	200/135	135/85
Cigarettes per day	None	10	10	None
Units of alcohol per week	6	30	40	10
Usual drink	Beer	Vodka	Lager	Wine
Hours of exercise	Football 3 hours Gym 3 hours	Gym 7 hours	None	Yoga 2 hours Walking 2 hours
Diet	Regular balanced diet	Eats snacks and salads Avoids fatty food	Eats a lot of burgers, chips and kebabs	Regular balanced diet

1. Who do you think is the most healthy and least healthy person out of the four people? Give clear reasons for your choices.

2. Describe the ways in which the remaining two members of the group appear to be healthy or unhealthy.

3. Identify three lifestyle factors that should be taken into account when interpreting the various health measurements.

People often need guidance and support to achieve health improvements

Overcoming difficulties in making health improvements

Making lifestyle changes to improve health and wellbeing can seem simple and straightforward, especially where there is a clear focus for this, such as doing more exercise to lose weight. However, as many people who have tried to lose weight will confirm, good intentions can be very hard to put into practice.

People trying to make lifestyle changes to improve their health and wellbeing tend to face a number of specific difficulties or challenges. These, and ways of addressing them, are outlined in Table 9.5.

Table 9.5 Difficulties in making lifestyle changes and ways of overcoming them

Area of difficulty	Ways of overcoming difficulties
Getting started	• Setting realistic goals • Seeking support • Accessing professional advice
Time commitment	• Setting regular time aside to exercise • Balancing exercise and home-life commitments • Balancing exercise and work commitments • Managing potential times when it is difficult to keep to the plan
Motivation	• Building up motivation to start • Keeping to plan after initial interest falls • Pushing through difficult times when little progress appears to be made

? Reflect

Have you ever tried to make changes to your lifestyle? Did you face any of the difficulties listed in Table 9.5? How did you overcome them?

Setting realistic targets

People seeking to make lifestyle changes as a way of improving their health and wellbeing need to set realistic targets for improvement. Targets must be safe, realistic and achievable. For example, it is important not to plan for unrealistically rapid weight loss that can only be achieved through 'crash dieting' or exercise binges. People who lose weight this way regain it quickly and can damage their physical health in the process. Instead, there should be a clear, logical plan with particular health improvement targets that can be achieved in a reasonable time scale. Health care workers tend to set short, medium and long-term targets, and build in regular reviews, so that service users can see their progress and address any difficulties they are having.

The methods chosen to achieve health improvement targets should be safe and, ideally, should fit in with an individual's current lifestyle. For example, improving physical fitness can be achieved in many different ways. Walking more, cycling to school or work, or going to an exercise class once a week are all relatively straightforward and won't disrupt a person's lifestyle too much. Setting out to run a marathon or swim the English Channel may result in a greater level of fitness but these aren't realistic or safe targets for most people! So, we can see that an individual is not likely to benefit from setting very ambitious targets.

Investigate

Think about the following aspects of your own lifestyle and identify a short and long-term health improvement target for each area.

Lifestyle area	Short-term target	Long-term target
Diet		
Exercise		
Weight		
Home and work environment		
Alcohol consumption		
Smoking		
Recreational drug use		
Sexual practices		
Personal hygiene		

It is important to view health improvement as a gradual process that requires commitment. Sudden changes in weight, fitness or behaviour are unlikely to be maintained. If you need to develop a health improvement plan for another person, remember to take their age and physical characteristics into account when conducting the health assessment. You will also need to ensure that the person agrees with the health improvement targets and is personally motivated to achieve them. If not, they'll never reach them.

Intervention strategies

Intervention strategies refer to the things that people do, with the support of health and social care workers, to change their lifestyle as a way of improving their health and wellbeing. These include:

- developing a healthy lifestyle plan that includes realistic short and long-term targets for health improvement

- identifying techniques that can be used to support individuals at various points as they try to change their lifestyle; for example, some people use hypnotherapy to support their efforts to stop smoking or acupuncture to help them to relax and reduce their alcohol consumption

- using face-to-face support such as counselling, social work or community nursing care to build relationships

- making use of medically prescribed and supervised products such as nicotine patches, **methadone** or calorie-controlled diets to enable people to take control of their smoking, drug or overeating problems.

 Key terms

Intervention: getting involved in something

Methadone: a medically prescribed substitute that is used to safely wean people off taking heroin

Types and sources of support available to promote healthy lifestyles

Forms of support

A healthy lifestyle is now seen as an essential foundation for positive health, development and wellbeing throughout an individual's life. A person who has decided to make lifestyle changes to improve their health and wellbeing is likely to need help and support to get started, keep going and to reach their goals. The person may be able to draw on both **formal** and **informal** sources of support (see below) or may have a preference for one particular source of support.

🔑 **Key terms**

Formal support: support based on a professional relationship

Informal support: support based on a personal relationship

Figure 9.4 Sources of formal support

Figure 9.5 Sources of informal support

Formal and informal providers of support may relate to an individual who wants to make lifestyle changes in different ways, depending on their different levels and types of training (or lack of it) and on the closeness of their relationship with the person. Whether formal or informal support and whatever the specialist area or skill level, the forms of support offered tend to be broadly similar. These include:

- listening carefully to what the person says about their efforts to change lifestyle

- using empathy to understand the person's motivation and difficulties

- providing encouragement to help the person to keep going and enable them to tackle any difficulties

- providing advice and guidance based on their own experience or specialist area of expertise.

Sources of formal support

Doctors and health specialists promote healthy lifestyles in a number of ways. They tend to use listening and empathy during consultations that assess health needs, diagnose illnesses and identify the causes of health problems, for example. As part of treatment and support, they are likely to encourage individuals to make lifestyle changes (explaining and reinforcing the health benefits). As part of this, they provide people with advice and guidance on ways of avoiding lifestyle-related health problems ('stop smoking', 'eat less fat and sugar', 'do more exercise') and on ways of maintaining optimum health and wellbeing.

Key term

Empathy: the ability to see and feel things from another person's point of view

Investigate

What kinds of support service are offered by your GP practice and school or college to people who want to make changes to their lifestyle?

Counsellors, teachers and health and social care workers can be sources of advice on healthy lifestyles

Counsellors and youth workers tend to be good at forming supportive relationships based on listening and empathy. Similarly, teachers, careers advisors and human resource department staff may be good sources of support in education and work contexts. A change of lifestyle may require information, guidance and practical advice on how to gain qualifications, change job roles or improve work–life balance, for example. There are many support groups, both locally and online, that offer advice, information and support from people who have already made lifestyle changes or who are in the process of trying to improve a specific aspect of their health and wellbeing. Joining such a group can make a person feel connected and supported at what may be a difficult, stressful or isolating time in their life.

People who are trying to make lifestyle changes can sometimes benefit from joining a support group

Sources of informal support

People often turn to their partner, family or friends when they need advice or support on personal matters. It is also important to note that an individual who wants to make lifestyle changes may need to consult those they live with, as the changes could impact on other people too. The close emotional connections and sense of trust we develop with partners, family members and close friends enables us to rely on these people for an honest opinion and genuine support when we need it.

Maintaining change

A person who is successful in changing their lifestyle and improving an aspect of their health and wellbeing next has to maintain this positive change. In particular, they need to develop strategies that help them to:

- keep to the plan

- maintain a positive outlook.

? Reflect

Who do you turn to when you need support or advice on personal matters? Why this person or group of people? Think about the reasons why you tend to seek support from them rather than from others.

Health and social care workers have developed a number of strategies to enable people to maintain their lifestyle changes. These include:

- using diaries and record-keeping forms to help the person monitor their own progress and their feelings about the plan or the targets they have to achieve

- encouraging people to attend support groups, or contribute to online forums

- helping service users to establish supportive 'buddy relationships' with others in a similar position

- recommending substitutes, such as nicotine patches or low-fat and low-calorie alternatives to particular foods

- implementing reward systems that score improvements (identifying a slimmer of the week, for example) or encouraging the person to treat themselves to a personal reward for making progress towards their targets

- holding review meetings that acknowledge difficulties and give positive feedback to the person for their efforts and the progress they have made. Review meetings also allow the health care worker and the service user to adjust targets if they reach them early or if they appear to be unrealistic.

Case study

Elsie Stevens is a 60-year-old woman who has recently retired from her job as a secretary. Elsie has decided that she needs to get fit to make the most of her retirement. She currently does no exercise at all and is two stones overweight. In her youth, Elsie was a keen swimmer and also enjoyed walking.

1. Suggest three types of exercise Elsie could take up to reduce her weight and get fitter. Explain how these particular choices would benefit Elsie and also fit into her lifestyle.

2. Plan a three-month exercise/activity programme for Elsie based on the range of opportunities and facilities available in your local area. Set out your programme in a table format.

The barriers to achieving a healthy lifestyle

What's stopping you being healthier?

A healthy lifestyle increases a person's chances of experiencing good health and wellbeing. Who wouldn't want this? People will generally choose health over illness and want to enjoy life, rather than feel ill and struggle with difficulties. So, what is stopping everyone from being healthier? In reality, achieving a healthy lifestyle isn't as easy or straightforward as it might appear. A number of factors can act as **barriers** to a healthy lifestyle.

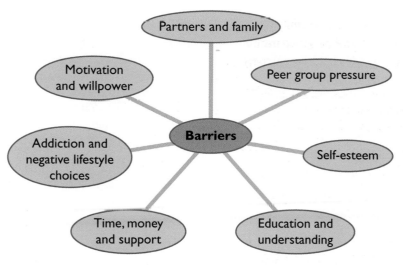

Figure 9.6 Barriers to a health lifestyle

Motivation and willpower

A person must really want to change their lifestyle to have any realistic hope of doing so. This is true of people who go on a diet to lose weight, who join a gym to get fit and lower their blood pressure, or who are trying to give up smoking or drinking. The people who succeed are those who have **motivation** and **willpower**. People are usually more motivated when they have a goal to work towards; something like losing weight for a wedding or training for a sponsored walk. People who believe that their achievements are under their own control tend to have stronger willpower.

> **Key term**
>
> **Barriers:** things that get in the way or which block achievement

> **Reflect**
>
> Are you someone with strong willpower or is this something that you struggle with when trying to live a healthy lifestyle? What other strategies do you use to motivate yourself to make lifestyle changes?

> **Key terms**
>
> **Motivation:** the desire or drive to take action
>
> **Willpower:** self-control over behaviour, usually for self-improvement purposes

Partner and family

People's partners and families are very important in shaping their attitudes and behaviour, and in providing support. Partners and families who are positive about and active in supporting lifestyle change can really help people to achieve their goals. A person who lacks the support of their family or partner (or who finds those close to them actually disagree with their planned changes) will feel undermined; they will require greater willpower and personal motivation to succeed. The situation can be made worse if the person is also unable to access support from health and social care services.

Peer group and media influences

Pages 244–245 outline the way in which peer groups and different types of media can inform and influence lifestyle choices. Peer group pressure and media influences can make unhealthy lifestyle choices seem more attractive – and easier to make – than healthy ones. These influences can undermine a person's good intentions, particularly during adolescence and early adulthood when people are keen to be accepted by their peers who may be following popular lifestyle trends. Drinking too much, experimenting with recreational drugs, eating fast food and engaging in unprotected sex may not seem so bad if everyone else in your peer group is doing the same thing and the media seems to encourage it.

Self-esteem, education and understanding

A person who has low self-esteem, who lacks education or who has a poor understanding about unhealthy lifestyles may be less able to make effective changes to their behaviour. Low self-esteem means not valuing yourself – if you feel worthless, why make an effort to look after your health? People with low self-esteem often feel that they don't deserve to have good health or positive feelings of wellbeing; they may even find it hard to imagine what feeling great might be like. Similarly, a lack of education and understanding about the benefits of a healthy lifestyle may undermine a person's motivation and willpower to make difficult lifestyle changes.

Lack of time and money

The most common reason for not making lifestyle changes is 'lack of time'. A person who lives a busy, hectic and pressured lifestyle may say that going to the gym or cooking fresh food is too time-consuming. They put off making what they can see are positive lifestyle changes until they have more time. This, of course, is not likely to happen.

> **? Reflect**
>
> *Have you ever challenged peers who have put you under pressure to make unhealthy lifestyle choices? How might your understanding of healthy and unhealthy lifestyles help you to resist peer group pressure in future?*

Going to the gym, buying better quality food or improving your home environment can involve spending money that some people just don't have. However, lack of money doesn't have to be a barrier to making some lifestyle changes. Consuming less alcohol, stopping smoking and avoiding recreational drug use all save money! However, when a person gives something up (like cigarettes) they often replace it with something else (like comfort eating or retail therapy).

Addiction and negative lifestyle choices

An addiction involves the continued use of substances such as drugs, alcohol or tobacco, despite being aware of the negative consequences. These might include damage to physical health, high risk of infection or dependency on the substance.

Addiction often leads to denial of the health risks and other negative consequences, and this prevents people from making lifestyle changes. Similarly, people may be unwilling to give up unhealthy habits (such as smoking) or activities that give them pleasure (drinking to excess) because they enjoy the short-term effects and don't believe that the long-term consequences for personal health will affect them. People in this position do not really want to change their lifestyles and are unlikely to value the benefits of making healthier choices.

On a more positive note, some people are able to overcome addiction and make lifestyle changes that benefit their health and wellbeing.

Health and social care play an important part in helping people to recover from addictions and negative lifestyle choices

10 | Human body systems and care of disorders

Learning aim A:
Understand the structure and function of main organs and major body systems, and their interrelationships

- ▶ Topic A.1 Structure and functions of main organs in the body

- ▶ Topic A.2 Structure of major body systems

- ▶ Topic A.3 Functions of major body systems

- ▶ Topic A.4 Relationships between major body systems

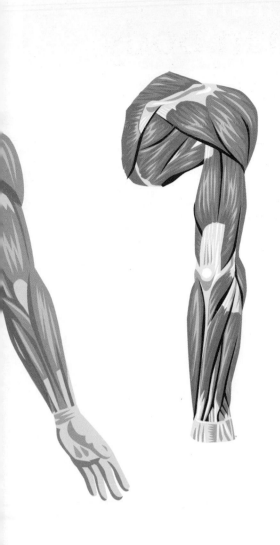
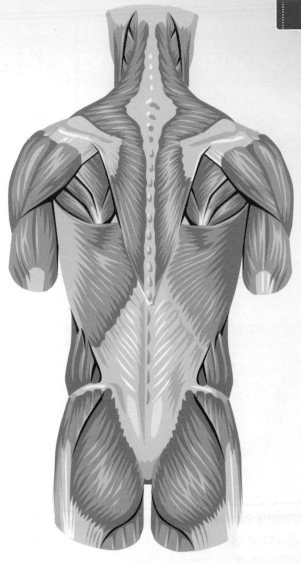
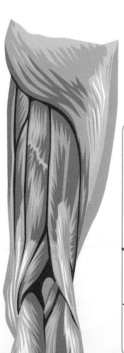
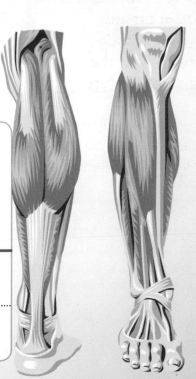

**Learning aim B:
Explore routine care
of disorders relating
to body systems**

▶ Topic B.1 Disorders relating to
body systems

▶ Topic B.2 Routine care of
disorders

Structure and function of main organs in the body

The human body

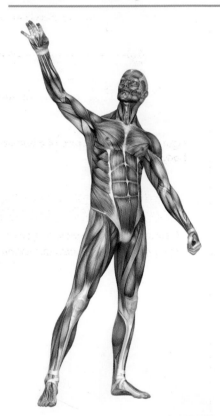

Figure 10.1 The anatomy of the human body

The human body is organised into cells, tissues, organs and body systems. You will not be assessed on your knowledge of cells and tissues but it is helpful to know something about them in order to understand the structure (anatomy) and function (physiology) of body organs and body systems.

Cells

Cells are the smallest (microscopic) elements of the body. The human body consists of many millions of cells that vary in size, shape and function. Each cell has three main parts:

- a *nucleus* that controls the way the cells works – as a nerve cell, a muscle cell or a blood cell, for example

- *cytoplasm*, a jelly-like substance containing the structures that enable the cell to function

- a *membrane* surrounding and protecting the cell.

Every cell in the human body has a specific function, such as being a brain cell (making the brain work) or a red blood cell (delivering oxygen to tissues).

Tissues

Tissues are made up of groups of cells that have the same structure and function. Bone tissue consists of bone cells, muscle tissue consists of muscle cells and blood tissues consist of blood cells, for example. There are four main types of human tissue:

- epithelial tissue makes up the membranes that cover internal and external surfaces of the body

- connective tissue has a supporting role and includes blood, bone and cartilage tissues

- muscle tissue is present in all muscles, including the heart

- nervous tissue consists of **neurons** that make up the nervous system.

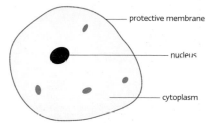

Figure 10.2 The structure of a human body cell

Investigate

Use library and other resources to investigate the structure and function of a specialised body cell. Draw a labelled diagram of the cell and explain its function in the body.

Key term

Neurons: *cells in the nervous system that process and transmit information*

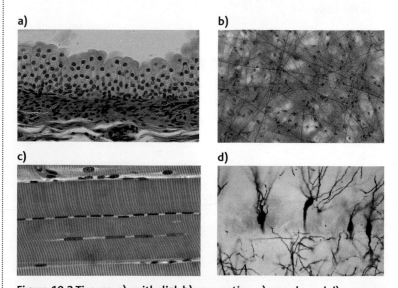

Figure 10.3 Tissues: a) epithelial, b) connective, c) muscle and d) nervous

Organs

Organs consist of different types of tissue that are grouped together in order to perform one or more specific functions in the human body. Figure 10.4 shows where some key organs are located throughout the human body.

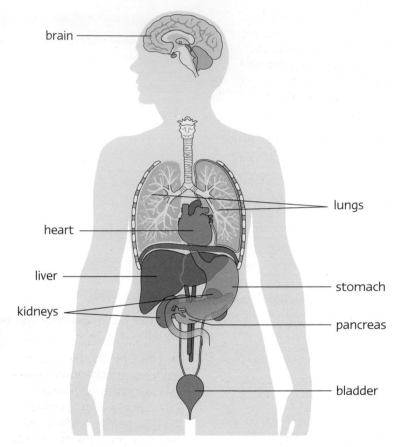

Figure 10.4 Human anatomy – location of organs in the body

The skin

The function of the skin is to protect the body, maintain body temperature, receive and communicate information from the person's environment – through touch, pain and pressure, for example – and to produce sweat that carries waste products out of the body (as well as having a cooling function).

The heart

The heart's vital function is to pump blood to the lungs and around the body. Blood delivers oxygen, nutrients, hormones and antibodies to different areas of the body, and removes waste products.

? Reflect

What do you already know about these different organs? Jot down one fact or piece of information about each. You will be able to add to this as you work through the chapter.

Case study

In 1995 Hannah Clark from Wales, then just two years old, had a heart transplant to treat a condition known as cardiomyopathy. Due to cardiomyopathy her heart had doubled in size and was likely to fail within a year.

Hannah underwent a pioneering surgery in which a donor heart was inserted into her body *alongside* her own heart. Hannah's new heart took on the task of pumping blood around her body, allowing her own heart, still beating, to rest. Following complications, Hannah's donor heart had to be removed 10 years later. When surgeons operated to remove the donor heart, they discovered that her own heart had recovered enough to function normally.

1. What would have happened if Hannah's own heart had failed before she had the transplant?

2. What vital role did the transplanted heart perform in Hannah's body?

3. Describe what a person's heart does when it functions normally.

The lungs

The two main functions of the lungs are to:

1. transport oxygen from the atmosphere into the bloodstream

2. remove carbon dioxide from the bloodstream and release it into the atmosphere.

A person's lungs are located in the chest (Figure 10.5) on either side of their heart.

Investigate

How many breaths per minute do you take at rest? If you can, monitor your normal breathing rate to see how often your lungs fill with air each minute. If this is difficult, ask a class colleague or friend to count the number of times your chest rises and falls in a minute as an alternative way of recording your breathing rate.

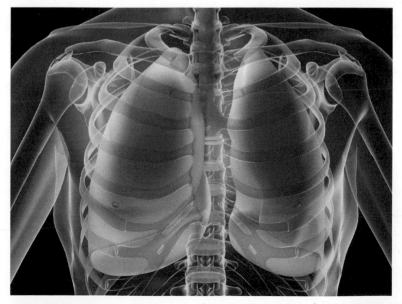

Figure 10.5 Lungs

The stomach

The stomach is basically a bag that stores and digests food. Digestive **enzymes** are released in the stomach to help this vital process. Solids are broken down and mixed with fluids. Partly digested food moves from the stomach into the small intestine where further enzymes are released to complete the digestion process.

Your assessment criteria:

1A.1 Identify the structure and function of three main organs in the human body

2A.P1 Describe the structure and function of the main organs in the human body

Case study

Television presenter Fern Britton caused controversy in 2008 when she revealed that her substantial weight loss was partly the result of having a 'gastric band' operation on her stomach. This type of surgery is based on a simple principle – when a person's stomach feels full they will stop eating.

The gastric band operation involves placing and tightening a silicone loop near the top of the person's stomach. When food enters the pouch that is created, the person feels full. The 'pouch' then slowly empties through the gap into the rest of the stomach, and appetite returns.

1. Create a diagram to show how a gastric band works.

2. People who have the gastric band operation normally lose weight. Why?

3. Investigate the risks and drawbacks to having a gastric band fitted.

> **Key term**
>
> **Enzymes:** *naturally occurring proteins that help chemical reactions to take place*

The bladder

The bladder's function is to store urine until it is excreted (removed) from the body. The bladder stretches when it fills and contracts when it is emptied.

The brain

The three main functions of the brain are to:

- receive and respond to information about the person's environment
- co-ordinate and control physical functions, such as breathing, heart rate, balance and movement
- make the individual self-aware and able to think about themselves and others.

A person's brain is located in their skull. It is a very complex organ that is the control centre for nervous system and the body as a whole.

Eyes and ears

The eyes and ears are sensory organs that receive information which is sent to the brain for interpretation. The eyes have muscles which allow them to move, so you can look in different directions. Muscles also help the eyes to focus light, so that you can see a clear image.

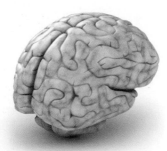

The human brain consists of a number of lobes, each with a particular function (such as vision, motor control or language)

The outer ears channel sound waves onto the ear drum. This vibrates, transmitting the sound waves further into the body until they become nerve impulses that can be interpreted by the brain. The inner parts of the ear also play an important role in a person's sense of balance.

The pancreas

The function of the pancreas is to produce hormones that control glucose levels in the blood, and to secrete enzymes into the small intestine that help the body to digest food.

The intestines

The alimentary canal extends from the stomach to the anus and the intestines make up part of this structure. The human intestines consist of two segments, the large and small intestine. The small intestine is a greyish purple colour, 35 mm in diameter and about 6–7 m long in an average adult. The main function of the small intestine is to break down and digest food. The large intestine is a dark red in colour and about 1.5 m long. It stores undigested food as faeces until these pass out of the body through the anus.

Investigate

Investigate the causes, symptoms and effects on the intestines of gasteroenteritis, Coeliac disease or irritable bowel syndrome. Produce a diagram or poster to explain how one of these health problems affects the normal functioning of the intestines.

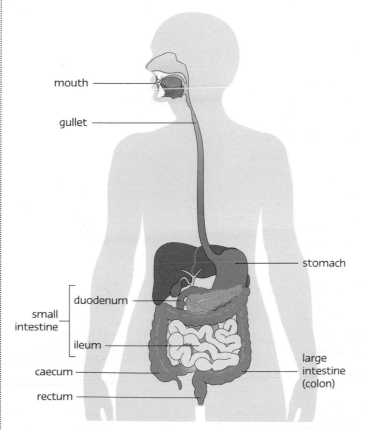

mouth

gullet

stomach

duodenum

small intestine

ileum

caecum

large intestine (colon)

rectum

Figure 10.6 The human intestines are part of the alimentary canal

The liver

The liver is the largest internal organ in the human body. It performs a number of functions including:

- storing iron and some vitamins

- removing drugs and alcohol from the blood

- helping to control levels of glucose in the blood

- producing heat to keep the body warm

- producing bile salts that break down fat in the small intestines.

The kidneys

The kidneys filter out and remove excess salt, water and waste products from the blood, producing urine. They keep the composition of the blood balanced by maintaining correct levels of minerals, salts and fluids. The kidneys are located behind the abdominal cavity, one on each side of the spine. The kidneys are bean-shaped, weighing between 115 and 170 g in adults, with the left kidney slightly larger than the right.

The testes and ovaries

The testes are the male reproductive organs that produce and store sperm cells, and that make the hormone testosterone. The ovaries are the female reproductive organs that produce and store eggs cells, and that make the hormones oestrogen and progesterone.

The uterus

The uterus, or womb, is a muscular structure that protects and feeds a baby as it is developing. During labour it contracts and pushes the baby down the birth canal.

Your assessment criteria:

1A.1 Identify the structure and function of three main organs in the human body

2A.P1 Describe the structure and function of the main organs in the human body

 Investigate

Find out about the causes and consequences of cirrhosis of the liver. Who is most at risk of developing this condition?

Case study

Two women living in Florida suffered severe health problems after receiving cosmetic injections from a fake doctor. One of the women received 40 injections of silicon and the other 20; both believed the treatment would enhance their appearance by giving them 'JLo' style bottoms. The women became seriously ill with internal organ failure and ended up in intensive care with damage to their livers, kidneys and lungs.

1. Where in the human body is the liver located?

2. What are the main functions of the lungs?

3. Identify two possible consequences of kidney damage.

Structure and function of major body systems

Major body systems

The human body consists of a number of major systems (Figure 10.7) that are connected. A body system is simply a group of organs that work together for a particular purpose.

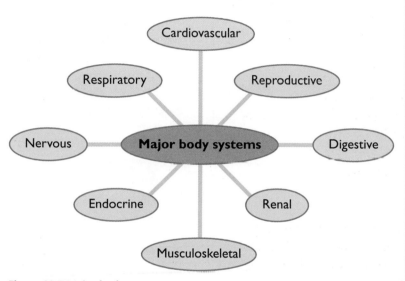

Figure 10.7 Major body systems

The cardiovascular system

The **cardiovascular** system consists of the heart, the blood and blood vessels. In basic terms, it is a pumping system; the heart is the pump and **arteries**, **veins** and **capillaries** are the tubes that carry blood around the body. The function of the cardiovascular system is to supply body tissues with oxygen and essential nutrients, and to remove waste products such as carbon dioxide.

Key terms

Arteries: *blood vessels that carry blood away from the heart*

Capillaries: *small blood vessels composed of a single layer of cells that connect arteries to veins*

Cardiovascular: *related to the heart and circulatory system*

Veins: *blood vessels that carry blood towards the heart*

Investigate

Use books or the Internet to find out how much blood is contained within the average adult's cardiovascular system. Have a guess before you carry out your research and compare this to what you discover.

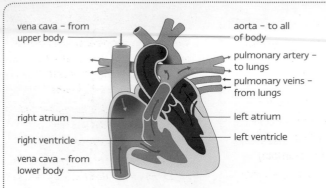

Figure 10.8 Annotated diagram of the heart

Figure 10.8 shows the structure of the heart. There are four chambers and a number of tubes (arteries and veins) that allow blood to be brought into and then pumped out of the heart. The right side of the heart pumps blood to the lungs to pick up oxygen. The left side of the heart then pumps the oxygenated blood through the arteries to tissues around the body. Deoxygenated blood returns to the heart through the body's network of veins.

The respiratory system

The **respiratory** system brings oxygen into, and takes carbon dioxide and water vapour out of, the human body.

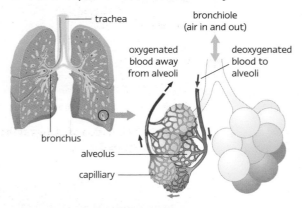

Figure 10.9 Annotated diagram of the respiratory system

Figure 10.9 shows the structure of the respiratory system. It looks like an upside-down tree! Oxygen in air enters the mouth and nose, and is then drawn down the trachea into the bronchus and bronchioles of each lung. It is then transferred into the blood through the alveoli sacs. Carbon dioxide travels the other way through the respiratory system. It passes out of the blood into the alveoli, back up the bronchioles, through the bronchus and trachea, and out through the mouth and nose.

The nervous system

The nervous system covers the whole of the human body. It consists of a network of specialised cells that receives, interprets and then responds to information about a person's internal and external environment.

Key term

Respiratory: *related to the process of breathing*

Investigate

Find the website below to watch and listen to an explanation of how the heart works as part of the circulatory system:

http://www.mayoclinic.com/health/circulatory-system/MM00636

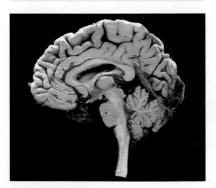

A cross-section of the human brain

There are two main parts to the nervous system. The **central nervous system** consists of the spine and brain. This part of the nervous system interprets information sent from the **peripheral nervous system**, which consists of nerves located throughout the body. Sensory nerves respond to internal and external stimuli by producing and passing on signals to the brain. The brain then processes and sends signals back to the muscles and glands of the body. A person's nervous system enables them to be physically active (walking, running, jumping, for example), aids perception by processing information from the five senses and also controls the way their body functions (reducing temperature, speeding up heart beat, blinking, for example).

The endocrine system

The **endocrine** system consists of glands (Figure 10.10) that produce and release hormones into the human body via the blood. The endocrine system controls metabolism, growth, development, puberty, tissue function and also plays a part in controlling mood.

The endocrine system works by releasing hormones in response to changes in the body. An endocrine gland will produce a hormone when it receives a signal that the body needs it, but will stop producing when there is enough of the particular hormone in the body – this is a negative feedback mechanism.

The digestive system

You are probably much more aware of both the structure and function of your **digestive** system than you are of your nervous or endocrine systems! The digestive system is responsible for the physical and chemical digestion, absorption and elimination of food materials. Figure 10.11 identifies the various parts of the digestive system.

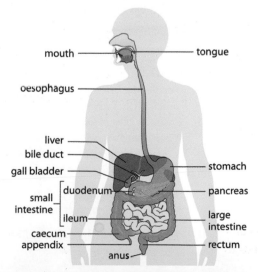

Figure 10.11 Annotated diagram of the digestive system

mouth — tongue
oesophagus
liver
bile duct
gall bladder
stomach
duodenum
small intestine
pancreas
ileum
large intestine
caecum
appendix
rectum
anus

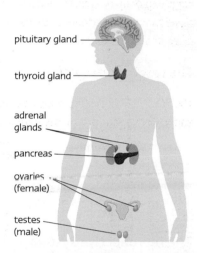

pituitary gland
thyroid gland
adrenal glands
pancreas
ovaries (female)
testes (male)

Figure 10.10 Location of glands in the endocrine system

First, food is ingested (taken into the mouth). It is chewed and softened by saliva. This starts to break the food down. When a ball of food is swallowed, it goes down the oesophagus to the stomach, partly through gravity and partly by way of a muscular action called peristalsis. When the food reaches the stomach, chemical digestion takes place as food molecules are broken down by enzymes and gastric juices. This partly digested food stays in the stomach for about five hours. It is then pushed into the small intestine for further chemical digestion. More enzymes and pancreatic juices break the food down into the components that the body needs and can absorb. This process takes about four hours. Between seven and nine hours after food was eaten, it reaches a stage where the nutrients can be extracted and the remaining undigested mass is moved into the large intestine as faeces. These are then eliminated via the anus.

The renal system

The renal system is the organ system that produces, stores and removes urine from the body. It consists of two kidneys, two ureters, the bladder and the urethra (see Figure 10.12).

The main role of the kidneys is to filter waste products and excess water to maintain the salt and pH balance of the blood and fluid balance in the body. The kidneys pass waste products and excess water through the ureters into the bladder. These wastes are excreted as urine.

The reproductive system

The male and female reproductive systems produce sperm and egg (ova) cells that, when combined, have the capacity to produce a child. The male reproductive system (Figure 10.13) consists of:

- two testicles (testes) that produce and store sperm, and produce male hormones

- the sperm tubes (vas deferens) that carry sperm from the testes to the penis

- the prostate gland and seminal vesicle that produce fluid which, when mixed with sperm, results in semen

- a penis that places semen inside the female vagina during sexual intercourse.

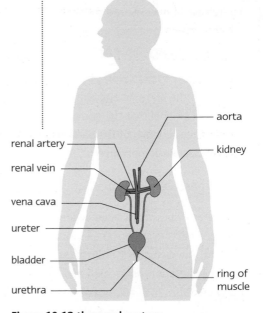

renal artery
renal vein
vena cava
ureter
bladder
urethra
aorta
kidney
ring of muscle

Figure 10.12 the renal system

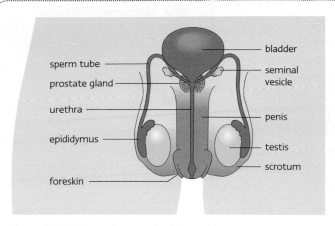

Figure 10.13 The male reproductive system

The female reproductive system (Figure 10.14) consists of:

- two ovaries that produce and store eggs (ova), and produce female hormones

- two fallopian tubes that transport the egg to the uterus

- the uterus where fertilisation takes place and in which the foetus develops; the cervix is the opening from the vagina into the uterus

- the vagina, where sperm is transferred into the female reproductive system.

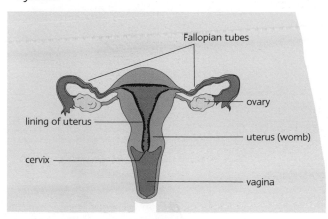

Figure 10.14 The female reproductive system

 Investigate

Find out why a woman's oviducts, or fallopian tubes, may become blocked or damaged and what the consequences of this might be.

Case study

Stacy was diagnosed with premature ovarian failure (early menopause) at the age of 25. This was very upsetting for her as she wanted to start a family. Using *in vitro*-fertilisation techniques, she was implanted with eggs donated by her twin sister that had been fertilised by her husband's sperm. When this procedure failed, Stacy's twin sister agreed to have one of her own ovaries removed and transplanted into Stacy. The surgery was successful and Stacy had her first menstrual cycle three weeks after the operation. She is now hopeful of being able to conceive a child.

1. Why is it now possible that Stacy might become pregnant?

2. Describe what happens when an ovary releases an egg during ovulation.

3. Where in the female body are the ovaries located?

Your assessment criteria:

1A.2 Identify the structure of one major body system

1A.3 State the function of one major body system

2A.P2 Describe the structure of major systems in the human body

2A.P3 Describe the functions of major systems in the human body

The musculoskeletal system

The musculoskeletal system consists of the bones of the human skeleton and the muscles that are attached to these bones (Figure 10.15). The function of this body system is to control movement. The bones of the skeleton also protect organs such as the lungs, heart and brain.

✎ Key term

Musculoskeletal: related to muscles and the skeleton

📋 Investigate

Find out what the main bones and muscles in a human leg are called and how they are connected to enable human beings to move effectively.

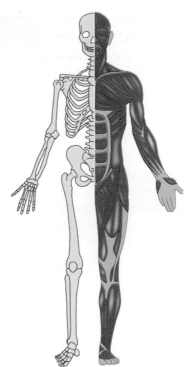

Figure 10.15 The human skeleton and main skeletal muscles

Relationships between major body systems

Your assessment criteria:

1A.4 Outline the relationship between three of the major body systems

2A.P4 Describe the relationship between major body systems

2A.M2 Explain how two major body systems interrelate

Interrelationship of body systems

The systems of the human body that you have learned about so far are linked. They interact to maintain life in an individual's body. The interrelationships between body systems are quite complex but Include, for example:

- the respiratory system supplying oxygen to the cardiovascular system which then pumps oxygenated blood around the body to keep cells alive

- the musculoskeletal system working closely with the nervous system to enable physical movement and co-ordination of limbs

- the digestive system working closely with the endocrine system to ensure that digestive hormones are secreted to allow the digestion of food and absorption of nutrients.

The respiratory system and the cardiovascular system

The respiratory system has two main functions: to collect oxygen from the air and to get rid of carbon dioxide made by the body. The respiratory system includes the lungs, trachea, nose and mouth. It moves air into and out of the lungs to allow the body to absorb oxygen and give out carbon dioxide.

> ### Key term
>
> **Interrelationship:** *a connection between two or more things*

The respiratory system works with the cardiovascular system to make sure every cell in the body has a supply of oxygen and can get rid of waste carbon dioxide.

Your assessment criteria:

2A.P4 Describe the relationship between major body systems

2A.M2 Explain how two major body systems interrelate

1. The lungs draw fresh air into the body (breathing).

2. Oxygen in the air moves into the blood (gaseous exchange).

3. The heart pumps the oxygenated blood around the body.

4. Oxygen moves from the blood to the body cells. Carbon dioxide made by the body cells moves into the blood.

5. The blood returns to the heart.

6. The heart pumps the blood to the lungs.

7. Carbon dioxide in the blood passes from the blood into the air in the lungs.

8. Air in the lungs is breathed out.

Figure 10.16 How the respiratory system works with the cardiovascular system

The musculoskeletal system and the nervous system

The musculoskeletal system is a framework of bones and tissues that allows the body to move. Movement happens when specific skeletal muscles contract and relax. Skeletal muscles in some parts of the body, like the arms and legs, are capable of voluntary movement. This means that a person is able to use them to deliberately raise their hand or flex their foot, for example. Other muscles, such as the heart muscle, move in an involuntary way and are not under a person's conscious control. In reality, movement of all muscles depends on the musculoskeletal system working closely with the nervous system. Skeletal muscles are controlled by the somatic nervous system; whereas the autonomic nervous system controls involuntary muscles. In both cases, impulses (electrical signals) that are sent through the nervous system trigger movement in the musculoskeletal system. The musculoskeletal system also helps the nervous system by protecting the nerves from damage.

Key terms

Autonomic nervous system: the part of the nervous system that controls the smooth involuntary muscles around the organs and the glands

Somatic nervous system: the part of the nervous system that controls voluntary, skeletal muscles which enable the body to move

The digestive system and the endocrine system

The endocrine system contains glands that release hormones which influence almost every cell, organ, and function of our bodies. The endocrine system is instrumental in regulating mood, growth and development, tissue function, and metabolism, as well as sexual function and reproductive processes, for example. There are close links between the digestive system and the endocrine system. For example, when we digest carbohydrates, they are transformed into sugars. The pancreas, part of the endocrine system, produces the hormone insulin to regulate how fast the carbohydrates are broken down; therefore, insulin regulates the amount of sugar in the blood in a certain amount of time (the blood glucose level).

Homeostasis

The human body has the ability to regulate and maintain a stable internal (physiological) environment. This is known as homeostasis. This ability gives the body the ability to respond to changes in the external environment. For example, when the weather is very hot or very cold, homeostatic mechanisms in the body compensate by making adjustments to the way the body functions. The liver, kidneys and brain are the main organs involved in homeostasis:

- the liver breaks down toxic substances and regulates carbohydrate metabolism

- the kidneys regulate water levels In the blood and excrete waste products, generally 'cleaning' the blood

- the hypothalamus in the brain is the control centre that responds to changes, such as variations in temperature, in the environment.

Homeostasis works through a negative feedback system. This means that, when changes are detected in the body's internal or external environment, the body takes action to maintain a constant internal environment (see Figure 10.17).

A range of physiological processes in the body are controlled through homeostasis. These include:

- body temperature

- blood pressure

- breathing depth and rate

- blood glucose levels.

Your assessment criteria:

2A.D1 Analyse how body systems interrelate to maintain one example of homeostasis in the human body

🔑 Key terms

Homeostasis: *the process by which internal systems of the body maintain a balance or stable state*

Negative feedback system: *a process the body uses to counter changes (e.g a rise in temperature) that might threaten its stable, internal environment*

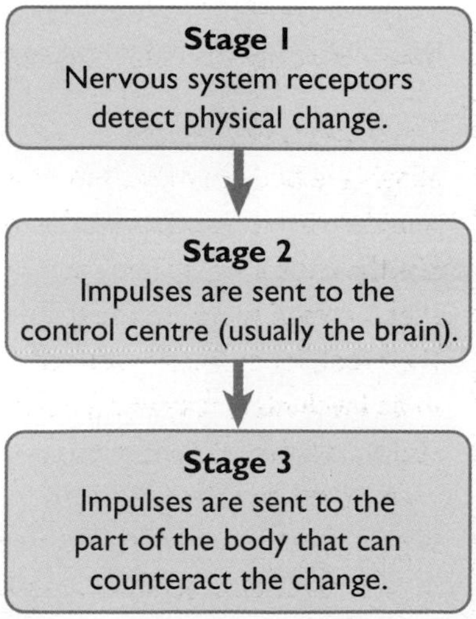

Stage I
Nervous system receptors detect physical change.

Stage 2
Impulses are sent to the control centre (usually the brain).

Stage 3
Impulses are sent to the part of the body that can counteract the change.

Figure 10.17 Negative feedback system

Maintenance of body temperature

Body temperature is controlled through a negative feedback system: changes in temperature are detected and corrective action is taken to keep core body temperature constant. This is vital to prevent the body's internal organs from overheating. The body will respond to:

- hot conditions by losing heat to keep the core cool
- cold conditions by retaining heat to keep the core warm.

Temperature receptors in the skin and around internal organs pick up and report changes in temperature to the brain. The brain then responds by switching on either the body's heat loss or heat retention mechanisms.

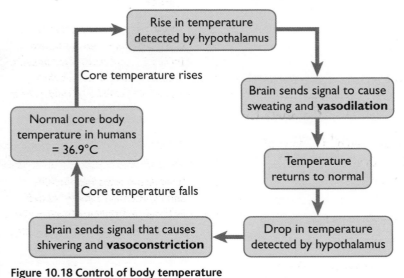

Figure 10.18 Control of body temperature

Your assessment criteria:

2A.D1 Analyse how body systems interrelate to maintain one example of homeostasis in the human body

A drop in normal body temperature triggers off a negative feedback system in the body

Case study

When Lianne, aged 18, left home to go to a birthday party, the weather was dry but a little windy. Lianne was wearing a short-sleeved top and jeans. She decided not to take a coat or a sweater, even though her mum warned her she would be cold. Lianne had a great time at the party and was almost the last to leave at 2.30am. As there were no buses, Lianne decided to walk home with a friend. She started feeling cold as soon as she began the three-mile walk. At first she rubbed her arms but then noticed she was shivering and that her hands and feet were getting colder and colder. After about 20 minutes' walking Lianne had warmed up a bit, but she didn't feel really warm until she was in bed at home.

1. How did Lianne's body react to the change in temperature when she left the warmth of the party?

2. Explain why Lianne's hands and feet became colder when she first started to walk home.

3. Describe how a negative feedback system worked to control Lianne's body temperature in this situation.

Maintenance of blood pressure

Control of a person's heart rate and blood pressure are linked. Heart beat is automatically controlled by the cardiovascular centre in the brain. The pumping action of the heart creates and maintains pressure in the person's arteries.

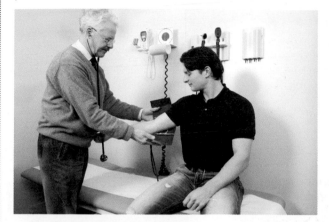

Blood pressure checks are a feature of many healthcare consultations

The rate at which a person's heart beats is affected by a number of factors including age, weight, fitness and whether they smoke. Rapid change in the heart rate is caused by excitement, fear and physical exertion. Receptors in the individual's **sympathetic nervous system** send messages to the control centre in the brain to increase heart rate in these circumstances.

Receptors in the **parasympathetic nervous system** send messages to the brain to decrease heart rate when the excitement, fear or physical exertion stops. In both cases, receptors detect changes in the levels of carbon dioxide and oxygen in the blood. A person's arteries widen to slow down the rate of blood flow in the body — lowering blood pressure — and narrow to increase blood pressure.

Maintenance of oxygen supply

A person's breathing is controlled by their brain. A negative feedback system uses nerve impulses to adjust the rhythm, depth and rate of breathing when receptors detect either a decrease or an increase in the amount of carbon dioxide in the blood:

- during exercise or exertion a person will have a high level of carbon dioxide in their bloodstream

- when resting and relaxed they will have a low carbon dioxide level.

Key terms

Parasympathetic nervous system: part of the autonomic nervous system (page 274) that slows heart rate, slows breathing and lowers blood pressure

Sympathetic nervous system: part of the autonomic nervous system (page 274) that raises blood pressure and heart rate and narrows the arteries when the body is under stress

Investigate

What do the terms 'hypertension' and 'hypotension' refer to? As well as finding a definition of each, make a list a three possible causes of each condition.

When carbon dioxide levels are high, receptors report this to the brain which quickens and deepens the person's breathing rate so that they breathe out more carbon dioxide and obtain more oxygen.

Good fitness and regular training are needed to keep the body supplied with oxygen during strenuous activities like running

Maintenance of blood glucose levels

Blood glucose level is also controlled by a negative feedback system – the pancreas is the control centre. It monitors how much glucose is in the bloodstream and whether there is sufficient insulin and glucagon to maintain a correct blood glucose level. A person's blood glucose level, and their negative feedback system, is affected by food:

- shortly after eating a meal a person will have a high blood glucose level

- when they are hungry they will have a low blood glucose level.

Your assessment criteria:

2A.D1 Analyse how body systems interrelate to maintain one example of homeostasis in the human body

 Investigate

What do the terms 'hypoglycaemia' and 'hyperglycaemia' refer to? Write a definition of each and identify how each can be treated.

Case study

Andrew was driving from Scotland to Portsmouth and hadn't eaten for over 10 hours. He was determined to complete his drive to a holiday cottage in France with as few stops as possible. When he got to the ferry he felt weak, tired and had poor concentration. He almost hit a post as he drove onto the ship! Andrew thought he'd better have something to eat as he had another long drive ahead of him when the ferry reached France. After eating a meal and drinking a cup of coffee, Andrew felt much less tired and much more alert. He also bought a sandwich and some chocolate to eat on the next leg of his journey.

1. Give a biological explanation for the way Andrew felt when he arrived at the ferry.

2. How would eating a meal boost Andrew's blood glucose levels?

Disorders relating to body systems

Disease, illness and malfunctioning body systems

The human body is often compared to a machine. When all of the parts are in good condition and working properly, the machine performs well. However, parts of the machine can break, get damaged or deteriorate. When this happens, the machine malfunctions. In medical terms, illnesses and diseases are the main causes of malfunctioning body systems. Different illnesses and diseases affect different body systems. Some are temporary and can be treated and even cured; others have long-term effects and can cause death.

Circulatory system disorders

The circulatory system is the system of organs that is responsible for passing nutrients, gases, hormones and blood cells around the human body. Relatively common disorders of the circulatory system include hypertension, coronary heart disease and deep vein **thrombosis**.

Hypertension

Hypertension, or high blood pressure, is usually defined as having a sustained blood pressure of 140/90 hg or higher. Over time this can weaken the heart and damage the walls of the arteries. High blood pressure can lead to blockages in arteries, or to the arteries splitting and haemorrhaging (bleeding). There are no obvious symptoms of high blood pressure. A doctor or a nurse uses a sphygmomanometer to measure an individual's blood pressure and diagnose hypertension. Risk factors for hypertension include:

- age and poor diet

- obesity and lack of exercise

- excessive alcohol consumption.

Key term

Thrombosis: a blood clot that forms within an artery

Investigate

Find out why hypertension is a worrying symptom in pregnancy. What condition can it be a sign of?

Coronary heart disease

Coronary heart disease (CHD) happens when a person's arteries become clogged with **atheroma plaques**. As the arteries narrow, oxygenated blood is gradually prevented from reaching the heart. Symptoms include:

- breathlessness
- chest pain
- **oedema**
- **cyanosis**
- weakness
- sweating.

Partial blockage of the arteries leads to angina or chest pain. Complete blockage leads to death of a section of heart muscle (heart attack). A person may develop CHD because of a genetic predisposition or because of lifestyle factors. Smoking, eating an unbalanced, fatty diet, lack of exercise, high blood pressure and high stress levels all increase the risk.

Deep vein thrombosis

A deep vein thrombosis (DVT) develops when a blood clot forms in one of the deep veins of the body, typically in one of the deep leg veins running through the muscles of the calf and thigh. The main symptoms are pain and swelling, sometimes accompanied by a feeling of warmth and a heavy ache in the affected part of the leg. Further serious complications may occur if a piece of the blood clot breaks off and moves through the arteries to block a blood vessel in the lung. This is called a pulmonary embolism (PE).

Approximately 1 in 1000 people in the UK is affected by DVT every year. Anyone can develop the condition, but the main risk factors are:

- increasing age
- previous venous thromboembolism (DVT and PE)
- family history of thrombosis
- certain medical conditions, such as cancer and heart failure
- inactivity (especially due to illness or after surgery)
- being very overweight (obese).

The risk of DVT can be reduced by:

- not smoking
- losing weight (if overweight)
- regular walking or other suitable exercise to improve (blood) circulation.

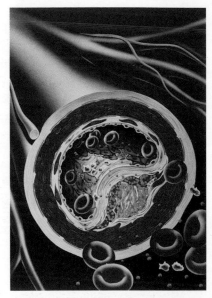

Coronary heart disease is caused by plaques, or fatty deposits, narrowing the artery wall and preventing blood flow.

Investigate

Using the British Heart Foundation website (www.bhf.org.uk) investigate the factors that cause coronary heart disease (CHD) and ways of preventing this. Produce a leaflet or poster about CHD summarising your findings.

Respiratory system disorders

The respiratory system consists of the lungs and airways that introduce oxygenated air into the body and remove deoxygenated air and waste gases from the body. Damage to the organs or tissues that make up the respiratory system can have a serious effect on a person's ability to breathe and carry out everyday activities. Bronchitis and asthma are examples of respiratory system disorders.

Bronchitis

Bronchitis is caused by inflammation of the bronchioles of the lungs. If left untreated, bronchitis is a disease that can cause irreversible damage to these parts of the respiratory system. Bronchioles are the tubes that link the larger bronchus to the alveoli where oxygen and carbon dioxide are transferred into and out of the blood.

Inflammation of the bronchioles can be caused by exposure to smoke, dust, air pollution or chemicals. Mucus is produced in response to this inflammation and gradually blocks the bronchioles. This causes tightness in the chest, breathlessness and wheezing, and coughing that is often painful. Repeated, hard coughing to remove the mucus can further damage the bronchioles, scarring and making them narrower.

People who suffer from chronic bronchitis often develop chest infections and go on to develop emphysema (a condition in which the structure of the alveoli begins to breakdown). Weight loss, drug therapies, exercise and stopping smoking may all help to relieve the symptoms of chronic bronchitis.

Asthma

Asthma is a condition that affects the respiratory system. It is an allergic response to **allergens** that cause irritation and inflammation in the bronchi or large air passages in the lungs. The bronchi become obstructed with mucous and an inflammatory response occurs in which the air passages narrow. This results in the person wheezing, coughing and struggling for breath.

Asthma is a condition that can be inherited, may be triggered by childhood infections and is associated with environmental factors, such as cigarette smoke, animal hair, dust mites and air pollution. A person may be prescribed a bronchial inhaler (usually brown, red or orange in colour) that they use regularly to prevent the swelling and inflammation that can trigger an asthma attack. Alternatively, some people carry inhalers (usually blue) can be used during an attack to relieve swelling and relax the muscles that are needed for breathing.

Your assessment criteria:

1B.5 State one common disorder related to each of three selected major body systems

2B.P5 Describe one common disorder related to each major body system

2B.M3 Explain in detail the effects of three common disorders on the major body systems

🔑 Key term

Allergen: any substance that causes an allergy

People with asthma use inhalers to prevent or relieve swelling and inflammation in their airways

Case study

Rachel, aged 22, was diagnosed with asthma after experiencing coughing, wheezing and sudden, unexpected breathlessness whilst out shopping. She was taken to hospital by ambulance. During the short trip, a worried paramedic gave her oxygen to help her breathing. Rachel found this very helpful. On admission to the accident and emergency department, Rachel produced a peak flow score of 70. This improved after she was given some medication but was still only 300 when she was discharged later in the morning. Rachel's GP has now prescribed preventer and reliever inhalers to help her cope with her asthma symptoms.

1. Identify three symptoms of asthma.

2. Explain why people who have asthma become breathless.

3. Describe the biological reasons why Rachel's peak flow score improved.

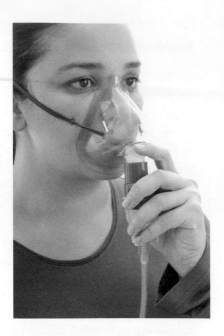

Nervous system disorders

The human nervous system is responsible for the co-ordination of different actions and sends signals all over the body. The central nervous system (CNS) consists of the brain and spinal cord. The peripheral nervous system consists of nerves or long fibres that connect the CNS to other parts of the body. Disorders of, or damage to, the nervous system can result in a person losing control of a part of their body or losing a specific function (such as speech) that relies on good nervous system function.

Stroke

A stroke occurs when a blood vessel in the brain becomes blocked or bursts, depriving part of the brain of sufficient oxygen. This loss of oxygen typically results in the failure of the brain to send or receive signals in the usual way. The effects of a stroke depend on which parts of the brain are affected by the loss of oxygen and often include loss of speech (sometimes temporarily), loss of movement on one or both sides of the body, confusion and memory loss. Coma and death can occur if the stroke affects the person's brainstem.

Sensory impairment

Damage to the nerves of the peripheral nervous system can result in a person experiencing loss of feeling in part of their body, such as their feet, fingers or legs. Damage to the sensory nerves can also cause a tingling feeling, numbness or a burning pain.

Your assessment criteria:

1B.5 State one common disorder related to each of three selected major body systems

2B.P5 Describe one common disorder related to each major body system

2B.M3 Explain in detail the effects of three common disorders on the major body systems

 Investigate

To find out more about stroke, go to the NHS Choices website (http://www.nhs.uk) and search for 'Stroke – Act F.A.S.T'.

Parkinson's disease

Parkinson's disease is a chronic neurological condition that affects the way the brain co-ordinates body movements. It can affect walking, talking and a person's ability to hold and use objects (such as cutlery). Parkinson's disease results from the loss of nerve cells in the brain. Without these cells, movement becomes progressively difficult. People with Parkinson's disease typically have a tremor, difficulty moving even slowly, and stiff or rigid muscles. Parkinson's disease is not fatal but can cause significant disability.

Multiple sclerosis

Multiple sclerosis (MS) is a neurological condition that can affect people at any age. It is caused by damage to a protective substance called myelin that surrounds the nerve fibres of the nervous system. Myelin helps messages travel quickly and smoothly from the brain to other parts of the body. When myelin is damaged, the messages get disrupted and mobility, balance and muscle problems occur. The precise cause of MS is not known and there is no cure at present – the condition is not fatal, but can reduce a person's quality of life. There are many treatments that can ease symptoms.

Digestive system disorders

The digestive system is responsible for breaking down food – and drink – into small units (nutrients) that can be absorbed by the body for use as energy and as building blocks for cells. Digestive system disorders occur when part of the digestive tract malfunctions or becomes diseased.

Bowel cancer

Bowel cancer is a disease of the intestines that typically starts in a part of the large bowel (colon or rectum). It is the third most common cancer in England. The signs and symptoms of bowel cancer include:

- blood in stools (faeces)

- unexplained changes in bowel habits (such as prolonged diarrhoea or constipation)

- unexplained weight loss.

The majority of cases of bowel cancer occur in those who are 65 years of age or older. Eating too much red or processed meat increases the chance of developing bowel cancer. However, a diet that is high in fibre and low in saturated fats can reduce the chance. Similarly, regular exercise can help to prevent the disease, whereas being inactive increases the risk. Alcohol consumption, smoking and a family history of bowel cancer also increase an individual's risk of developing the disease.

Investigate

Go to NHS Choices, search for 'Parkinson's disease' and watch the short video called 'Karen's story' to find out about the impact this condition can have on a person's life.

Cholecystitis

Cholecystitis is a condition that occurs when a gallstone (a small 'stone' usually made of cholesterol) becomes trapped in a duct or opening of the gallbladder, causing the gallbladder to become inflamed (swollen). The gallbladder stores bile, a digestive fluid produced by the liver to help break down fatty foods. A common symptom of acute cholecystitis is severe, sharp and constant pain in the upper right of the abdomen which may worsen when the person breathes deeply or when the abdomen is touched. A fever of 38°C (100.4°F) and above is also common.

Antibiotics may relieve the symptoms, though surgical removal of the gallbladder may also be required in some cases. Without treatment this condition can have serious complications, including death of gallbladder tissue leading to serious infection or the gallbladder may split (perforate). An immediate referral to hospital should always be made if acute cholecystitis is suspected.

Irritable bowel syndrome

Irritable bowel syndrome (IBS) is a common condition of the digestive system. It usually starts when a person is between 20 and 30 years of age, causing bouts of stomach cramps, bloating, diarrhoea and constipation. Symptoms typically develop when a person experiences stress or after eating certain foods. The symptoms and their severity vary greatly between individuals.

The cause of IBS is unknown. Disruption in the normal digestion process, particularly a change in the body's ability to move food through the digestive system, and increased sensitivity to pain from the gut are thought to be possible causes. There is currently no cure for IBS, but symptoms can be managed through diet and lifestyle changes and anti-inflammatory medication.

Renal system disorders

The renal, or urinary, system consists of the organs, tubes, muscles and nerves that work together to create, store and carry urine. This includes two kidneys, two ureters, the bladder, two sphincter muscles, and the urethra. Ageing, injury or illness can cause renal system disorders.

Urinary tract infection (UTI)

UTIs are very common, particularly in females. They usually result from a bacterial infection. UTIs in males are much less common and need medical investigation because there may be an underlying physical cause, such as narrowing of the urethra or prostate gland problems. UTIs can be very painful and uncomfortable, but usually pass within a few days, being easily treated with antibiotics.

Investigate

Go to NHS Choices, search for 'Irritable bowel syndrome' and watch the short video about Ansar's experience of living with irritable bowel syndrome for 20 years.

The signs and symptoms of a UTI include:

- pain or a burning sensation when urinating
- the need to urinate more often
- pain in the lower abdomen.

It is important that a person sees their GP if the symptoms suddenly worsen or last for more than five days. The risk of developing a UTI can be reduced by:

- maintaining good personal hygiene (especially of the genital area)
- emptying the bladder after sex
- drinking cranberry juice.

Renal failure

One of the main functions of the kidneys is to remove waste from the body. Urea is a waste product that is extracted from the blood and passes along the ureter to the bladder for elimination in urine. However, if kidney function is impaired or fails, waste products like urea build up in the blood.

Acute renal (kidney) failure can occur if the blood supply to the kidneys is insufficient, if there is a fall in overall blood pressure, or if severe dehydration, a lack of salt or a blockage in the proper drainage of urine from the kidneys occurs. Chronic renal failure can occur if urine doesn't drain from the kidneys properly, if the kidney tissue becomes inflamed or because of complications associated with diabetes.

Symptoms include:

- nausea, vomiting and diarrhoea
- high blood pressure
- sudden inability to drain urine
- fluid retention such as swollen ankles
- tiredness
- loss of appetite
- weakness.

Acute renal failure can usually be treated by drugs and short-term dialysis (cleaning) of the blood. Chronic renal failure generally requires long-term dialysis, drug treatment and eventually a kidney transplant.

Investigate

To find out more about urinary tract infections (UTIs), go to the NHS Choices website (http://www.nhs.uk) and search for 'Urinary Tract Infection'.

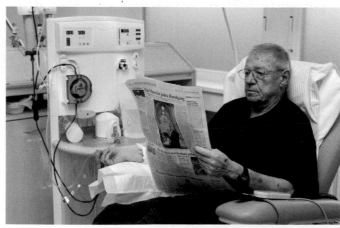

A person with renal failure may need kidney dialysis for the rest of their life, unless they have a kidney transplant

Endocrine system disorders

The endocrine system consists of a network of organs and glands that are responsible for producing, storing and secreting the hormones that help to maintain and control vital functions such as growth, reproduction and maintenance of energy levels. Endocrine system disorders result from disruption to this system.

Diabetes

Diabetes occurs as a result of a person's blood glucose (sugar) levels being too high. A person's blood glucose levels can be too high because:

- their pancreas produces little or no insulin (Type 1 diabetes)

- the cells in their body do not respond properly to the insulin they produce, which may also be at lower levels than normal (Type 2 diabetes)

- pregnancy is affecting the way their body functions (Gestational diabetes)

- illness or medication are affecting the way their body functions (Secondary diabetes).

Insulin is a hormone produced by the pancreas to enable glucose to enter the cells and be used as energy. A sufficient supply of insulin is needed to control blood glucose levels.

Symptoms of diabetes include:

- increased thirst

- frequent urination

- weight loss

- itchiness around the genitals

- recurrent skin infections.

Diabetes can be an inherited condition, though lifestyle and viruses also play a part in its development. Approximately 2.3 million people have diabetes in the United Kingdom. Poor diet, obesity and other lifestyle problems have resulted in an increase in Type 2 diabetes over the last 20 years. Most people can manage their diabetes and stay healthy by limiting the sugar and fat content of their diet, and taking regular exercise. In some cases, people also need to monitor their blood glucose levels and take insulin.

People with type 1 diabetes need to regularly inject insulin to treat their condition

 Investigate

To find out more about type 1 and type 2 diabetes, go to the NHS Choices website (http://www.nhs.uk) and search for 'Diabetes'.

Thyroid gland disorders

The thyroid gland is located in the neck. It releases hormones into the bloodstream that control the body's growth and metabolism. An overactive thyroid speeds up the body's metabolism, affecting heart rate, body temperature and conversion of food into energy. Symptoms of an overactive thyroid include:

- nervousness and anxiety

- hyperactivity

- unexplained or unplanned weight loss

- goitre (a swollen thyroid gland which is located in the neck).

Overactive thyroid is a relatively common disorder. It can start at any age, typically between 20 and 40 years of age, and is ten times more common in women. Treatment generally involves taking medication to control the production of thyroid hormones. In a few cases surgery may be needed to remove some or all of the thyroid gland.

The thyroid gland can also be underactive in some people, producing insufficient hormones for the body to function effectively. Common signs and symptoms of an underactive thyroid include:

- tiredness

- weight gain

- feeling depressed

- sensitivity to cold temperatures

- dry skin and hair

- muscle aches.

An underactive thyroid is not usually a serious health condition and can easily be treated with hormone tablets that boost the person's thyroxine hormone levels. An underactive thyroid is not always easy to detect as the signs and symptoms may be confused for other issues and conditions. If untreated, however, it may lead to problems such as goitre (swelling of thyroid gland), heart disease, mental health problems and infertility. Thyroid function blood tests, organised by a GP, are used to measure an individual's hormone levels. In their first week of life, babies have a routine heel-prick to give a blood sample to screen for an underactive thyroid.

Reproductive disorders

Reproductive system disorders affect the structure and function of an individual's reproductive organs.

Investigate

Watch the video of an endocrinologist explaining what causes an overactive thyroid on the NHS Choices website (http://www.nhs.uk). You can find it by searching for 'overactive thyroid'.

Cervical cancer

Cervical cancer is a relatively uncommon disorder of the cervix (the entrance to the womb from the vagina). Over many years the cells lining the surface of the cervix undergo changes. In some people, these cells can become cancerous.

There are often no obvious symptoms in the early stages of cervical cancer. If symptoms do occur, the most common is abnormal bleeding which should be checked by a GP. Almost all cases of cervical cancer are caused by a type of virus (Human papillomavirus, HPV) that is spread during sex. Women should undergo regular cervical smear tests to detect early signs of the disease. A cervical smear test involves taking a small sample of cells from the cervix and checking for abnormalities under a microscope. Treatment depends on the stage of the cancer and may involve surgery (removal of some cervical tissue, or of the whole womb), radiotherapy or chemotherapy.

Testicular cancer

Testicles are an important part of the male reproductive system because they produce sperm and the hormone testosterone which plays a major role in male sexual development. Testicular cancer is a relatively uncommon reproductive disorder, accounting for approximately 1 per cent of all cancers in men and usually affecting younger men (aged 15–44 yrs). The main symptoms are:

- most commonly, a painless lump or swelling in the testicle(s)
- a dull ache in the scrotum (the sac of skin containing the testicles)
- a feeling of heaviness in the scrotum.

The cause(s) of testicular cancer are unknown, but a family history of testicular cancer or having had an undescended testicle(s) at birth both increase a person's chance of developing the disease. Fortunately, it is one of the most treatable cancers (with chemotherapy or surgery to remove the affected testicle) and there is a good outlook for sufferers.

Infertility

There are many reasons why a couple may not be able to produce a baby. Both a woman's inability to conceive and a man's inability to impregnate a woman with healthy, active sperm are called infertility. Infertility can result from problems with either the man or the woman's reproductive system but can also occur for no obvious physical reason. Typical reasons for infertility include, for example:

- hormone imbalance (male or female)
- blocked fallopian tubes (female)
- low sperm count (male)
- erectile dysfunction (male).

Investigate

The fertility unit at your local hospital has decided to update the information they give to people who use their services. The most common question asked by couples who come for a consultation is: 'Why can't we produce a baby?' The second most popular question is: 'How can you help us to have a baby?' You have been asked to:

- *produce an information leaflet that explains the causes of infertility*

- *describe forms of treatment that are used to help infertile couples to conceive.*

Use the Internet, libraries and other resources to obtain suitable information. You should then use your findings to design and produce a clear, easy-to-follow information leaflet.

Sexually transmitted infections

Each year sexually transmitted infections (STIs) affect about one million men and women in the United Kingdom. STIs are caught through unprotected sex with an infected person. A person can become infected with an STI after a single act of unprotected sex with another infected person. Young sexually active people are most at risk. The most common sexually transmitted disease is chlamydia which can cause serious problems, such as pelvic inflammatory disease (PID) and inflammation of the fallopian tubes (oviducts) if it is not treated. However, it isn't fatal and people recover after treatment. Other STIs include:

- gonorrhoea

- genital warts

- herpes

- public lice ('crabs')

- HIV (human immunodeficiency virus).

People who do not use condoms and spermicides during sex run a higher risk of catching sexually transmitted diseases.

Investigate

Use medical reference books or a website such as www.teenagehealthfreak.com or www.avert.org to find out more about the causes, symptoms and longer-term consequences of a range of sexually transmitted infections.

Musculoskeletal disorders

The musculoskeletal system gives the body support, stability and movement. Musculoskeletal disorders affect the body's muscles, joints, tendons, ligaments and nerves.

Osteoarthritis

Osteoarthritis is the most common form of arthritis in the UK, affecting mainly women and those over 50 years old. The key characteristics of osteoarthritis are:

- mild inflammation of tissues in and around joints (usually knees, hips and hands)

- damage to cartilage (the smooth surface covering of bones that allows joints to move easily and without friction)

- bony growths that develop around the edge of joints.

Osteoporosis

Osteoporosis is a bone disease in which the mineral density and strength of a person's bones is reduced. This increases the risk of a person experiencing bone fractures. Osteoporosis tends to be found in women who have experienced the menopause, but is also common in men and women over the age of 75.

Routine care of disorders

Care needs

This topic focuses on the types of care needs of people who have bodily malfunctions. It also outlines health and safety and risk factors associated with providing care.

People who develop physical health problems because one of their body systems malfunctions may require treatment and care at home or in hospital. A person's care needs may include:

- monitoring of their physical condition for signs of change (deterioration or improvement)

- pressure-area care to prevent ulcers and other skin problems from developing

- ensuring that they are warm and comfortable

- education, support and encouragement to eat a healthy diet, exercise, stop smoking or take prescribed medication, for example

- monitoring of their blood glucose levels (for example, if they are diabetic)

- ensuring they are as physically active as they can be to minimise the risk of thrombosis

- protection from infection and from any other health and safety hazards within the home or care setting.

Your assessment criteria:

1B.6 Identify the routine care given for one common disorder for each of three selected major body systems

1B.7 Carry out and record over a period of time one routine observation that can be used to support care

2B.P6 Describe the routine care given for one common disorder related to each major body system

2B.P7 Carry out and record over a period of time one routine observation that can be used to support care, interpreting your results in relation to norm values

2B.M4 Discuss the impact of routine care given to individuals, with reference to a selected example

2B.D2 Recommend and justify appropriate routine care for a selected individual with a common disorder

---

⚲ Key term

Thrombosis: *a blood clot that forms within an artery*

A person's need for care will be affected by:

- lifestyle factors, such as whether they smoke, exercise, misuse drugs or alcohol, and consume a balanced diet

- environmental factors, such as their housing conditions, the area where they live and whether they have support from other people

- inherited factors, such as their family history and whether they have inherited any genetically transmitted diseases or disorders

- exposure to infections, including whether they are carrying an infection (such as MRSA or HIV) which may affect their ability to recover from health problems.

Regular monitoring and support of disorders

Health care workers who provide care for those with physical and mental health problems try to do so in ways that meet individuals' needs without reducing their independence. A balance has to be found between enabling individuals to care for themselves and providing sufficient support; the importance of encouraging individuals to do as much as possible for themselves to maintain their independence, self-care skills and physical abilities should not be underestimated. Good practice includes asking an individual what they can do for themselves and only then providing assistance where they clearly cannot carry out self-care tasks independently.

As part of a monitoring and support role, health and social care workers may carry out:

- blood, urine and other tests to diagnose disorders (such as hypertension, diabetes or urinary tract infection) and monitor physical functions

- provide and demonstrate the use of adaptive equipment and mobility aids to maximise an individual's self-care skills and independence, if they have been affected by stroke, osteoporosis or Parkinson's disease, for example

- advising and supporting, physiotherapy, creative activities or other forms of treatment to promote and maintain physical and mental health (as part of treatment for cancer, multiple sclerosis or renal failure, for example)

- prescribe and monitor the management of a person's medication – for thyroid disorders, coronary heart disease or infertility, for example

- support an individual to self-administer medication (such as tablets, injections or topical creams) for conditions like diabetes, asthma and deep vein thrombosis.

Mobility support and help with personal care are part of the routine care of many disorders

Table 10.1 Ways of meeting individual needs

Type of care need	Examples of care or assistance that may be required
Dietary needs	• Helping with the choice and consumption of a healthy, balanced diet for people who are acutely ill or chronically sick (all conditions) • Providing information and guidance on special diets (e.g. for people with IBS) • Assistance with eating and drinking (perhaps following a stroke) • Monitoring a person in case they choke on their food (for example, after a person has had a stroke)
Monitoring of condition	• Regular measurement of blood pressure and pulse (if a person has hypertension or coronary heart disease) • Blood and urine tests (for urinary tract infection, diabetes or deep vein thrombosis) • Examination and observation of a physical condition (asthma, for example) • Specific tests or scans to check on a condition and a person's response to treatment (e.g. for infertility, thyroid disorder or osteoporosis)
Pressure-area care	• Monitoring and examination of skin condition (for people with diabetes or who have had a stroke) • Regular movement or turning to ensure skin doesn't break down (for immobile multiple sclerosis, stroke and osteoporosis sufferers) • Treatment and monitoring of any areas of dry or broken skin to minimise and cure problems resulting from immobility or illness (such as stroke, multiple sclerosis or renal failure)
Prevention of hypothermia	• Monitoring of body temperature to ensure it is within the normal range • Management of the environment to ensure adequate warmth • Ensuring appropriate clothing is available and is worn, both inside and outside of care setting
Maintenance of blood glucose levels	• Regular blood tests to check blood glucose levels • Monitoring to ensure a healthy diet and low sugar intake • Treatment of diabetes using insulin if prescribed
Reduction of thrombosis risk	• Regular exercising of limbs to ensure adequate blood flow (such as when a person has DVT) • Raising of a limb (e.g. leg) if person is unable to self-mobilise, to prevent formation of blood clots • Treatment using anti-coagulant drugs to prevent blood clots forming

Self-monitoring of disorders

Wherever possible health and social care workers should ask the individuals they work with to self-monitor their own conditions and to do what they can to meet their own care needs. For example:

- a person with diabetes may be able to self-monitor their blood glucose levels, give themselves insulin and manage their diet

- a person with a sexually transmitted infection or multiple sclerosis may be encouraged and supported to make lifestyle changes to improve their health status or to maximise their ability to live independently

- developing the ability to self-administer medication is important for people who have long-term conditions such as under-active thyroid, osteoarthritis and diabetes, for example

- maintaining an appropriate environment to avoid hypothermia and to minimise the risk of developing infections.

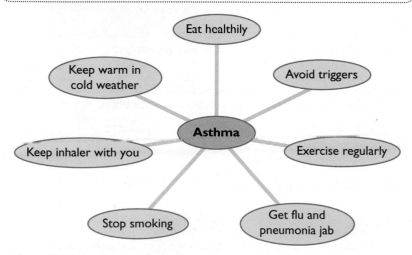

Figure 10.19 Routine care for asthma

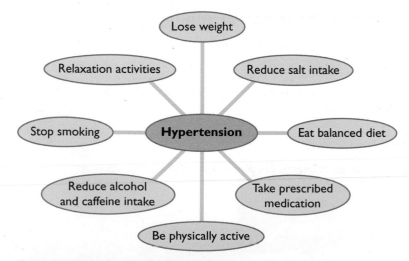

Figure 10.20 Routine care for hypertension

Figure 10.21 Routine care for diabetes

The impact of care

The purpose of providing care and support for people with physical health problems is to relieve pain and suffering, and improve the quality of individuals' lives. For example, effective care can have a positive impact in terms of:

- improving an individual's mobility

- reducing pain and discomfort

- easing an individual's breathing difficulties

- stabilising a person's blood sugar levels and minimising the risks associated with diabetes

- boosting a person's mood, sense of wellbeing and self-confidence by reducing the threat felt from serious or ongoing illness

- enabling a person to maintain their personal and social relationships, and minimising any feelings of being burdensome.

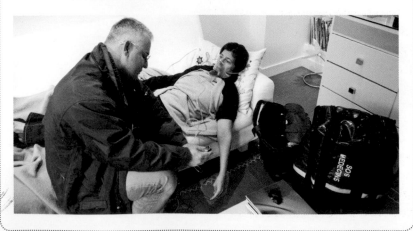

However, being in receipt of care and support for physical health problems isn't always something people welcome or see in a positive way. The negative impacts of care include:

- the financial costs associated with receiving treatment, paying for adaptive equipment or making lifestyle changes

- having to find time to carry out procedures (such as dialysis), travel to appointments and self-monitor for changes in condition

- the side-effects of treatment (especially medication, chemotherapy or radiotherapy) and the consequences of surgery on physical health and wellbeing.

Carrying out and recording routine observations

There are many different methods of measuring physical health, but they are all based on the same basic idea – the health care practitioner measures and records data on an aspect of health and then compares the individual's 'score' against a standard scale. In order to interpret the results of any physical measurement procedure, a health care practitioner has to take into account the individual's age, sex and lifestyle. This is important because a pulse rate of 100 beats per minute would be fast for an adult but normal for a baby, for example.

Taking temperature

Normal body temperature is between 36.5°C and 37.2°C. A person's temperature will vary throughout the day and changes according to their activity level, clothing, whether they are ovulating (if female) and the weather, for example. Regardless of conditions, a thermometer is needed to measure body temperature accurately. A health practitioner would usually place a thermometer under a person's armpit or in their mouth to record their temperature. Core temperature is measured by placing a thermometer in the person's anus. Specialist equipment such as ear thermometers and thermometers strips (which are placed on the forehead) can also be used to measure body temperature if an individual is too young, too unwell or is unable to hold a thermometer in their mouth or under their arm for some other reason.

Taking a pulse

A person's pulse rate indicates how fast their heart is beating. It can be felt in any artery and is a wave of pressure caused by blood being pumped through the arteries by the heart. For adults, the average (or normal) resting rate is usually between 70 and 80 beats per minute. Babies and young children normally have a faster pulse rate than adults.

? Reflect

Do you know how to take a temperature and pulse? Try taking your own temperature (if you have a thermometer available) and your pulse. Compare your own measures against the averages for adults.

 Reflect

How might each of the following factors have an impact on an individual's pulse rate:

- stress

- blood loss

- drugs

- strenuous exercise

- age

- infection

- sleep?

In conscious people, it is usual to take a person's pulse at the radial artery, which can be found in the wrist. In unconscious people, the carotid artery, which can be felt at the neck, may be used. A person's pulse rate increases when they exercise, when they are emotionally upset, or if they develop a form of heart or respiratory disease. Unfit people, smokers and overweight people have a faster resting pulse rate than normal.

Measuring respiration rates

A person's respiration or breathing rate is simply the number of times they take a breath per minute. A healthy adult would be expected to have a breathing rate of 16–18 breaths per minute. Babies and children have a faster breathing rate that slows as their lungs grow and develop to maturity. Breathing rate can be measured by:

- observing and counting the number of times a person's chest rises and falls in 1 minute

- putting your cheek close to the person's nose and mouth (if they are unconscious, for example) and counting the number of breaths you feel on your cheek.

Measuring blood pressure

Health care professionals routinely measure blood pressure, as well as pulse rate. Blood pressure measurement is a direct way of checking heart function (and an indirect way of assessing physical fitness).

Blood pressure is measured with an instrument called a sphygmomanometer or 'sphyg' for short. Some health care professionals use automatic electronic sphygs which display the results on a screen. The other way of measuring blood pressure is to use a manual sphyg, but this is less accurate.

 Investigate

Measure your own, or another person's, pulse rate (using the radial pulse) for 1 minute. Compare the resting pulse rate with the pulse rate taken after some brief exercise.

Investigate

Observe a friend or relative for a few minutes to measure their breathing rate. It's probably best to do this by watching their chest rise and fall rather than feeling their breath on your cheek!

When a person's blood pressure is checked, two measurements are taken by the sphyg:

- systolic blood pressure – the maximum pressure of the blood in the arteries when the heart beats

- diastolic blood pressure – the continuous pressure that the person's blood puts on the arteries between heart beats.

A person's blood pressure is recorded as two numbers. The systolic measure comes first, followed by the diastolic measure. An average healthy young adult will have a blood pressure reading of about 120/80 mm Hg (millimetres of mercury), but blood pressure rises with age and body weight.

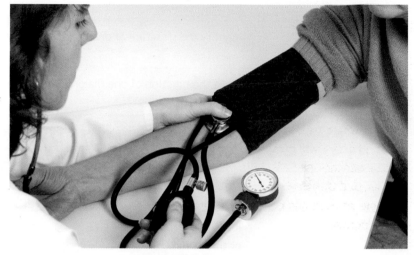

A person's blood pressure fluctuates throughout the day and night. It increases when the person is active and decreases when they are inactive, resting or sleeping. Consistently high blood pressure (hypertension) is linked to a higher risk of heart attacks and

Health care workers are trained to take blood pressure using manual sphygmomanometers like this

strokes. Low blood pressure (hypotension) may be an indicator of heart failure, dehydration or other underlying health problems.

Case study

Edwin recently turned 50 years of age. He was concerned about this birthday because he's always believed that people over the age of 50 suffer from ill health. His parents died of heart and lung diseases when they were in their late 50s. Edwin tries to live a healthy life. However he does smoke 10 cigarettes per day, drinks in moderation and rarely exercises. He was worried enough about his health to go to a private clinic to have a range of health checks carried out. These revealed that his:

- blood pressure is 190/110 mm Hg

- breathing rate is 28 respirations per minute

- pulse is 92 beats per minute.

1. Should Edwin be pleased or worried about the results of his health checks?

2. Describe how Edwin's pulse rate would have been measured.

What kind of blood pressure problem(s) would be cause for concern in someone like Edwin?

 Investigate

Find out what effect each of the following can have on a person's blood pressure:

- *a diet high in fat and salt*

- *regular exercise*

- *stress*

- *cigarette smoking*

- *malnutrition (lack of food).*

Assessment checklist

To achieve level 1, my portfolio of evidence must show that I can:

Assessment criteria	Description	✓
1A.1	Identify the structure and function of three main organs in the human body	
1A.2	Identify the structure of one major body system	
1A.3	State the function of one major body system	
1A.4	Outline the relationship between three of the major body systems	
1B.5	State one common disorder related to each of three selected major body systems	
IB.6	Identify the routine care given for one common disorder for each of three selected major body systems	
1B.7	Carry out and record over a period of time one routine observation that can be used to support care	

To achieve a pass grade, my portfolio of evidence must show that I can:

Assessment criteria	Description	✓
2A.P1	Describe the structure and function of the main organs in the human body	
2A.P2	Describe the structure of major systems in the human body	
2A.P3	Describe the functions of major systems in the human body	
2A.P4	Describe the relationship between major body systems	
2B.P5	Describe one common disorder related to each major body system	
2B.P6	Describe the routine care given for one common disorder related to each major body system	
2B.P7	Carry out and record over a period of time one routine observation that can be used to support care, interpreting your results in relation to norm values	

To achieve a merit grade, my portfolio of evidence must show that I can:

Assessment criteria	Description	✓
2A.M1	Explain the function of component parts of one major system in the human body	
2A.M2	Explain how two major body systems interrelate	
2B.M3	Explain in detail the effects of three common disorders on the major body systems	
2B.M4	Discuss the impact of routine care given to individuals, with reference to a selected example	

To achieve a distinction grade, my portfolio of evidence must show that I can:

Assessment criteria	Description	✓
2A.D1	Analyse how body systems interrelate to maintain one example of homeostasis in the human body	
2B.D2	Recommend and justify appropriate routine care for a selected individual with a common disorder	

11 | Services in health and social care

Learning aim A:
Understand the provision of health and social care services

- ▶ Topic A.1 Provision of health and social care services
- ▶ Topic A.2 Current and relevant legislation

Learning aim B:
Explore factors that affect access to health and social care services

- ▶ Topic B.1 Factors that affect access to health and social care services

Learning aim C:
Examine partnership working in health and social care

- ▶ Topic C.1 Partnership working in health and social care

Provision of health and social care services

Introduction to this chapter

Health and social care services in the UK are provided for a number of different client groups, including children, older people and people with disabilities. Individuals within these and other client groups receive a diverse range of services to meet complex health and social care needs. Gaining access to *appropriate* services and receiving *effective* care from care providers are key issues for many people. This chapter will explore the way health and social care services are provided, factors that affect access to services and partnership working between health and social care service providers.

Your assessment criteria:

1A.1 Outline the provision of health and social care services

2A.P1 Describe the provision of health and social care services

Structure of health and social care services

A range of health and social care services is provided throughout the United Kingdom for people with physical and mental illnesses, physical disabilities and sensory impairments, as well as those with learning disabilities and social support needs. You probably know about a number of health, social care and early years services in your local area. There may be a hospital, health centre, family doctor service, a nursery or a residential home near to where you live, for example. You (or a member of your family) may have used some of these services recently.

Local care services are provided by different types of care organisation and by self-employed care workers. One way of understanding how care services are provided is to look at how they are organised into **primary**, **secondary**, **tertiary** and **informal care** providers.

Key terms

Informal care: *forms of physical and psychological care, practical support and assistance provided voluntarily by the partners, relatives and friends of individuals in need*

Primary care: *general health care provided in community settings*

Secondary care: *health and social care services that are generally provided for people with more complex or emergency care needs in hospital or residential settings*

Tertiary care: *highly specialist care usually provided on an in-patient basis for people with complex needs*

? Reflect

Can you think of examples of a primary, a secondary and a tertiary care service in your local area?

Primary care

Primary care is the term given to essential frontline services that are targeted at individuals within their local community. Practitioners who provide primary health care include GPs (family doctors), opticians, dentists, health visitors and midwives.

Your assessment criteria:

1A.1 Outline the provision of health and social care services

2A.P1 Describe the provision of health and social care services

2A.M1 Discuss the differences in the different types of health and social care provision, with reference to examples

Primary health care services focus on general health assessment, diagnosis and non-emergency treatment services. Primary health care is provided for all client groups in community settings, such as health centres, clinics and service users' homes. Many primary health care providers also offer health education and specialist care services aimed at tackling health problems like smoking, obesity and stress.

Some people need to use primary health care services regularly because they have a **chronic** health problem or a disability that requires continuing treatment or monitoring. However, most people use primary health care services on an occasional basis for minor illnesses.

Secondary care

Secondary care refers to the types of medical, nursing and therapeutic care provided by hospital-based specialists and by social care workers in various settings (see Figure 11.1 on page 304). People who work in secondary care settings generally aren't the first point of contact for a service user. The secondary care worker will usually receive a **referral** from a primary care worker asking them to see an individual who has a specific health or social care need.

? Reflect

Think about the range of care services you have used. Divide your list into health, social care and early years services.

? Reflect

Make a list of the types of events or situations that can result in the need for urgent care or specialist treatment from secondary health care services.

🔑 Key terms

Chronic: long-term or enduring health problems

Referral: a request by one care professional for care services to be provided by another care professional

Most secondary health care is provided by **NHS Trust hospitals**. These are government-funded organisations that have a legal responsibility to provide health care services in a local area. There are a number of different kinds of hospital:

- *District General Hospitals* provide a wide range of secondary health care services for the whole population of an area. For example, they provide services for seriously ill adults and children who need an operation or treatment from specially trained doctors and nurses.

- *Local community hospitals* usually provide a reduced range of treatments for a smaller number of people in a limited area. They often have facilities for people to be seen as out-patients and have far fewer beds than district general hospitals.

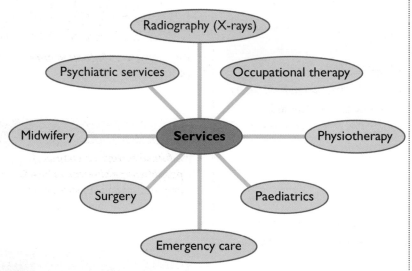

Figure 11.1 Examples of secondary health care services for client groups

Key term

NHS Trust hospitals: *hospitals that provide health care services in England and Wales on behalf of the National Health Service*

Investigate

Using information available through the Internet, leaflets or booklets produced by your local NHS Trust, investigate the services offered by your nearest NHS Trust hospital. What kinds of specialist care and treatment are provided for children? Does the hospital specialise in any other kinds of health care service? Summarise your findings in either a poster or a leaflet.

Case study

Ashok is nine years old. Last Christmas Ashok was admitted to a children's hospital when he fell over on his new roller-blade skates. Ashok broke his ankle and banged his head hard against the pavement. He stayed in the children's hospital for three days whilst tests were done and his ankle was put in plaster. Ashok felt frightened and lonely in hospital and was glad to go home after his short stay.

1. What care needs did Ashok have a result of his accident?

2. What effect did being in hospital have on Ashok's emotional wellbeing?

3. List as many childhood illnesses as you can think of and try to identify the kinds of care or treatment that are provided to deal with them.

Tertiary care

Tertiary care is a third level of highly specialist care, usually for people who have been referred by primary or secondary care workers. Examples of tertiary care services include dementia day care centres, nursing homes, residential care homes, hospices, fostering services and specialist medical services such as renal (kidney) and oncology (cancer) units. There are also a number of national teaching hospitals and specialist units in the United Kingdom that provide highly specialist tertiary care for patients from all over the country. Their expertise is available to both in-patients and out-patients. These include, for example, Great Ormond Street Hospital for Sick Children, the Royal Homeopathic Hospital in central London and Broadmoor Hospital, a secure psychiatric hospital in Berkshire.

Informal care

A variety of informal care services are provided by the very large number of unpaid people who look after their partners, children, relatives, friends or neighbours who have care needs. Because they are not trained, employed or paid to provide care, these people are known as informal carers and they are part of the **informal sector**.

Types of care provision

A second way of understanding how care services are provided is to identify the three different types of organisation providing services. These are:

- statutory provision

- private and independent provision

- voluntary provision.

Statutory provision

By law, the government has to provide some types of care services. The laws that state this are called 'statutes' and this is where the term 'statutory' comes from. Examples of statutory care organisations include the National Health Service (NHS) and local authorities (local councils). The NHS provides statutory health care services for people of all ages throughout the United Kingdom. Local authorities provide social care, social work and some early years services to people in their area, usually through an adult social services department and a children and families department.

An example of informal care provision

 Key term

Informal sector: this consists of people who provide care to friends and relatives on a voluntary basis

? Reflect

Do you know of anyone who is an informal carer? What kinds of care, assistance or support do they provide?

A number of government organisations within England, Wales, Scotland and Northern Ireland are responsible for planning, funding and regulating health and social care services. These are discussed below.

England

Following the Health and Social Care Act (2012), the NHS in England was reorganised. The organisations that make up the NHS now include the following:

- The Department of Health (www.dh.gov.uk) is responsible for planning and funding health and social care provision.

- Public Health England works with local authorities and other organisations on public health issues and protection.

- NHS Trusts provide and deliver NHS services. These can be NHS Foundation Trusts, which have some independence from central government control and are accountable to the local population, or NHS hospital trusts.

- Clinical commissioning groups, made up of GPs, carers, members of the public and other health and care professionals, are responsible for commissioning services for their local population. They work with local authorities to ensure there are sufficient services to meet local care needs.

- Monitor (www.monitor-nhsft.gov.uk) is the independent regulator of Foundation Trusts.

- The Care Quality Commission regulates and inspects providers of health and social care services to ensure a safe, quality service is provided.

- The NHS Commissioning Board (www.healthandcare.dh.gov.uk) supports clinical commissioning groups and is responsible for allocating and accounting for NHS resources. It is also responsible for ensuring that the public and patients are involved in NHS planning for improvements in quality.

Scotland

The devolved parliament in Scotland has been responsible for NHS Scotland since 1999. There are 14 area Health Boards in Scotland. In each area, an NHS Board oversees the NHS locally. Within each Board, Community Health Partnerships manage primary and community services. Healthcare Improvement Scotland checks that providers meet national care standards.

An example of a secondary care provider

Your assessment criteria:

2A.M1 Discuss the differences in the different types of health and social care provision, with reference to examples

2A.D1 Compare national provision of health and social care services to local provision

Wales

The Welsh National Assembly has been responsible for NHS Wales since 1999. Local Health Boards (LHB) commission services and manage the NHS locally. NHS Trust providers, independent contractors and other provider organisations provide services at a local level throughout Wales. Community Health Councils hold NHS Wales to account for the way in which it delivers services and Healthcare Inspectorate Wales (HIW) checks that providers meet national care standards.

Northern Ireland

The Northern Ireland Assembly has been responsible for health and social care care in Northern Ireland since 2007. The Department of Health, Social Services and Public Safety (DHSSPS) is responsible for health, social services and public safety. The Regulation and Quality Improvement Authority (Northern Ireland) checks that providers meet national care standards.

Private and independent provision

The private and independent care sector is made up of care businesses and self-employed care practitioners. Examples of care businesses include private hospitals, domiciliary (home) care companies and care homes. Examples of independent self-employed practitioners include dentists, counsellors and osteopaths, for example. **Private sector** care providers usually charge people a fee for the health and social care services they

provide and work to make a profit. Many of the services they provide aren't available in the **statutory sector** and are specialist, non-emergency services. Cosmetic surgery and osteopathy services are examples.

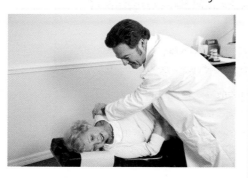

An example of a private sector provider

Voluntary services

The voluntary care sector consists of a large number of charities, local support groups and not-for-profit organisations. **Voluntary sector** organisations:

- provide care services because they see a need for them

- are independent of government

- don't have a legal (or 'statutory') duty to provide care services

- don't try to make a profit and often don't charge for their services

- often recruit workers who are unpaid volunteers.

Your assessment criteria:

1A.1	Outline the provision of health and social care services
2A.P1	Describe the provision of health and social care services
2A.M1	Discuss the differences in the different types of health and social care provision, with reference to examples

---

🔑 Key terms

Department of Health: *the government department responsible for planning and coordinating statutory health care provision*

Private sector: *this consists of care businesses and practitioners who charge for their services*

Statutory sector: *this consists of NHS and local authority organisations that are funded and run by the government*

Voluntary sector: *this consists of registered charities and not-for-profit organisations*

📋 Investigate

Find out where your nearest NHS Hospital is. What is the name of your local authority?

MENCAP is an example of a voluntary sector organisation that recruits volunteers to work with people who have learning disabilities. The *Salvation Army* works with homeless people, while the *Samaritans* provide telephone helpline services to people experiencing mental distress. Voluntary sector organisations often provide social care and early years services.

Care providers in each of the main care sectors make an important contribution to the overall provision of care services in the UK. A care provider usually focuses on providing either health care, social care or early years services. However, in practice, care providers from different sectors (or from different parts of the same sector) often work together to help clients with complex needs. This is called **multi-agency working**.

Case study

Sophie is 17 years of age and has Down's syndrome. Sophie's condition has affected her health and personal development throughout her life and will mean that she has life-long care and support needs. Dr Hill is Sophie's GP. He works at a local NHS health centre. Alison Rasheed is a learning disability social worker, employed by the local authority. Alison organises and monitors the special education and social care services that Sophie uses. Sophie attends the Stepping Stones day centre on three days each week, where she takes part in a range of education and leisure activities. The centre was established and is still managed by MENCAP, a voluntary organisation. Sophie's parents also pay for her to attend a riding school that provides classes for people with learning disabilities. Sophie is still very reliant on her parents for day-to-day care and support. They provide practical and emotional support in a variety of ways to encourage Sophie to develop her daily living skills.

1. Which of the health and social care workers working with Sophie are employed by the statutory sector?

2. Identify the voluntary sector care service that Sophie uses.

3. Which of the services mentioned is part of the private sector?

4. What type of care do Sophie's parents provide for her?

Your assessment criteria:

 1A.1 Outline the provision of health and social care services

 2A.P1 Describe the provision of health and social care services

2A.M1 Discuss the differences in the different types of health and social care provision, with reference to examples

Key term

multi-agency working: *involves care workers from different care organisations or agencies working together*

Investigate

Do you know of any private health or social care practitioners or care businesses offering services in your local area? Make a list of local private sector providers and identify the kinds of services each offers.

Investigate

Can you name three voluntary organisations that provide care services in your local area?

Current and relevant legislation

The legal framework of care

All care homes in England are now regulated by the Care Quality Commission

The provision of health and social care services in the United Kingdom is affected by a range of laws. These laws have been passed to allow or require care organisations to provide services and to function in particular ways.

The National Health Service Act (1948) established, for the first time, a free health service that everyone in the UK was entitled to use. The Family Allowance Act (1945) introduced the first forms of child benefit to support families with children, while the National Insurance Act (1946) and the National Assistance Act (1948) established what has since become the welfare benefits system that provides financial support to those in need.

There have been many more pieces of legislation affecting the provision of care services in the United Kingdom since the birth of the so-called 'welfare state' in 1948. Much of the legal framework of care was passed to create and manage statutory health and social care services. More recently, legislation has been passed to enable and require statutory services to work more effectively with independent sector (private and voluntary) organisations and to regulate standards of care provision.

Key terms

Legislation: written laws

Regulate: to apply rules to an issue or to bring under the control of law

Investigate

The NHS Choices website (http://www.nhs.uk) contains a summary and video about the birth of the NHS. Go to the website and use the search term 'the birth of the NHS' to find out more.

Health and Social Care Act (2008)

The Health and Social Care Act (2008) focuses on the **integration** and regulation of health and social care provision. The Act affects the:

- availability of services

- resources that must be provided to service users

- rights of service users within services

- provision of basic **service-level agreements** by care organisations.

The Act didn't introduce *new* health or social care services, but it does require health and social care service providers to *work together*. It also introduced a system of regulation of health and social care services in order to monitor and maintain national minimum standards of service provision. Under the Act, regulated activities now include:

- provision of health care to patients by a National Health Service Trust or National Health Service Foundation Trust

- provision of ambulance services, for transporting patients for the purpose of treatment by a National Health Service Trust or an National Health Service Foundation Trust

- provision of health care to patients by a Primary Care Trust

- management of NHS Blood and Transplant Services.

The Health and Social Care Act (2008) created the Care Quality Commission as the main regulatory body of health and social care services in England.

Your assessment criteria:

1A.2 Outline one effect of current and relevant legislation on the provision of health and social care services

2A.P2 Outline how current and relevant legislation affects the provision of health and social care services

Key terms

Integration: bringing together and mixing or combining

Service-level agreement: the part of a contract where the service level (for example, ambulance response times, number of beds provided or length of activity sessions) is defined

Investigate

You can find out more about the work of the Care Quality Commission by visiting their website (http://www.cqc.org.uk). You can also use the site to look up the inspection reports about local hospitals or care homes.

The provision of ambulance services is covered by the Health and Social Care Act (2008)

Mental Health Act (1983)

Prior to the Mental Health Act (2007), The Mental Health Act (1983) was the main piece of law affecting the treatment of adults experiencing serious mental disorders in England and Wales. The Mental Health Act (2007) updated previous legislation by seeking to safeguard the interests of adults who are vulnerable because of their mental health problems, ensuring that they can be monitored in the community by care practitioners and admitted to hospital if they don't comply with treatment. The Mental Health Acts of 1983 and 2007 also protect the rights of people who use mental health services in a number of ways. Both Acts give individuals the right to appeal against their detention in hospital and give them some rights to refuse treatment. The 2007 Act particularly gives individuals detained in hospital the right to refuse certain treatments, such as electroconvulsive therapy, and ensures that a person can only be detained in hospital if appropriate treatment is available for them.

Care Quality Commission Regulations (2009)

The Health and Social Care Act (2008) established the Care Quality Commission as the regulator of all health and adult social care services in England. The Care Quality Commission is responsible for ensuring that all health and social care providers are registered and are delivering quality care when providing regulated activities. The Commission's powers as the care standards registration authority include:

- being able to issue financial penalty notices of up to £50,000 for regulatory breaches

- the power to suspend the registration of care providers who do not meet expected standards.

? Reflect

What are the pros and cons of people having a right to refuse treatment for mental illness? Would you want to be able to say 'no' to medication or other forms of treatment if you became mentally unwell?

Factors that affect access to health and social care services

Promoting access to care services

A person may need one-off or continued access to health and social care services because they require:

- care or social support due to health or social problems

- treatment or therapy for physical or mental illness

- developmental support for learning disabilities

- advice or guidance on health or welfare issues.

A range of services are provided nationally and locally to meet the health care, social support and development needs of individuals and local communities. Individuals who require care services can gain access to them through the referral system. There are three main types of referral:

- **Self-referral** occurs when an individual applies for a care service themselves. Making a GP (family doctor) appointment, phoning NHS Direct for advice and information, or going to an opticians for an eye-test are all examples of self-referral to health care services.

- **Professional referral** happens when a health or social care worker puts someone in touch with another care practitioner who can best meet some or all of their health care or social support needs. An example of a professional referral is when a GP refers a patient to a counsellor for therapy.

- **Third-party referral** is when a person who is not a care practitioner applies for a care service on behalf of someone else. For example, if a person phoned their local social services department to request domiciliary services for a neighbour, this would be a third-party referral.

Typically, people in the UK gain access to primary care services through self-referral. Access to secondary and tertiary care services generally requires a professional referral, though there are many exceptions to this. A number of factors influence access to health and social care services and also affect the referral process (see Figure 11.2).

Key terms

Professional referral: a request by one care professional for care services to be provided by another care professional

Self-referral: a direct request by an individual for health or social care services

Third-party referral: referral to care services by someone who isn't a care professional, such as a friend, relative or employer

Reflect

Have you experienced one or more of these types of referral in order to obtain health or social care services? Try to identify a time when you benefited from a referral.

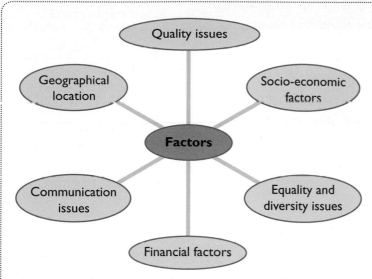

Figure 11.2 Factors affecting access to services

Geographical location

An individual's ability to access the health and social care services they need can be affected by where they live and where the services are located. Health and social care services that are available near to where people live are much easier to access than those that are not. Access to services is a particular problem for people who live in rural (country) areas and is made even worse for people who rely on public transport. Poor transport links, not having access to a car and living some distance from specialist health or social care facilities can mean that the geographical location of services limits access.

Socio-economic factors

A variety of socio-economic factors, including education, health awareness and an individual's lifestyle choices, can affect an individual's use of health and social care services. Few people know about the complete range of health and social care services available in their area. However, individuals who develop their knowledge and understanding of health issues, who have good personal health awareness and who generally make positive, healthy lifestyle choices are more likely to know about and use care services than individuals who lack health knowledge and awareness or who have an unhealthy lifestyle.

Equality and diversity issues

Health and social care services should be equally available and accessible to everyone in the United Kingdom. It is illegal to discriminate against or treat people less favourably on the basis of their race, culture, gender, sexuality or age.

> **? Reflect**
>
> *How far do you have to travel to obtain primary and secondary health care services? Are they located near to where you live or do you face a lot of travelling to get to them? Think about how this affects the way you make use of health care services.*

However, equality and diversity issues can still impact on the ability of people to access and use care services if the diverse needs of a local community are not recognised. For example, members of some religious groups require appointments that do not clash with prayer times and will only receive care from same-sex carers. Sensitivity to gender, sexual orientation, age and ethnicity is important in making care services accessible to individuals from diverse backgrounds.

Communication

Communication issues are closely linked to issues of diversity and respect. In areas where there are large numbers of people from minority ethnic communities, health and social care authorities try to ensure that language barriers are overcome by providing multi-lingual signs, interpreters and bilingual staff. However, health and care information is not always available in the languages that some people speak or in the formats needed by people who have eyesight or hearing problems.

Individual health and social care practitioners need to be aware of how they communicate with service users to ensure that everyone can use services effectively and see staff as respectful. This might involve avoiding jargon and acronyms (better not to say, 'Have you had a UTI recently?', but to explain in full), using age-appropriate language when working with children and young people, and using a person's preferred title (saying 'Mrs James' rather than 'Audrey', for example).

People from minority groups or different cultures, or with hearing or visual impairments, sometimes struggle to obtain care services that meet their cultural, language and communication needs. People will not use care services if they are unable to make themselves understood or if staff lack sensitivity to their particular needs. Adapting to the particular needs of individuals whose first language is not English or who use alternative methods of communication (such as sign language) is a way of overcoming this possible barrier to accessing care services.

Your assessment criteria:

1B.3 Identify factors that positively affect access to health and social care services

1B.4 Identify factors that negatively affect access to health and social care services

2B.P3 Describe factors which positively affect access to health and social care services

2B.P4 Describe factors which negatively affect access to health and social care services

2B.M2 Assess how factors affect access to health and social care services

2B.D2 Make recommendations on how to improve access to health and social care services for a selected individual

Key term

UTI: an abbreviation of 'urinary tract infection'

Financial

Health, social care and early years services are sometimes only available to people if they pay some or all of the cost. For example, in England, if you do not qualify for free services, you have to pay NHS prescription, eye test and dental charges; but if you fall into an exempt group you will receive these free of charge. The financial cost of these and other services can act as a barrier to care for some people. For example, when free eye testing for people over 65 was withdrawn in 1989 there was a dramatic fall in the number of older people having eye tests. The British Medical Association claimed that this led to serious eye diseases and potential causes of blindness going undetected. These free eye tests have now been reintroduced.

A range of health, social care and early years services provided by private sector companies and independent practitioners are available to people who can afford to pay the **fees** for these services. Some people pay into insurance schemes or are given health insurance by their employers to cover these costs. However, many people who would have to pay out of their own pocket are put off by the cost of private sector fees. So, the availability of local NHS and social services, or private funding, has a big influence on whether or not a person can access services.

Other indirect costs, such as the cost of transport to and from appointments, and the loss of income when receiving treatment, can also affect an individual's access to care services. As a result, financial barriers do prevent some people from obtaining some forms of health, social care and early years services that they would otherwise benefit from.

Quality of care provision

People often want to know which care services are 'best' and which might help them most. Care organisations that provide high quality, person-centred services and which have a positive reputation within a local community are more popular than those that don't prioritise individuals' needs or which don't have a good reputation. The quality of care provision in an organisation is closely linked to the way that service users are treated by the health and social care workers who deal with them. Service users expect their rights, wishes and preferences to be respected by health and social care workers and to have their dignity protected. People want to access and use services that meet their expectations in these areas and will avoid services that don't.

 Investigate

How much would you have to pay for a prescription and an eye test if you were not eligible for free services? Find out what the current fees are for these things and think about how such fees might impact on your use of services if you had to pay for them.

 Key term

Fees: *payments for services*

Partnership working in health and social care

Working in partnership

This topic focuses on the different ways in which care organisations work in partnership with each other and with service users in the health and social care sector.

There is an increasing emphasis on **partnership working** within the health and social care sector. Partnership working means that different types of care provider work together. It is likely that health and social care workers with different professional backgrounds (and care organisations or agencies from different parts of the health care sector) are working together to provide services for people in your local area. A health or social care worker might become involved in partnership working through:

- **multi-agency working**
- **multi-disciplinary team** working.

Figure 11.3 Primary care teams are examples of partnership working

Your assessment criteria:

1C.5 Identify professionals who might work in partnership in health and social care

2C.P5 Describe how professionals could work together in partnership in health and social care, using selected examples

Key terms

Multi-agency working: *collaboration between different care organisations*

multi-disciplinary team: *a care team consisting of practitioners from different care professions*

Partnership working: *ways of working together with practitioners from other care professions or other care organisations to provide a joint service*

Purposes of partnership working

The main aim of partnership working is to improve the quality and efficiency of service provision. This can be achieved by:

- using a holistic approach to assessment and care delivery

- identifying and working towards common aims

- integrating health and social care workers into multi-disciplinary teams to maximise expertise

- reducing the duplication of service provision

- ensuring a consistent approach is taken within an area of care practice

- pooling and sharing resources.

Some of the benefits of partnership working include:

- better and quicker access to care services and to the expertise of a range of health and social care workers

- earlier identification of and response to an individual's health, social care and developmental problems

- better links between service providers

- more cost-effective, saving money that can be spent on other services

- more efficient and effective local care services.

Multi-agency working

Health and social care organisations, or agencies as they are sometimes called, work together by setting up:

- **integrated services** using multi-disciplinary teams in which a range of separate services merge together and work in a collaborative way to meet the needs of a particular client group. Community mental health care, child protection and drug and alcohol services usually involve multi-agency working.

Your assessment criteria:

2C.P5 Describe how professionals could work together in partnership in health and social care, using selected examples

2C.M3 Explain the potential benefits of partnership working in health and social care to service users

---

🔑 **Key term**

Holistic: an approach that takes into account the 'whole' person

---

📋 **Investigate**

Sure Start Children's Centres are an example of partnership working in action. Using the Internet and local resources, investigate how partnerships are an important feature of the work of your local Sure Start centre. Try to find out which agencies and care workers are involved, what they do and what they are aiming to achieve. Produce a summary diagram or a brief report to illustrate your findings.

🔑 **Key term**

Integrated services: this is a group of care practitioners providing different but complementary care services

• multi-agency panels in which practitioners employed by a variety of different care organisations meet regularly to discuss individuals with complex needs who would benefit from multi-agency input. Child protection panels are an example of this type of multi-agency service.

Figure 11.4 Practitioners involved in multi-agency working

Statutory health care, early years and social care organisations often work closely with voluntary organisations in their area to:

• identify and assess care needs in the population

• fund and make referrals to voluntary sector services

• obtain information about the experiences of service users and their carers in the local area.

Investigate

What do you know about each of the work roles featured in Figure 11.4? Find out about the ones you haven't heard of before. Write a sentence or two about how each may contribute to an multi-agency child protection team.

Case study

Peter is 64 years of age. He has mental health problems, diabetes and had a serious heart attack a year ago. Peter tries to be as active as he can. He attends a MIND day centre on three days each week, goes to an exercise group at his GP practice for people recovering from heart problems and enjoys socialising with other residents in the small private sector care home where he lives. Peter has a social worker who co-ordinates the care he receives. The people who work with Peter meet a couple of times each year to discuss his needs and what they can do as a team to help him.

1. Identify the different forms of care Peter receives.

2. The organisations and practitioners involved in Peter's care come from all care sectors. Say which organisation belongs to which sector.

3. How does Peter benefit from a partnership approach to his care?

Difficulties of partnership working

It is both government policy and good practice for health and social care organisations to work co-operatively to provide services for individuals as efficiently and effectively as possible. Partnership working between care organisations is usually based on a *local partnership agreement* that sets out the goals and procedures for the partnership organisations. However, despite the best intentions to provide high quality care and support for service users, partnership working can be challenging. There are a number of reasons for this, including:

- professional tensions that can develop when health and social care workers have different priorities or want to adopt different approaches to supporting an individual

- poor communication between care organisations and agencies that can sometimes lead to duplication of services or a person's needs remaining unmet because everybody assumes that somebody else is dealing with the situation

- manipulation of care workers by service users to obtain more support, medication or other resources, or to distract attention away from safeguarding issues

- logistical problems in organising or delivering sufficient care or in providing the right kind of care skills and expertise

- financial constraints imposed by different care organisations that are reluctant to spend their own budget without matched partnership funding

- the breakdown of service provision when organisations fail to take responsibility for delivering their part of a partnership agreement.

Partnership working is an increasingly important feature of health and social care work. It is most effective when organisations and the care workers they employ:

- adopt a person-centred approach to care

- communicate clearly and share information in an appropriate and timely way

- ensure that trust, openness and honesty are a feature of all working relationships

- create a work environment in which there is mutual respect between different workers.

Your assessment criteria:

2C.D3 Assess the potential difficulties of partnership working in health and social care

 Discuss

As part of a small group or with a class colleague, try to identify reasons why a doctor or nurse and a social worker might want to adopt different approaches to supporting a low-income family with a disabled child.

Assessment checklist

To achieve level 1, my portfolio of evidence must show that I can:

Assessment criteria	Description	✓
1A.1	Outline the provision of health and social care services	☐
1A.2	Outline one effect of current and relevant legislation on the provision of health and social care services	☐
1B.3	Identify factors that positively affect access to health and social care services	☐
1B.4	Identify factors that negatively affect access to health and social care services	☐
1C.5	Identify professionals who might work in partnership in health and social care	☐

To achieve a pass grade, my portfolio of evidence must show that I can:

Assessment criteria	Description	✓
2A.P1	Describe the provision of health and social care services	☐
2A.P2	Outline how current and relevant legislation affects the provision of health and social care services	☐
2B.P3	Describe factors which positively affect access to health and social care services	☐
2B.P4	Describe factors which negatively affect access to health and social care services	☐
2C.P5	Describe how professionals could work together in partnership in health and social care, using selected examples	☐

To achieve a merit grade, my portfolio of evidence must show that I can:

Assessment criteria	Description	✓
2A.M1	Discuss the differences in the different types of health and social care provision, with reference to examples	☐
2B.M2	Assess how factors affect access to health and social care services	☐
2C.M3	Explain the potential benefits of partnership working in health and social care to service users	☐

To achieve a distinction grade, my portfolio of evidence must show that I can:

Assessment criteria	Description	✓
2A.D1	Compare national provision of health and social care services to local provision	☐
2B.D2	Make recommendations on how to improve access to health and social care services for a selected individual	☐
2C.D3	Assess the potential difficulties of partnership working in health and social care	☐

12 | Creative and therapeutic activities in health and social care

Learning aim A:
Explore different creative and therapeutic activities used in health and social care and their benefits

▶ Topic A.1 Different creative and therapeutic activities used in health and social care

▶ Topic A.2 Benefits of creative and therapeutic activities

Learning aim B:
Understand how professionals support and encourage individuals who take part in creative and therapeutic activities

▶ Topic B.1 The role of professionals in supporting and encouraging individuals

Learning aim C:
Be able to plan and implement appropriate creative and therapeutic activities in a health and social care setting

▶ Topic C.1 Plan and implement appropriate activities

Different creative and therapeutic activities used in health and social care

Introduction to this chapter

Creative and therapeutic activities are a common feature of treatment plans in health and social care settings. They are used by a variety of different health and social care workers to meet the physical, intellectual, emotional and social needs of people who use care services. Health and social care workers need to have a good understanding of the benefits of different activities, the roles of professionals who use them in care settings and of the factors that influence the selection, planning and implementation of activities in care practice.

Your assessment criteria:

1A.1 Identify three creative and therapeutic activities suitable for individuals or groups in one health and social care setting

2A.P1 Describe three creative and therapeutic activities suitable for individuals or groups in two different health and social care settings

Creative and therapeutic activities

This topic introduces you to a range of creative and **therapeutic** activities used in the health and social care sector. Creative and therapeutic activities are used to:

- help people to acquire, improve and practise a range of physical and intellectual skills and abilities

- enable people to explore and express feelings they may not be able to put into words

- provide opportunities for people to socialise and form relationships.

Creative and therapeutic activities can be used to meet an individual's physical, intellectual, emotional or social needs.

Key term

Therapeutic: *another term for 'healing'*

Reflect

Make a list of creative activities that you have experienced. For each activity, jot down a few words or a phrase that explains the impact on you of participating in the activity. If you had to choose one of these creative activities as a way of 'de-stressing', which one would it be?

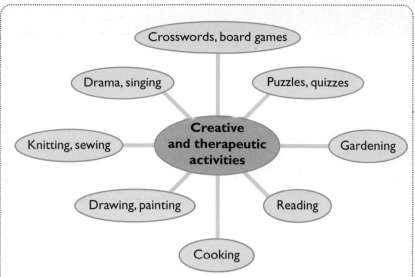

Figure 12.1 Some creative and therapeutic activities

Art and craft activities

Expressive art, photography and craft activities are widely used in settings such as residential care homes, day centres, pre-school groups, children's and family centres. Painting, pottery, photography, making cards and producing collages are popular activities with people of all ages. Art, craft and photography are creative activities that allow people to use their intellectual and physical skills. In some settings, people with mental health problems, learning difficulties or terminal illness use **art therapy** services to explore and express feelings that they find it difficult to talk about.

Creative activities can help learning and development, as well as being therapeutic for children

? Reflect

When was the last time that you took part in an art or craft activity – on your own or as part of a small group? How did it feel to be creative? Did you find it relaxing, exciting, challenging or daunting? Compare your experiences and thoughts with those of a class colleague.

🔑 Key terms

Art therapy: the use of art techniques to improve physical, mental, emotional or spiritual wellbeing

Expressive: a way of communicating thoughts or feelings

Performing arts: drama and music

Drama, role play and music are used in a wide variety of health and social care settings, including hospitals, specialist units for people with learning disabilities and mental health problems, residential care settings for older people and specialist schools. Performing drama or music can help individuals, couples, families or groups of people to express and explore their thoughts, ideas and relationships.

Drama and role play activities can be used to enable people to express difficult or distressing feelings in a safe, supported way

Drama can involve creating and acting in plays, purely for the pleasure of taking part in theatrical activities. However, in care settings **drama therapy** is normally used to help an individual or a group of people to:

- solve a problem

- find out some inner truths about themselves

- explore and correct unhealthy ways of relating to or communicating with others.

Role play and drama can be used to distance a person from the painful issue they want to address – it allows them to 'act out' their thoughts and feelings in a safe and therapeutic way.

Your assessment criteria:

1A.1 Identify three creative and therapeutic activities suitable for individuals or groups in one health and social care setting

2A.P1 Describe three creative and therapeutic activities suitable for individuals or groups in two different health and social care settings

Key term

Drama therapy: the use of theatre techniques to help people to achieve personal growth and promote health

? | Reflect

Can you think of any topics or experiences that a person may find it easier to explore through drama and role play rather than by talking?

Case study

Amanda works in a day centre for young people with emotional and behavioural problems. Some of the people who use the day centre have been referred by the Police or the courts. Amanda has found that they often have low self-esteem, find it hard to talk about their feelings and struggle to be tolerant of others. She uses a drama activity called 'The Empty Chair' to help small groups of these people to improve their self-awareness and their ability to relate to others.

Six people, including Amanda, sit on chairs in a circle. There is also a seventh empty chair to Amanda's right. When everyone is seated Amanda says the activity is about describing people. She tells the group members that if they think she is describing them they should move to occupy the empty chair. The person on the left of the new empty chair then has to carry on by saying, 'There is an empty chair to my right, please sit with me if you are ...' They then describe an obvious physical feature (such as being tall or black, or having long hair).

After a few rounds, Amanda then asks about personal qualities and attributes. For example, she might say:

- 'Sit with me if you are a good friend.'

- 'Sit with me if you are a trusted daughter.'

- 'Sit with me if you are a kind son.'

Next, she moves on to ask about feelings, for example, saying:

- 'Sit with me if you have been happy recently.'

- 'Sit with me if you have been very angry this week.'

- 'Sit with me if you have been lonely lately.'

She then helps the group to talk about these feelings and to try to understand why they get them, and how to cope with the way they feel.

1. How might 'The Empty Chair' activity be therapeutic for the young people at the day centre?

2. Which aspects of their PIES (physical, intellectual, emotional, social) needs does the activity address?

3. Why do we describe 'The Empty Chair' as a drama or role-play activity?

Music can be used in a variety of different ways in health and social care settings. A care practitioner might encourage and support an individual to play an instrument or listen to their favourite music because it brings them pleasure, is relaxing and enables them to maintain their skills and interests, for example. However, **music therapy** is used for therapeutic purposes in the same kind of way as drama therapy. Music therapy can be used to:

- improve learning

- reduce stress

- build self-esteem

- help communication

- support exercise.

Music therapists work in settings where people with learning disabilities, mental health problems, sensory impairments and physical disorders receive care.

Sport and exercise

Physical activities such as dancing, swimming and keep-fit exercise (stretching, pilates or using gym equipment, for example) are used in day care, hospital and community settings. They can be used to help people to:

- relax and de-stress

- communicate without using words

- express difficult emotions

- improve or maintain their physical strength, suppleness and skills.

Key term

Music therapy: the use of music to meet a person's health and wellbeing needs

Investigate

Go to the Nordoff Robbins music therapy website (www.nordoff-robbins.org.uk) and investigate what music therapy involves. Using the 'Frequently asked questions' feature, find out:

- *how music therapy can help people*

- *what a typical music therapy session might involve*

- *what the difference is between music therapy and the other uses of music for therapeutic purposes.*

Movement therapy is a specialist use of movement and exercise activity (usually dance) in care settings. It focuses on strengthening the mind–body connection so that a person can achieve better physical and mental wellbeing. It is used to help and support people with learning and physical disabilities, people experiencing mental health problems, people with sensory impairments and children and young people who have behavioural and emotional problems.

Other forms of exercise include walking and cycling, as well as joining in sports such as football, tennis and cricket in a controlled and supported way. These promote physical fitness and a sense of wellbeing, provide opportunities for people to develop relationships and teamwork-related social skills, for example, and can be therapeutic in terms of relieving stress.

Yoga and massage

Yoga is a combination of breathing exercises, physical postures and meditation. It is used in day care centres, residential homes and other community settings with people who have a wide range of physical conditions and emotional problems. Yoga encourages relaxation and is very helpful for people who are feeling stressed. Some simpler aspects of yoga can be practised immediately by complete **novices**. A trained and experienced yoga teacher would be needed for more difficult, demanding and complex yoga activities.

Massage involves manipulating the soft tissues of the body using gentle movements and pressure. Massage is used to:

- promote relaxation and decrease stress

- improve physical functioning

- promote physical health and wellbeing.

Massage is typically used to help people who have stress-related problems or difficulties with pain.

Key terms

Massage: *physical manipulation of someone's body for medical or relaxation purposes*

Movement therapy: *the therapeutic use of movement (often dance) to support and help people who have emotional, social, intellectual or physical problems*

Novice: *a beginner*

Reflect

Identify a form of exercise (sport or keep-fit, for example) or movement (dancing, for example) that you currently take part in or have participated in at some time in the past. Make some notes on:

- *what you do physically when you take part in this activity*

- *how you feel during and after taking part in the activity*

- *how, if at all, this activity has a therapeutic effect on you.*

Horse-riding and animals as therapy

Therapeutic horse-riding, or adaptive riding, is provided to help people with a range of physical, intellectual, emotional and social problems. Adaptive riding is particularly popular with people who have physical disabilities or learning difficulties. As well as learning to ride a horse, the disabled person can also:

- experience companionship

- learn leadership and decision-making skills

- boost their self-confidence and self-esteem

- learn to take and accept responsibility.

Horse-riding can also be used for leisure and recreation as well as therapy. The skills needed to build a relationship with a horse can be applied to relationships with people, physical fitness can be improved and general enjoyment gained from controlling and working with the horse.

Care settings such as mental health units, nursing homes for older people and early years settings for disabled children may also use animals within their treatment programmes. Animal-assisted therapy aims to improve the functioning and PIES needs of people using care services. Many different types of animals are used to provide comfort, encourage nurturing, reduce loneliness and provide a way of meeting others. People with learning difficulties, such as autism, behavioural problems and mental distress have been shown to benefit from forms of animal-assisted therapy.

Games and quizzes

Games include a wide variety of different pastimes, from playing cards or board games, doing crosswords or Sudoku, to watching or playing sports such as football, rugby or athletics. People can participate in games in different ways – as a player or observer, for example. Games can be played individually or in groups. Health and social care settings tend to have a variety of board games available for patients or residents who want some intellectual stimulation and social activity.

 Investigate

Go to the website of the English Federation of Disability Sport (www.efds.co.uk) and investigate one form of sport adapted for disabled people. As well as identifying the range of sports available for disabled people, try to make a list of the barriers that can prevent disabled people from participating in sport. Produce a poster or summary diagram outlining the opportunities and barriers for disabled people taking part in sport.

Games that require people to solve problems, be competitive or to use strategies to beat an opponent (or another team) can be very involving and exciting. Taking part in games can meet an individual's physical, intellectual, emotional and social needs, depending on the game and the way the person participates.

Taking part in a quiz is a fun and stimulating way of allowing people to use their intellectual abilities and social skills. Quizzes require people to recall knowledge and solve problems. They are often used as a way of bringing people together in small groups to develop and practise their communication and social skills. Getting questions right and scoring points can boost self-esteem. Sharing ideas and bonding with team members can also promote social skills and social relationships.

Gardening and multi-sensory stimulation

Horticultural therapy uses gardening to promote human wellbeing. A horticultural therapist may use all of the phases of gardening, from preparing soil and sewing seeds, to watering plants, through to cropping fruit and vegetables to promote an individual's health and wellbeing. An individual may enjoy gardening on their own or may enjoy being part of a group or team of people involved in a gardening project.

Investigate

Go to the Thrive website (www.thrive.org.uk) and read the section called 'About Thrive' – here you can download a copy of the leaflet called 'Using gardening to change lives'. Use the information you obtain to explain in a poster or leaflet how gardening can be a therapeutic activity for people with care needs.

Key term

Horticultural therapy: the use of gardening to improve health and wellbeing

These activities and projects can be adapted to meet the PIES and care needs of people with a variety of health and development problems.

Snoezelen are controlled, multi-sensory, therapeutic environments. Specially designed rooms are used to deliver sensory stimulation to an individual's different senses; sound, colour, textures and scents can be used to stimulate the person and give them pleasure. Multi-sensory stimulation is used with people of all ages who have brain injuries and older people with dementia. This therapy has been shown to have short-term effects on emotion and behaviour. One of the main advantages of multi-sensory stimulation is that it doesn't rely on verbal communication. This can be very important to people with autism, brain injuries or dementia-related illnesses.

Multi-sensory stimulation in a snoezelen

Cookery

Cooking can be both creative and therapeutic. It involves planning, preparing and cooking food to make a dish that the person – by themselves or with others – will enjoy. Cooking can be used as part of therapeutic activity to help a person to develop their thinking skills (about ingredients, cooking methods and temperatures, for example) and physical skills (chopping, stirring, cleaning and balancing). It can also be a good way of building a person's self-esteem as they may achieve a sense of satisfaction at completing a recipe or making a meal, and may receive praise and thanks from the people who join in eating! Cooking is part of the activity programme in many different types of care setting. Appropriate facilities, equipment and supervision are needed to ensure that safety and hygiene rules are observed.

? Reflect

Why do you think it would be necessary to carry out a risk assessment before a cookery session could become part of an activity programme in a care setting?

Benefits of creative and therapeutic activities

The benefits of creative and therapeutic activity

This topic will explain how taking part in creative and therapeutic activity can be beneficial for people who use care services. Creative and therapeutic activities are used for specific purposes in health and social care settings. **Participation** in such activities should meet the physical, intellectual, emotional or social needs of an individual. When these activities are used as part of a treatment programme they must be carefully chosen and organised in ways that are appropriate to an individual's particular needs.

Your assessment criteria:

1A.2 Outline the benefits of three creative and therapeutic activities for individuals or groups in one health and social care setting

2A.P2 Describe the benefits of three creative and therapeutic activities for individuals or groups in two different health and social care settings

> **Key term**
>
> **Participation:** another term for 'taking part'

Physical needs and benefits

People who use health and social care services often do so because they have physical health problems and physical care needs. These include, for example:

- **mobility** problems resulting from painful joints, fractures or conditions that cause physical weakness

- **dexterity** problems resulting from damaged muscles and inflamed tendons

- balance and co-ordination problems resulting from tremors and other involuntary muscle movements

- circulatory and respiratory problems that result in fatigue, breathlessness and lack of stamina

- weakness or paralysis of limbs as a result of **strokes**, brain injury or accidents

- loss of a limb as a result of an accident, infection or cancer.

Figure 12.2 Activities with physical benefits

People who have physical needs may use creative and therapeutic activities as a way of:

- learning new physical skills

- reducing the symptoms of their physical problems (with improved cardio-vascular function, for example)

- maintaining, adapting or improving their existing physical skills (such as dexterity) or movement abilities

- maintaining or improving their physical and hand–eye co-ordination

- maintaining or improving physical strength and fitness.

Your assessment criteria:

1A.2 Outline the benefits of three creative and therapeutic activities for individuals or groups in one health and social care setting

2A.P2 Describe the benefits of three creative and therapeutic activities for individuals or groups in two different health and social care settings

🔑 Key terms

Dexterity: *the ability to use your hands in a skilful way*

Mobility: *the ability to move freely in a co-ordinated way*

Stroke: *a condition that results from an interruption to the oxygen supply to the brain when blood vessels become blocked or burst*

❓ Reflect

Which of the activities in Figure 12.2 might appeal to you if you needed to improve your physical strength and fitness after a period of illness? Think about what you would hope to gain from the activities you choose.

Cooking, gardening, movement, exercise, horse-riding and team games can all be used to help people to learn new physical skills and to promote their physical fitness, for example. To promote both their physical health and their social skills, people with learning disabilities or mental health problems are sometimes encouraged to take part in team games (such as football) or outdoor adventure activities, such as long-distance walking, climbing and camping trips. Exercise, indoor and outdoor movement programmes and gym use are increasingly being prescribed as treatment for people who have heart or respiratory problems. Occupational therapists and physiotherapists also use adapted equipment and exercise programmes to help stroke patients practise and relearn basic physical skills, such as walking, using the toilet and holding cutlery.

Intellectual needs and benefits

People who have learning disabilities or brain injuries (caused by accidents, drug or alcohol misuse, or by conditions such as Alzheimer's disease) have **cognitive** problems and intellectual care needs. These include, for example:

- problems with confusion and memory loss

- learning difficulties that result from conditions such as Down's syndrome

- mental health problems that can cause distress, problems with decision-making and difficulties with motivation, concentration and communication

- communication and language problems.

People who have intellectual care needs may use creative and therapeutic activities as a way of:

- learning new thinking and problem-solving skills

- regaining lost skills

- becoming more organised and independent

- maintaining, adapting or improving existing thinking and memory skills

- expressing their thoughts and imaginative ideas.

> **Key term**
>
> *Cognitive: related to thinking, reasoning and remembering*

Gardening can have physical, intellectual, emotional and social benefits, depending on how an individual wants to participate in this type of activity

> **Investigate**
>
> *Using the Internet, investigate reminiscence therapy. Find out what this involves – how it is carried out with older people who have cognitive problems and what the benefits are. Produce a leaflet or poster summarising your findings.*

Looking at old photographs can bring back happy memories for people with dementia and other cognitive impairments

Emotional needs and benefits

People who experience physical illness, mental distress or social problems are also likely to have a range of emotional needs. These can be the result of:

- relationship breakdown or the loss of loved ones

- loss of health, skills or abilities as a result of a condition, illness or negative life event

- low self-confidence and poor self-esteem as a result of being unwell or less capable than previously

- mood swings and marked changes in behaviour as a side effect of medication or treatment

- hopelessness, depression or anger in response to the frustration of not getting better.

People who have emotional care needs may use creative and therapeutic activities as a way of:

- learning how to explore, control and express their feelings

- developing or boosting their self-esteem and self-concept

- maintaining, adapting or improving their motivation and coping strategies

- expressing distressing or troubling thoughts and feelings

- developing new interests.

Your assessment criteria:

1A.2 Outline the benefits of three creative and therapeutic activities for individuals or groups in one health and social care setting

2A.P2 Describe the benefits of three creative and therapeutic activities for individuals or groups in two different health and social care settings

? Reflect

Identify a couple of creative or therapeutic activities that you might choose to take part in as a way of boosting your self-confidence or that might help you to overcome a personal setback in your life. What would you choose to do that might be emotionally beneficial?

Social needs and benefits

People have social needs when they lack supportive relationships, become isolated or don't have the skills needed to establish and maintain good relationships with others. People who use health and social care services may also have social needs because they:

- feel lonely, isolated and frightened when they are admitted to a care setting where they don't know anyone

- have no contact with family, a poor relationship with family members, or lack friends who can provide them with support

- have a mental health problem, learning difficulty or a condition such as Alzheimer's disease that makes trusting and communicating with other people difficult.

Creative activities can have important social benefits, helping participants to make and maintain relationships and use their social skills

Creative and therapeutic activities, such as drama, music and dance, as well as taking part in games and craft activities, provide participants with opportunities to:

- meet and interact with others

- develop friendships

- become part of supportive social networks.

? | Reflect

Analyse the possible benefits for a group of older people who have limited social contact of taking part in a weekly quiz at a local day centre. Identify the PIES benefits that could result from taking part in this type of activity.

Case study

Edward is three years of age. He attends the Stepping Stones pre-school nursery for a few hours twice a week. Edward's mum was reluctant to enrol him at first but was persuaded by a neighbour that Edward would benefit from attending. Edward really loves going to the nursery and looks forward to meeting his new friends, playing with a variety of different toys and games, and painting. He particularly likes listening to stories read by the nursery teacher or one of the nursery nurses. Since starting at the nursery six months ago, Edward has become more self-confident, talks a lot more and has learned a lot of different things. When asked what he likes best about the nursery, Edward always says 'my friends who play with me'. Edward seems to prefer playing indoors and rarely uses the climbing equipment, toys and facilities that are available in the small play area outside.

1. Identify two creative or therapeutic activities that Edward takes part in at the nursery.

2. Analyse one of these activities and explain, using PIES, the benefits this could have for Edward.

3. What have been the main social benefits of attending the nursery for Edward?

4. Assess the suitability of the creative and play activities available to Edward.

5. How do you think the activities available at Stepping Stones could be improved to meet Edward's health, wellbeing or development needs?

Your assessment criteria:

2A.M1 Assess the suitability of creative and therapeutic activities for an individual or group, with reference to a case study

2A.D1 Make recommendations to improve creative and therapeutic activities for an individual or group, with reference to a case study

Case study

Gerald is 77 years of age. He has recently been receiving treatment for anxiety and depression. Gerald became isolated and mentally unwell last year when his wife died of cancer. Gerald's social worker has been trying to persuade him to attend a day centre and lunch club where he can meet other men and women of a similar age who also live alone and lack social support. On his first visit to the day centre Gerald reluctantly took part in an art group, played cards with a couple of other service users and helped to cook the lunch. Gerald said that he enjoyed playing cards but that he'd 'rather do something a bit more practical' than art or cookery. Gerald is a keen gardener and used to work as a builder before he retired.

1. Identify two creative or therapeutic activities that Gerald took part in at the day centre.

2. What PIES benefits could these activities provide for Gerald?

3. Assess the suitability of the creative and therapeutic activities available to Gerald on his first visit to the day centre.

4. How do you think the activities available at the day centre could be improved to meet Gerald's health and wellbeing needs?

The role of professionals in supporting and encouraging individuals

Who uses creative and therapeutic activities?

Creative and therapeutic activities have to be carefully planned and implemented in ways that are safe, empowering and enjoyable for people who use services. Health and social care workers from a number of different disciplinary backgrounds use creative and therapeutic activities as part of treatment plans. These include:

- **occupational therapists** (OTs), technical instructors and occupational therapy assistants who plan and implement **purposeful activities** for individuals

- physiotherapists and physiotherapy assistants who use forms of exercise, massage and yoga to help people with mobility and other physical problems

- hospital play specialists who use a variety of play activities to promote the learning and development of children and young people who are in hospital

- nursery nurses and nannies who use a variety of play activities to promote the development and wellbeing of young children

- doctors, nurses and social workers who may suggest an individual takes part in specific activities as part of a broader **treatment plan**

- activity assistants (sometimes also called activity co-ordinators) employed in residential care settings to promote and support social activities among residents.

Your assessment criteria:

1B.3 Outline the role of professionals who plan and implement activities in one health and social care setting

2B.P3 Describe the role of professionals when planning and implementing activities in one health and social care setting

2B.M2 Compare and contrast the role of two professionals when planning and implementing activities in two different health and social care settings

2B.D2 Evaluate the impact of professional support on a selected individual participating in creative and therapeutic activities

Key terms

Occupational therapist: *a practitioner who helps people to engage as independently as possible in activities (occupations) that enhance their health and wellbeing*

Purposeful activity: *meaningful activity, which enables a person to achieve a goal and which meets one or more of the individual's needs*

Treatment plan: *a professional's plan for treating a patient*

Health and social care workers such as occupational therapists, hospital play workers and activity assistants focus most of their time and attention on planning and implementing creative and therapeutic activities. Other practitioners, such as doctors, nurses and social workers, may suggest or use creative activities as part of an individual's treatment plan but will not focus most of their time on this.

Ways professionals support activities

Health and social care workers use different strategies to encourage and support people to take part in creative and therapeutic activities:

- planning and running a range of creative and therapeutic activities to meet the differing needs of diverse groups of individuals

- identifying, selecting and adapting appropriate activities to meet individuals' specific needs

- motivating people to try new activities, follow their interests and to use their skills and abilities as best they can

- giving praise, promoting positive thinking and setting achievable goals to help to motivate people

- offering support when individuals require it, helping people to have a positive experience of creative activities

- offering practical help to enable people to access different activities, and use the facilities and equipment that are available

- providing resources such as art materials, photography equipment, yoga mats or access to music or computer equipment, for example

- ensuring service users' health, safety and security by risk assessing activities and monitoring the way that people participate – it is vital that people who use creative and therapeutic activities can do so safely.

Your assessment criteria:

1B.3 Outline the role of professionals who plan and implement activities in one health and social care setting

2B.P3 Describe the role of professionals when planning and implementing activities in one health and social care setting

2B.M2 Compare and contrast the role of two professionals when planning and implementing activities in two different health and social care settings

2B.D2 Evaluate the impact of professional support on a selected individual participating in creative and therapeutic activities

Investigate

Use the NHS careers website (www.nhscareers.nhs.uk) or the College of Occupational Therapy website (www.cot.co.uk) to investigate the role of occupational therapists and the way they use purposeful activities to promote health and wellbeing.

Activity

Produce a poster entitled 'You can do it!' that invites and motivates a group of teenagers or older people to take part in an art, craft or a dance group. Your poster should be positive, encouraging and supportive.

Principles, values and inclusion

Health and social care workers who plan and use creative and therapeutic activities should ensure that they:

- use an anti-discriminatory approach in their work

- promote equality of opportunity for each person who uses services

- empower individuals through the activities they use

- promote independence and self-care skills

- maintain confidentiality about individual's needs and personal circumstances

- respect diversity by acknowledging cultural differences and personal beliefs.

Good care practice should be inclusive of individuals with diverse needs and backgrounds. Providing a variety of creative activities in a care setting is a good way of ensuring that the needs, abilities and interests of all service users are catered for. Health and social care workers who use creative and therapeutic activities in their work can support inclusion through:

- providing opportunities for the development of friendships via activities that have a strong social focus

- promoting and supporting interaction between participants so that people use and develop their communication skills

- supporting and encouraging people to try activities that offer them new experiences and opportunities for personal development and expression.

? Reflect

Identify examples of creative and therapeutic activities that could be used to:

- *develop friendships between a group of isolated older people*

- *enable teenagers with learning disabilities to practise using their communication skills*

- *provide an adult with physical disabilities with a new experience of physical activity*

- *encourage a group of toddlers (aged two to three years) to express themselves.*

⚷ Key term

Inclusion: being part of the group

Case study

Jayne Marshall is an occupational therapist working at Edward Watson House, a day centre for older people. Most of the people who use the day centre have a diagnosis of dementia or depression. Jayne and her colleagues use a variety of different creative activities in individual and group sessions at Edward Watson House. The activities currently on offer include painting and drawing, pottery, knitting and making soft toys. Many of the people who attend also like to take part in cookery sessions, making cakes and preparing lunch. Jayne also supervises a walk around the local park once a week. The regular walkers use this as an opportunity for exercise, to take photographs of trees, birds and park scenes and sometimes to have a picnic if the weather is good. Jayne tries to encourage conversation and friendships between the people in all of the groups she runs. She has noticed that this has a positive effect on some people's confidence and can lift their mood if they are feeling down.

1. Identify an example of the PIES benefits associated with three of the creative activities that are on offer at Edward Watson House.

2. Describe two important care values that Jayne should use when undertaking creative and therapeutic activities with the people who use Edward Watson House.

3. Explain how Jayne tries to support inclusion when she uses creative activities with people at Edward Watson House.

Creative activities can be intellectually absorbing and a really good reason to spend time with other people

Plan and implement appropriate activities

Planning appropriate activities

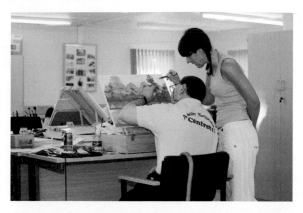

This topic focuses on planning and **implementing** creative and therapeutic activities and the factors that affect this process. A range of factors should to be taken into account when planning appropriate creative and therapeutic activities in health and social care settings. For example, the planning of any form of activity must take account of:

- legal factors

- the needs of the individuals involved.

Adhering to legislation, regulations and guidelines

Creative and therapeutic activities have many potential benefits for people who use care services. However, there are also some **hazards** and **risks** involved in these activities. Health and social care workers who use creative and therapeutic activities in practice need to know about and work within a range of safety-related **legislation**, **regulations** and guidelines that are designed to protect people from harm.

A number of health and safety laws and regulations affect the way that materials can be used and are stored in health and social care settings

Your assessment criteria:

1C.4 Describe three factors that affect the selection, planning and implementation of creative and therapeutic activities

2C.P4 Describe factors that affect the selection, planning and implementation of creative and therapeutic activities in one health and social care setting

Key terms

Implementing: *putting something into practice*

Hazard: *anything that can cause harm*

Legislation: *written laws also known as 'statutes' and Acts of Parliament*

Regulations: *detailed legal rules*

Risk: *the chance of harm being done by a hazard*

The Health and Safety at Work Act (1974)

The Health and Safety at Work Act (1974) is the key piece of health and safety law affecting care settings in the United Kingdom. A care organisation is responsible for providing:

- a safe and secure work environment
- safe equipment
- information and training about health and safety.

Health and social care workers have a responsibility to:

- work safely within the care setting
- monitor their work environment for health and safety problems that may develop
- report and respond appropriately to any health and safety risks.

Risk assessments, health and safety training and a range of health and safety equipment must be provided to ensure that creative and therapeutic activities meet the requirements of this law.

Control of Substances Hazardous to Health (2002)

The Control of Substances Hazardous to Health (COSHH) Regulations (2002) state that all hazardous substances must be correctly handled and stored to minimise the risks they present. The COSHH file that must be kept in each care setting provides details of:

- the hazardous substances that are present
- where they are stored
- how they should be handled
- how to deal with any spillage or accident involving each substance.

Any toxic or potentially dangerous substance, such as glue, paints and cleaning solvents, for example, would be listed in the COSHH file and handled according to COSHH regulations.

The Reporting of Injuries, Diseases and Dangerous Occurrences Regulations (1995)

In care settings, health and social care workers are expected to report diseases, illnesses and conditions that are infectious or which present a significant risk to health, safety or hygiene. The Reporting of Injuries, Diseases and Dangerous Occurrences Regulations (RIDDOR) (1995)

🔑 Key terms

Risk assessment: a careful examination of what could cause harm to people

Toxic: poisonous

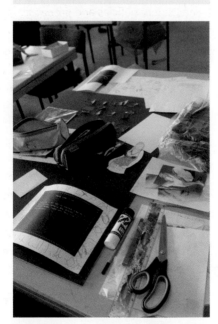

A risk assessment must be carried out before scissors, knives and other tools can be used in care settings

📋 Investigate

Go to the Health and safety Executive website (http://www.hse.gov.uk) to find out more about COSHH, RIDDOR and other health and safety regulations that apply to care settings.

identify a range of situations that must, *by law*, be recorded and reported to the **Health and Safety Executive**. These include:

- death in the workplace

- injuries that lead to three or more days off work (i.e. on sick leave)

- a range of infectious diseases and illnesses including malaria, tetanus, typhoid, typhus, measles and salmonella.

The aim is to identify situations that are dangerous so that measures can be taken to prevent them from happening again. Failing to follow food safety regulations or misusing equipment in art and craft activities are examples of occurrences that should be reported under RIDDOR.

Organisational policies and codes of practice

Care organisations produce detailed policies, procedures and codes of practice relating to health and safety issues in the care workplace. Health and social care workers are expected to be familiar with the health and safety policies and procedures that apply in their own care setting. They are often given specific health and safety training during their induction period and through regular refresher courses. Failure to follow organisational policies and codes of practice can lead to disciplinary action, and even dismissal, if an individual's care practice is thought to be dangerous to others.

Making risk assessments

Health and social care organisations are, by law, required to carry out formal risk assessments of their care settings. Risk assessment aims to identify hazards and potential risks to the health, safety and security of employees, people who use care services and visitors to a care setting. Hazards that might be present in creative and therapeutic activity include:

- toxic and flammable materials such as glue, paint, solvents and detergents

- equipment such as scissors, knives or other sharp implements

- electricity, gas or wood fires

- physical contact (such as tackling when playing sports or other games).

Key term

Health and Safety Executive: the government body that enforces health and safety laws

Reflect

What specific types of hazard might exist in a nursery or early years child care setting? Think about aspects of or objects in the environment that may be a hazard to young children.

Risk assessment recognises that a range of care activities and equipment, and the way a care setting is organised can be hazardous, but that steps can be taken to minimise or remove the risk to people of experiencing harm. The law doesn't expect health and social care workers to completely remove all risks but to protect people as far as *reasonably practicable*. The ultimate aim of a risk assessment is to ensure that people take part in creative and therapeutic activities without coming to any harm.

Health and social care workers who use creative and therapeutic activities sometimes undertake risk assessments on behalf of the care organisation that employs them. A care worker should always think about hazards and risks whenever they plan or participate in activities with people who use services.

Assessing individual needs

Health and social care workers who use creative and therapeutic activities in care settings have to plan their work carefully. One of the first tasks is to assess the care needs of an individual to ensure that their participation in creative and therapeutic activities is appropriate and beneficial. Health and social care workers should focus on an individual's physical, cognitive (intellectual), social and emotional needs. Assessment might cover, for example:

- the physical needs of the individual, including their stage of physical growth and development, physical fitness, any mobility, balance or other physical problems, and any requirements they have for physical assistance and support

- the sensory needs of the individual, including any hearing or visual impairment, speech or communication problems and any requirements the person has for assistance, support or specialist equipment

- any developmental needs that may affect an individual's physical and communication skills, and their intellectual abilities

- the individual's communication needs, especially if they have speech or hearing problems or if their first language is not English; some people may require additional support to enable them to communicate effectively

- whether the person is socially isolated – an individual may be less able or less willing to participate in some creative activities if they have few existing social contacts or sources of support

- any learning disability as this will affect an individual's ability to make decisions, establish relationships, communicate and be independent.

Your assessment criteria:

1C.4 Describe three factors that affect the selection, planning and implementation of creative and therapeutic activities

2C.P4 Describe factors that affect the selection, planning and implementation of creative and therapeutic activities in one health and social care setting

? | Reflect

How could you find out about an individual's activity interests, experiences and skills if English was not their first language? Think about different strategies that you could use to communicate with the person so that you were able to assess their needs appropriately.

Activities that meet an individual's needs, which help them to learn, maintain or regain skills, or which improve their relationships or self-esteem are likely to be beneficial and therapeutic.

Choosing activities

In addition to assessing the care needs of an individual, a health or social care worker should consider a range of factors that are likely to have an impact on the individual's preferences and suitability for different types of creative activity.

The **selection** of activity for an individual or group of people will be affected by the:

- nature of the care (and activity) setting

- potential benefits of participation (and how these meet individuals' needs)

- individuals' preferences

- age of participants

- individuals' intellectual and physical abilities

- communication skills needed to participate

- culture and gender of participants

- health and fitness of participants

- availability of resources and facilities

- time and cost restrictions that may apply.

Key term

Selection: choice

Care workers may need to assist an individual to participate in their chosen activities

The nature of the setting

The type of care setting (residential or day centre) has a significant impact on the types of creative and therapeutic activities that can be provided. For example, general hospitals have few outdoor facilities. However, there may be specially designated rooms for art, craft and other creative activities and even a gym or fitness room where some forms of therapeutic exercise can take place.

By contrast, a day centre may have many specially designed and equipped rooms that enable specialist creative and therapeutic activities, ranging from cookery and art to woodwork and car maintenance, to take place. It is always important to think about health and safety and risk management issues, as well as the restrictions that the nature of a care setting imposes when considering and choosing creative and therapeutic activities for service users.

Potential benefits

Pages 333 to 338 describe how creative and therapeutic activities can have physical, intellectual (cognitive), emotional and social benefits for an individual. A health or social care worker should **analyse** both the individual's needs and the potential benefits of an activity before they propose it as part of a treatment programme. There will be a clear benefit to the individual if the activity enables them to develop, improve or regain any physical, intellectual, emotional or social skills or abilities.

Interests and preferences

An individual's interests and preferences for taking part in particular activities are probably the most important factors affecting choice. It is bad practice to choose activities for an individual without consulting them. Ignoring what the individual would like to do in favour of your own preference for them is likely to be counter-productive as they may not wish to participate in (or be motivated by) your choice of activity. The person has to be motivated for the activity to have any therapeutic benefit. This means that they:

• have to want to do it

• can see the benefits for them

• are likely to enjoy it and are capable of taking part.

Health and social care workers often have to provide information, and offer encouragement and support, before people have enough confidence to take part in creative and therapeutic activities.

Your assessment criteria:

1C.4 Describe three factors that affect the selection, planning and implementation of creative and therapeutic activities

2C.P4 Describe factors that affect the selection, planning and implementation of creative and therapeutic activities in one health and social care setting

---

🔍 **Key term**

Analyse: to consider in detail

❓ **Reflect**

What are the drawbacks of choosing activities for people to participate in? Why might this not lead to any therapeutic benefits for the individual?

Age

An individual's age may affect their interests, skills and abilities. Younger children and older adults who have dexterity or mobility problems may find certain activities – such as yoga or horse-riding – difficult. However, they may be more interested in other activities that match their stage of development better. Many activities, such as music, cookery and art, can be adapted and presented in age-specific ways so that they match an individual's age-related level of ability, knowledge and interest.

Abilities

An individual's physical and intellectual abilities may affect their opportunities and motivation to take part in some creative and therapeutic activities. For some people, this occurs because they have not yet developed the abilities that are needed to read books, play music or use computers, for example. However, other people who have physical disabilities or learning difficulties may find it difficult to participate in creative activities because of their specific physical or intellectual needs. In these circumstances, activities and equipment may need to be adapted to enable an individual to participate. Occupational therapists are often asked to assess the activity needs of disabled people and to find ways of adapting activities and equipment to enable individuals to participate. A careful analysis of an individual's abilities should be carried out before any creative or therapeutic activities are suggested or used as part of their treatment plan.

Communication skills

Communication skills are essential to establish good relationships and enable interaction between people. An individual's age, intellectual ability, sensory impairment or cultural background could affect their ability to communicate with others. Children and people with learning disabilities tend to have less well-developed communication skills than adults, for example. A person whose first language is not English may also require some communication support in order to participate fully in some creative activities that rely on speech and the use of language.

 Reflect

How could an activity like painting be adapted to meet the needs, skills and abilities of a young child (3–4), an adolescent (14–15) and an older person (65)?

Investigate

Most sports can be adapted to enable disabled people to participate. Investigate the website of the English Federation for Disabled Sport (www.efds.co.uk) and find out how disabled people participate in a range of sports activities.

Culture and gender

A person's cultural background affects their values, lifestyle and beliefs. A person's gender can affect how they think about and manage physical contact with other people. Culture and gender may influence, for example, the way a person uses or reveals their body and their expectations about touch and proximity. Mixed sex massage, swimming or exercise classes may be unsuitable for men and women who hold certain religious beliefs, for example. Similarly, cooking may be a therapeutic activity if it enables an individual to prepare, cook and eat food that expresses their cultural identity. It is always important to assess whether an activity, or the way it is presented and run, could offend an individual because of their gender or cultural background.

Consider how a person's gender is likely to influence the types of activities that interest and motivate them. It is important not to **stereotype** men and women, but males are more likely to want to participate in football than flower arranging, for example. Similarly, many girls and women may be drawn to art, cooking and yoga in a way that many men may not be. However, it is important to get to know an individual's needs and preferences for different types of activities because it is possible that they may not conform to expected gender patterns. The way an activity is presented or carried out should take into account gender differences so that one gender isn't put off or excluded from taking part.

Health and fitness

Some creative and therapeutic activities require participants to have a higher level of health and fitness than others. Many people who are frail or unwell can carry out activities that require little physical strength or stamina, such as listening to music, watching television or reading a book. However, more strenuous activities such as taking part in sport, swimming or even walking around a local park may be inadvisable for people who have physical health problems. Assessing the physical demands of an activity is an important part of the risk assessment process.

Resources and facilities

As we have seen, the nature of a care setting is likely to affect the resources and facilities that are available for creative and therapeutic activity. Some care settings allocate rooms, staff, equipment and other resources to support creative and therapeutic activities.

Your assessment criteria:

1C.4 Describe three factors that affect the selection, planning and implementation of creative and therapeutic activities

2C.P4 Describe factors that affect the selection, planning and implementation of creative and therapeutic activities in one health and social care setting

Key term

Stereotype: *a way of categorising a person or a group that is simplified and often misleading*

Reflect

List the advantages and disadvantages of planning and providing gender-specific activity groups, such as 'Cooking for Men' or 'Women-only swimming' sessions. Are there circumstances where a gender-specific group could be more beneficial to the participants than a mixed group?

In other settings, such as residential homes and hospitals, areas of the care setting (such as the lounge or kitchen area) may need to be adapted or used only occasionally for these activities. It is important to find out what resources and facilities are available before suggesting or planning any activities for service users.

Health and social care settings often have a range of resources available for use in creative and therapeutic activity sessions. These include:

- specialist helpers
- art and craft materials
- musical instruments
- CD players, cameras and computers
- puzzles, books and games
- cookery ingredients and equipment
- appropriate clothing and protective equipment.

Specialist resources that may be required for activities involving people with physical or sensory disabilities or other specific needs include:

- large-print items
- left-handed scissors
- easy-grip tools
- talking books
- non-slip mats
- touch-screen computers.

Time and cost

The amount of time needed to participate in a creative or therapeutic activity may affect how appealing it is to service users. Activities that fit into people's everyday routines (knitting or crochet) or which are relatively short in duration (such as playing cards or board games) are usually more appealing than those that require a lot of preparation (such as pottery or dress-making) or which disrupt everyday life (for example, long walks and visiting the theatre).

Similarly activities that are free or low cost – because they don't require people to purchase equipment or entry tickets – are more accessible than those that require people to spend money to participate. Health and social care organisations often have only a small budget for creative and therapeutic activities, so it is important to think about cost early in the planning process.

Using creative and therapeutic activities in practice

The ability to plan and implement creative and therapeutic activities is best developed by practical experience. To demonstrate that you are able to select, plan and implement a creative or therapeutic activity for an individual or group you will need to undertake several linked tasks:

- assessing the PIES needs of an individual or group

- identifying one or more creative or therapeutic activities that could be used to meet these needs

- carrying out a risk assessment to identify and minimise potential hazards and risks to those who will participate in the proposed activity

- planning and explaining how you would carry out the creative activity in a health or social care environment, including identifying any equipment or assistance required

- evaluating the effectiveness of your planned activity in terms of how well it met the needs of the individual or group involved and recommending any improvements that could be made.

Stages in planning creative and therapeutic activities

Figure 12.3 identifies a range of issues that you should consider when planning and implementing a creative activity. It is best to work through the tasks identified below in stages so that your preparation is thorough, person-centred and considered. Remember that the aim of any creative or therapeutic activity is always to meet the participants' health, wellbeing or development needs.

Your assessment criteria:

1C.5 Plan one creative and therapeutic activity for service users of one health and social care setting

2C.P5 Select, plan and implement one individual or one group creative and therapeutic activity for service users of one health and social care setting

2C.M3 Assess the selection, planning and implementation of the creative and therapeutic activity

2C.D3 Recommend improvements to the planning and implementation of the creative and therapeutic activity

Step 1 – Matching an individual with an activity
- Identify an individual and describe their needs.
- Identify a creative or therapeutic activity for them.
- Describe the benefits to the individual of participating in the activity.

Step 2 – Planning the activity
- Outline how you will carry out the activity.
- Identify any materials or resources needed.
- Decide when and for how long the activity will run.
- Identify and deal with any health and safety issues.

Step 3 – Carrying out the activity
- Obtain tutor and workplace consent to run the activity.
- Implement your planned activity.

Step 4 – Evaluating the activity
- Describe what went well and what didn't.
- Explain how well the activity met the individual's needs.
- Describe how you would change or improve the activity or your approach to it.

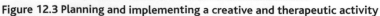

Figure 12.3 Planning and implementing a creative and therapeutic activity

Assessment checklist

To achieve level 1, my portfolio of evidence must show that I can:

Assessment criteria	Description	✓
1A.1	Identify three creative and therapeutic activities suitable for individuals or groups in one health and social care setting	☐
1A.2	Outline the benefits of three creative and therapeutic activities for individuals or groups in one health and social care setting	☐
1B.3	Outline the role of professionals who plan and implement activities in one health and social care setting	☐
1C.4	Describe three factors that affect the selection, planning and implementation of creative and therapeutic activities	☐
1C.5	Plan one creative and therapeutic activity for service users of one health and social care setting	☐

To achieve a pass grade, my portfolio of evidence must show that I can:

Assessment criteria	Description	✓
2A.P1	Describe three creative and therapeutic activities suitable for individuals or groups in two different health and social care settings	☐
2A.P2	Describe the benefits of three creative and therapeutic activities for individuals or groups in two different health and social care settings	☐
2B.P3	Describe the role of professionals when planning and implementing activities in one health and social care setting	☐
2C.P4	Describe factors that affect the selection, planning and implementation of creative and therapeutic activities in one health and social care setting	☐
2C.P5	Select, plan and implement one individual or one group creative and therapeutic activity for service users of one health and social care setting	☐

To achieve a merit grade, my portfolio of evidence must show that I can:

Assessment criteria	Description	✓
2A.M1	Assess the suitability of creative and therapeutic activities for an individual or group, with reference to a case study	☐
2B.M2	Compare and contrast the role of two professionals when planning and implementing activities in two different health and social settings	☐
2C.M3	Assess the selection, planning and implementation of the creative and therapeutic activity	☐

To achieve a distinction grade, my portfolio of evidence must show that I can:

Assessment criteria	Description	✓
2A.D1	Make recommendations to improve creative and therapeutic activities for an individual or group, with reference to a case study	☐
2B.D2	Evaluate the impact of professional support on a selected individual participating in creative and therapeutic activities	☐
2C.D3	Recommend improvements to the planning and implementation of the creative and therapeutic activity	☐

INDEX